CAESAR'S GREATEST VICTORY

The Battle of Alesia 52 BC

JOHN SADLER AND ROSIE SERDIVILLE

CASEMATE

Oxford & Philadelphia

Published in the United States of America and Great Britain in 2016 by
CASEMATE PUBLISHERS
10 Hythe Bridge Street, Oxford OX1 2EW, UK
and
1950 Lawrence Road, Havertown, PA 19083, USA

Hardcover Edition: ISBN 978-1-61200-405-1
Digital Edition: ISBN 978-1-61200-463-1

A CIP record for this book is available from the Library of Congress and the British Library

Printed in the United Kingdom by TJ International

For a complete list of Casemate titles, please contact:

CASEMATE PUBLISHERS (UK)
Telephone (01865) 241249
Fax (01865) 794449
Email: casemate-uk@casematepublishers.co.uk
www.casematepublishers.co.uk

CASEMATE PUBLISHERS (US)
Telephone (610) 853-9131
Fax (610) 853-9146
Email: casemate@casematepublishers.com
www.casematepublishers.com

*Front cover: Vercingétorix devant César (Vercingetorix faces Caesar), by Lionel Royer. Courtesy of Musée
Crozatier, Le Puy-en-Velay, France.*

For Khaled al-Assad, who showed us that true history can be worth dying for

During this period . . . more than 400,000 of the enemy were slain by Gaius Caesar and a greater number were taken prisoners. Many times had he fought in pitched battles, many times on the march, many times a besieger or besieged. Twice he penetrated into Britain, and in all his nine campaigns there was scarcely one which was not fully deserving of a Triumph. His feats about Alesia were of a kind that a mere man would scarcely venture to undertake, and scarcely anyone but a god could carry through.
Velleius Paterculus, *Roman History*, II, 47

CONTENTS

ACKNOWLEDGEMENTS

You can blame Ladybird Books, those omnipresent hardback companions of our early youth (ours and many others), particularly *Julius Caesar and Roman Britain*, for John's obsession with the Roman army. Most of his childhood summers were spent at High Shield in the shadow of the Wall where it reaches across the escarpment of the Whin Sill, so much a part of the landscape, it seemed impossible to imagine the place before Hadrian's big idea. It is grossly unfashionable to suggest that Empire might be a 'good thing' – *what did the Romans ever do for us?* But they did do rather a lot and Northumberland would have had little or no tourism otherwise, so providing us with a heritage base was something the Romans definitely did do for us up here.

John's early introduction to Roman and Romano-British archaeology as a lad cemented the craze and he owes a lifelong debt to such local titans as John Gillam, George Jobey and 'Jock' Tate, Barbara Harbottle, the late Alex Bankier and the still-very-much-living John Day and Beryl Charlton. And there were the models; Billy Bulmer's lovingly crafted scale reconstruction of the wall itself, of milecastles, turrets, forts and bath houses in the old Museum of Archaeology (now part of the Great North Museum). Since that time we have both walked the Wall countless times and John has taught about the Roman Army for many years at Newcastle University's Centre for Lifelong Learning; thanks are also due to Colm O'Brien, Max Adams and other colleagues there.

John has followed Caesar and Vercingetorix along the whole route of the campaign of 52 BC and it is one of the most compelling military odysseys you can undertake. The whole thing hangs on a series of knife edges; for the first time Caesar faced a brilliant opponent with a thorough grasp of tactical realities, every bit as single minded and ruthless.

For Rosie, the introduction came in a gentler clime. Growing up at one end of the Icknield Way she was raised on tales of the Celts and their resistance to Rome. They won a partial victory those ancient ones – the Roman road is called Icknield Street, they never got their hands on the road... Better still, her Irish family happily informed her that the Romans never got their hands on the Emerald Isle – they were scared off. A limited truth as it turned out but that was for later. Then she saw the film *Carry on Cleo* and her view of Rome was set forever. *Infamy, infamy, they've all got it in for me.* Julius Caesar has never looked the same since Kenneth Williams played him.

This book could not have been completed without the assistance of the following people: Jez Hunt, Paul Martin and Dave Silk, staff at the Literary and Philosophical Society Library Newcastle upon Tyne, at the Society of Antiquaries of Newcastle upon Tyne, Newcastle Central Library, Sebastian Pitoizet and colleagues at Museo-Parc Alesia, and lastly to Clare Litt of Casemate for another successful collaboration.

As ever, the authors remain responsible for any errors of omissions and whilst every effort has been made to trace copyright holders of any quotations and illustrations included throughout the text, the authors would be pleased to hear from anyone who may, inadvertently, have been overlooked or incorrectly identified.

John Sadler and Rosie Serdiville
Northumberland, spring 2016

A NOTE ON SOURCES

Any description of the events in Gaul in 52 BC, in particular the politics and society of Celtic Gaul has to deal with one fundamental problem: the Gauls did not leave a written record, theirs was an oral society. What they have left us are physical remains: their art, their artefacts and the landscapes they inhabited. If we want a written record we have to rely on Caesar, he's the only one there who put pen to paper. This is frustrating as we only get the view from that side of the hill written by one with a very firm agenda and a particular audience in mind. Caesar and Rome needed Gaul, if only because they needed to top up their supply of Gaulish slaves by 15,000 a year. We have used other sources, drawing on the insights offered by archaeology, anthropology and the medieval renditions of the oral tradition recorded by Irish monks in the medieval period.

Later sources such as Plutarch's *Fall of the Roman Republic*; *Six Lives*, *The Parallel Lives & Lives of the Noble Greeks and Romans* and Suetonius' *Lives of the Twelve Caesars* offer us valuable insights.

We may also refer to Appian, *History of Rome*; Cassius Dio, *Roman History*; Diodorus Siculus, *Library* and *World History*; Frontinus, *The Strategemata*; Paterculus, *History of Rome*; Strabo, *Geography*; Velleius Paterculus, *Roman History*. Tacitus, in his *Germania* (he was writing about Agricola's time of course toward the end of the first century AD) offers some useful snapshots. For Roman military science, as ever we fall back on Vegetius, *Epitome of Military Science*.

Caesar has many biographers; most recently Adrian Goldsworthy's work deserves to become a modern classic. Both Dr Peter Inker and Dr Nic Fields have produced excellent modern accounts of the siege of Alesia though, for such a significant event with such telling resonances, it is generally 'under-written'. We hope to bridge that gap.

CHRONOLOGY

390 BC	The Celts sack Rome
154 BC	Massalia (Marseilles) petitions for Roman assistance
122 BC	Rome first allies with the Aedui. They fight and defeat the Allobroges
66 & 62 BC	Revolt of the Allobroges
61 BC	The Aedui request Roman assistance, the Helvetii are restless
59 BC	Caesar is consul and appointed governor of the provinces of Cisalpine Gaul and Dalmatia. Transalpine Gaul is added to his portfolio on the death of the governor
58 BC	The Helvetii march as Caesar takes up his appointment; he checks their advance and inflicts a major defeat. At the end of the summer he trounces Ariovistus' Germans
57 BC	Caesar campaigns against the Belgae
56 BC	Caesar campaigns against the Veneti and takes what is now south-west France
55 BC	Caesar defeats a major Germanic incursion, bridges the Rhine and mounts an exploratory raid on Britain
54 BC	Second and larger expedition against Britain
53 BC	More fighting against the Belgae
52 BC	Vercingetorix revolt, massacre of Roman citizens at Cenabum (Orléans), Caesar is wrong-footed but reacts with customary vigour, Vercingetorix unites most of

Gaul, promises total war, Caesar besieges and storms Avaricum (Bourges), he tracks Vercingetorix to the Arvernian *oppidum* of Gergovia, Caesar is rebuffed with loss. After marches and counter-marches, Caesar inflicts a reverse on Vercingetorix who retreats to re-group in the Mandubii *oppidum* of Alesia, the siege and attempted relief follow, leading to the defeat of the relief and surrender of Vercingetorix

51 BC	Winter raids, mopping up and the siege of Uxellodunum
50 BC	Minor mopping up in Gaul
49 BC	Caesar crosses the Rubicon and sparks the Civil War
45 BC	Defeat of the Republicans
44 BC	Caesar is assassinated on the Ideas of March

INTRODUCTION: MOMENT OF DECISION, THE MAN IN THE RED CLOAK

You all do know this mantle,
I remember the first time ever Caesar put it on
'Twas in a summer's evening in his tent
That day he overcame the Nervii...
Shakespeare, *Julius Caesar*, II. ii.

An officer serving in one of his [Caesar's] subsequent wars tries to explain this
magnetic sentimental relationship between Caesar and his men when speaking of
a brief period in which he was separated from his army – 'they missed the sight
of their commander, his vigour and wonderful good spirits. He held his head high
and radiated confidence'.

Michael Grant, *Julius Caesar.*

One of the great moments from 20th-century literature – Caesar accepting Vercingetorix's surrender at Alesia. The gallant, inevitably red-headed Gaul hurls his shield at Caesar's feet. Who howls as it stubs his toe. Goscinny and Uderzo have begun *Asterix and the Chieftain's Shield*. Except Anthony King got there first, using one of France's national symbols (Asterix) to consider the political place in history of another (Vercingetorix).[1] What made this so key a moment in both French and European history? There are many who would argue it was the moment when nationhood first became possible, the moment when a decentralised society was torn apart and rearranged.

It is the tipping point, the crisis of battle on a sultry September afternoon in what is now Burgundy. At this pivotal moment the whole conquest of Gaul hangs by a thread. For Gaius Julius Caesar, general of Rome, and his opponent the Arvernian nobleman Vercingetorix, the stakes could not possibly be higher. For fertile Gaul and mighty Rome itself the stakes could not be higher. It is make or break, win or lose. The winner will take all and the loser will be very lucky if he survives. Rarely does history offer us such a dramatic flourish.

> Both sides realised that this was the very moment for putting their utmost effort into the fight – the Gauls must despair of saving themselves unless they broke through the Roman defences and the Romans, if they held firm, were looking forward to the end of all their labours.[2]

Another Arvernian noble, Vercingetorix' cousin Vercassivellaunus, has massed his forces, possibly as many as sixty thousand fighters,[3] north-west of the main siege lines, hidden in the dead ground by the hunched shoulder of Mount Rea. As the battle ebbs and flows on the flat plain below, the Gauls pour down the shallow slope. No mad Homeric rush this time, they've learned new tricks. This is all about tactics and not just for local glory. The advantage of high ground in this sector allows the attackers to unleash a storm of arrows and javelins onto the defenders, covering or suppressing fire as we'd call it today; a steel-tipped deluge.

Two under-strength legions, one commanded by G. Antistius Reginus and the other by G. Caninius Rebilus, were all that stood between the relief force and the *oppidum*. They were outnumbered probably by ten to one. Steep odds, made stiffer by the new drill the Gallic warriors had clearly been practising, their own version of the Roman *testudo*. Those hard-pressed legionaries, crouched behind their own *scuta* (shields) as arrows thump and ricochet, watch their enemies, formed in typical dense masses of infantry, coalesce into disciplined phalanxes, front and flanks crashing their long shields. Those in the centre raised theirs to form a moving fortress, the defenders' javelins biting and shearing as the unit moved inexorably forward.

Each unit contained a section of pioneers tasked with bridging the field defences: they were to neutralise the obstacles, pack ditches with fascines then tumble gabions of earth against the palisades. The tortoises marched on, inexorably it must have seemed, their numbers vast, smashing home along a wide frontage of the ramparts. This was a skilled and scientific assault, not the furious rush the legions had beaten back a hundred times. These Gauls were very serious: 'Our men were now running out of weapons and strength'.[4]

Caesar, from his command post, immediately saw the seriousness of the threat. He ordered his second-in-command, the vastly experienced Titus Labienus,[5] to take an ad hoc battle group of six cohorts: 'He told him that if it was impossible to hold his ground he should withdraw his forces and then launch a counter-attack – but this was only to be done in an emergency'.[6] The legate would have to move these troops across the valley from his own command post on Mount Bussy and be ready, if need be, to launch a pincer movement against the flanks of the enemy attacking the embattled camp.

It was also time for that 'touch of Harry in the night'. The good, and in Caesar's case, great, commander, knows that while he needs to keep firm control over events and not indulge in either micromanagement or foolish risks, there is a point when his personal charisma *matters*. That decisive moment when he must be ready to share the dangers with his men where the pressure is greatest. The general, his famous red cloak billowing behind and accompanied only by his personal bodyguard, cantered down from Mont Flavigny. He paused first on the plain, treating his men there to a burst of bellicose oratory, fresh heart and new confidence flowing with his words. The soldiers of Rome are led by Julius Caesar in person, defeat is unthinkable and here he is, the *bald whore-monger* and magician who has led them to victory after victory; who time and again, has beaten the odds, whose sublime confidence is their talisman.

Atop the palisades the legionaries are fighting for their lives, every sinew of training and ounce of stamina they possess fully committed. Their enemies came on in waves, like the ceaseless lines of breakers beating on the shore, long swords slashing and cleaving, each man who went down instantly replaced by another. This was the soldiers' battle, blinded by sweat and the steam of thousands of packed fighters, the pervasive sweet odour of blood, the stench of piss and shit, no man able to see beyond his own immediate front. Jab at the enemy on your right, up into his exposed side as he raises an arm for the swing, drive the short thrusting blade home, twist, withdraw, stamp on him as he goes down, get ready for the next. There are plenty more.

The crisis isn't yet passed.

CHAPTER I

AN ANCIENT CITY IN GAUL

Why man, he doth bestride the narrow world
Like a colossus; and we petty men
Walk under his huge legs, and peep about
To find ourselves dishonourable graves
Shakespeare, *Julius Caesar*, I, ii.

He himself was no philosopher and no mystic, but he was instinctively a gambler
who never paused to tremble at the odds but relied on his capacity to force them
to his will. Luck is never far below the surface of his 'Commentaries'
Michael Grant, *Julius Caesar*.

The hotel in Alise-Sainte-Reine has plastic cloths on the tables and you
eat what's put in front of you. It was *le proprietaire*'s daughter, moonlighting
during the school lunch hour, who served us wine. All local and like the
food, quite splendid. The modern town, as pleasing and nondescript as
any rural halt in Burgundy, stands 50 kilometres north-west of Dijon in
the Côte-d'Or. Today, you drive from Veneray-les-Laumes then branch
off onto the minor road D103J. It is mostly open farmland, rolling and
well wooded, the French are still wedded to *la chasse*. The little town
stands on the plain of Laumes at the foot of Mont Auxois, this flat-
topped escarpment is the (generally) accepted site of both Vercingetorix'
last stand and the later Gallo-Roman *oppidum*.

Alise has done rather well out of Vercingetorix, his patrician statue
crowns the plateau on the dramatic western scarp of the fortress. It

is said the name *Alise* may derive from an Indo-European description indicating 'a rocky height' linked to the cult of the Celtic god Alisanos. The origin could also have its roots in a spring that rose in the heart of the settlement.[1] *Sainte Reine* comes later, a Christian martyr, beheaded there in 252 AD. The place is still very French – no ex-pat gentrification here. Paint is flaking, plentiful supplies of old tractors and their tyres still lounge about with that scruffy, careless charm that provincial France does rather better than anyone else.

The commune has had to work hard to maintain its historical significance. As with most battles in the ancient world, exact locations can be hard to pin down and the distinction has serious implications for tourism. Meticulous as ever, Caesar provides a good topographical description:

> The actual stronghold of Alesia was in an extremely lofty position on top of a hill, apparently impregnable except by means of a siege. On two sides the foot of this hill was washed by rivers, and for about three miles there stretched a plain in front of the town. Close by in every other direction more hills of equal height girded the town.[2]

There have been those who have disputed the location over the last forty years but the town holds its ground.

Caesar was writing for a popular 'dime novel' audience. They'd never been to Burgundy and weren't that desperately interested in detailed topographical descriptions. His readers wanted action, drama, and deeds of glory. Caesar was a first rate story-teller. He knew his audience and his measured account, always in the third person, is dryly under-stated, the boasting discreet and inferred. He gives credit to his men. He doesn't generally disparage or demean the enemy. After all, his achievement is far greater if his enemy is respected. You always know who's going to win of course. Like Montgomery a couple of millennia afterwards, Caesar can always claim complete mastery of the battlefield, can always make the enemy dance to his tune.

Plus of course, the ultimate (resounding) victory always helps. Unlike Monty or any other modern generals, Caesar had no literary rivals nor did he have journalists looking over his shoulder. There were no correspondents 'embedded' with the legions, tastefully mucked up to convey what it was 'really' like. It was easier for Caesar to be the consummate seducer. The only contemporary written source we have, the only voice we ever hear is his. It was very disobliging of Vercingetorix not to leave a memoir, after all he had six years in imprisonment, plenty of time. Many military memoirs, if indeed we regard Caesar's work as a personal rather than general history, are stilted and formal, couched in 'staff college' language, devoid of description or drama. Caesar knew better, he had a novelist's touch; pace and action flow, he is still a rattling good read.

The battle for Alesia was a decisive moment in world history. It determined whether Rome would finally conquer Gaul or whether Vercingetorix would throw off the yoke and a swathe of independent Celtic tribal territories could endure. Failure would have been a total defeat for Julius Caesar, not just in Gaul but in the Senate. His career would have been over. His innumerable enemies would have pulled him down, there would have been no Civil War, no dictatorship, no liaison with Cleopatra. Rome might never have become an empire beyond the Mediterranean littoral.

It was the Waterloo of its day. The final defeat of Napoleon Bonaparte in 1815 ended a century of economic and military conflict between Britain and France. Wellington's victory settled that argument and bought Britain a century of world dominance. It still wasn't tactical perfection, not by a long way. Wellington made some serious mistakes, happily Napoleon made rather more and there were plenty of witnesses and commentators falling over themselves to write up accounts of the battle. Caesar had to wait near a hundred years before Tacitus and Plutarch would be heard. Cicero, at least, was contemporaneous and had the advantage of a brother who actually took part in the campaign. However, time sweeps many mistakes under the literary historical carpet.

Caesar's campaign of 52 BC frequently hung in the balance. Vercingetorix was a far more formidable and nimble opponent than any he'd so far encountered in Gaul; bold, charismatic and imbued with strategic insight of the highest order. The Romans were caught totally off-guard and it seemed all too likely their grip on Gaul, which Caesar had imagined secure, would be prised free. At Gergovia, the unbeaten Caesar suffered his first and only significant defeat (which he cannily blamed on reckless subordinates).

Nonetheless, the Siege of Alesia itself was one of the most astonishing military undertakings of all time. Caesar's interior siege lines (*circumvallation*) stretched for 18 kilometres and were surrounded by an outward facing line (*contravallation*) 3 kilometres longer, complete with palisades, towers, ditches, minefields and outposts. This work was completed in less than three weeks. Vercingetorix' refuge proved a trap and, despite an energetic defence and the arrival of a huge relief army, there was to be no escape. It's not wise to give a general of Caesar's capacity a second chance.

In the 19th century, when leaders such as Vercingetorix and the German Arminius had been adopted as nationalist icons, the Romans were seen as conquerors – bloodthirsty oppressors. Those who resisted were elevated to totemic status. The great statue that dominates the plain of Alise-Sainte-Reine is an image of noble defeat. The romantic loser always has its appeal, Mark Anthony and Cleopatra are more interesting than Augustus. Richard III has a far bigger fan club than Henry VII. Mindless psychopaths like Jesse James and Ned Kelly bask in Robin Hood status.

It is part of our overall objective to place the campaign, siege and battle into a wider context. It had profound consequences for the social and political development of what is now France. Indeed you could argue that the concept of a unified nation could never have been brought to fruition without dismantling the Celtic model of society. When it came to creating an identity for modern France, Alesia and the symbol that would be Vercingetorix would be a valuable resource.

Alesia must also take its place in the history of warfare. It forms an example of classic asymmetric tactics, which fails only when one of the main protagonists abandons his own dictum of mobility and harassment to 'place his faith in fortresses': thereby surrendering the initiative and virtually ensuring his own defeat.

Caesar's swashbuckling brand of empire-building appealed to many Romans. Generally they did pretty well out of his exploits. His physical robustness won plaudits:

> He was highly skilled in arms and horsemanship, and of incredible powers of endurance. On the march he headed his army, sometimes on horseback, but more often on foot, bareheaded both in the heat of the sun and in rain. He covered great distances with incredible speed, making 100 miles a day in a hired carriage and with little baggage, swimming the rivers which barred his path or crossing them on inflated skins, and very often arriving before the messengers sent to announce his coming.[3]

His enemies were equally vehement. Rome's outstanding orator, Marcus Tullius Cicero moved that he should be branded as a war criminal and handed over to the Gauls themselves for punishment, rare to hear so early a condemnation of what we now class as war crimes. Of course, Cicero had his own motivations, and we should apply the same pinch of salt to his motives that expend on Caesar's.

The Gallic Wars, 58–51 BC, marked a pivotal epoch in the expansion of Rome, a monument to Caesar's towering military genius. Although he portrays his invasion as being more of a preemptive or defensive action, most historians agree that the wars were fought primarily to boost Caesar's political career and to pay off his more insistent creditors. Still, Gaul was of significant military importance to Rome. Celts and Romans had a history of antipathy going back to the sack of Rome in 390 BC. Conquering Gaul allowed Rome to secure the natural frontier of the Rhine and to launch probes against Britain. It is possible that without Caesar there could have been no Claudian invasion.

Following his initial consulship in 59 BC, Caesar engineered an appointment to Cisalpine Gaul (the region between the Alps, the Apennines and the Adriatic – modern-day northern Italy), and Transalpine Gaul ('Gaul beyond the Alps' – modern-day Switzerland and Alpine France). Although the pro-consular term of office was normally limited to twelve months, Caesar was able to secure his post in Gaul for an unprecedented period of ten years. With a pro-consular mandate or *imperium*, he had absolute authority within these provinces. One by one Caesar defeated Gallic (Continental Celtic) tribes including the Helvetii, the Belgae, and the Nervii, and secured pledges of alliance from many others. These impressive military successes brought an enormous amount of wealth into the Republican coffers. Caesar himself amassed a vast fortune, completing reversing his earlier dire circumstances. Inevitably, wealth and renown also brought enemies.

Caesar had bought some measure of security with the First Triumvirate, an informal alliance linking him to Gneaus Pompey and Marcus Licinius Crassus. This happy arrangement came to an end in 54 BC, with the death of Julia − Caesar's daughter and Pompey's wife − in childbirth and of Crassus, who was killed after his own Waterloo, the battle of Carrhae in Parthia. Without this vital bond to the influential Pompey, dedicated Republicans like Cato the Younger began a vitriolic campaign against Caesar − accusing him of plotting to overthrow the Republic and become 'king' − the Republicans' recurrent nightmare.

In the winter of 54–53 BC, the previously quiescent Eburones, led by their chieftain Ambiorix, rebelled and virtually annihilated *Legio XIV* (the Fourteenth Legion) under Quintus Titurius Sabinus in a carefully orchestrated ambush in the wild northern region. This was a major blow to Caesar's strategy. Worse, he'd lost more men than he could afford to and the political situation in Rome prevented any hope of early reinforcement. The rising of the Eburones was the first clear Roman defeat in Gaul and inspired further insurrections. Caesar's personal leadership status wasn't dimmed by Sabinus' debacle. His speed and incisiveness in reacting to and overcoming the fallout was, by any standards, impressive.

It took almost a year, but Caesar managed to regain control of Gaul and pacify the natives. However, the unrest in Gaul was far from over. Those factions within the tribes who wanted Rome ejected had finally reached the ascendancy. It was time to negotiate another alliance, one large enough to defeat Rome. A general council was summoned at Bibracte by the Aedui, once Caesar's loyal supporters. Only the Remi and the Lingones preferred to keep their alliance with Rome intact. The council declared Vercingetorix, a prince of the Arverni, overall commander of the combined Gallic armies. This seems to have been a formal and very limited role, rather like that of the Irish *Ard Righ* or the Saxon *Bretwalda*: a post that was primarily a war leader, but which might be converted by the canny to something closer to an overlord.

Caesar was then in winter quarters in Cisalpine Gaul, blissfully unaware of the storm brewing. The first sign of trouble came from the Carnutes, who murdered all the Roman settlers in the city of Cenabum (modern Orléans). This outbreak of violence was followed by the slaughter of all Roman citizens, merchants and officials in the major Gallic cities. On hearing this unwelcome news, Caesar hastily rallied his army and crossed the Alps, still deep in snow, into central Gaul. This was accomplished in record time and Caesar was able to achieve a measure of surprise and partly regain the initiative. Only partly as, most commentators agree, Vercingetorix was to prove the most resolute adversary he would ever face.

Caesar now took the bold decision to split his forces, sending four legions under the experienced Titus Labienus to take on the Senones and Parisii in the north while he himself set off in pursuit of Vercingetorix with six legions and allied Germanic cavalry. After the successful siege of Avaricum (Bourges), where Caesar stormed the place at an opportunistic moment and the luckless population was made to fully understand what defeat now entailed, he headed south. Vercingetorix had not allowed his field army to intervene and withdrew into the Auvergne. This was classic asymmetric tactics, refusing to take on the stronger opponent, relying on a quasi-guerrilla campaign of attrition.

The two armies met by the hill fort of Gergovia, where Vercingetorix held an immensely strong defensive position. He would not be drawn into a general engagement. Caesar was checked and forced to retreat to avoid utter defeat. Throughout the summer, several extended skirmishes were fought between opposing cavalry forces with Caesar finally succeeding in scattering the Gallic army. Vercingetorix decided that the timing was not right to instigate a major pitched battle and fell back to regroup in the Mandubii fortress of Alesia. Spotting a major blunder, Caesar seized his opportunity. The scene was now set for the decisive contest and the siege of Alesia proved to be an epic finale, worthy of Homer or Xenophon.

The Gauls found themselves surrounded by a complex system of fortified siege lines. The defenders remained active but couldn't pierce the lines. As a massive relief force was mustering, Caesar caused a second outward facing line to be thrown up, forming an impenetrable ring. When the Gallic reinforcements arrived, both sides recognised this was the endgame. After a long, hard-fought battle where the result hung in the balance, Caesar emerged victorious. Next day Vercingetorix surrendered and the Gallic Wars were effectively over, one of the most dramatic episodes in the history of warfare and a key moment in Rome's imperial expansion.

It is still hotly disputed whether Alise-Sainte-Reine is the site of the siege. It looks right, and it is broadly in the right region but there have been and remain other contenders. The two leading alternatives are Chaux-des-Crotenay in the Juras and Alaise in Franche-Comte. In 2012, the new heritage centre opened in Alise-Saint-Reine. A pretty significant statement of intent, it took a decade to build and cost around sixty million pounds or seventy-five million Euros.

It is impressive. The central rotunda houses the principal interactive exhibition and the old reconstructions of Caesar's lines of *circumvallation* have been thoroughly refreshed. Not only is this a first-class introduction to both the campaign and battle but it is a very solid affirmation of civic pride and certainty. It is immediately reminiscent of a similar investment by English Heritage, which gave the visitor centre at Bosworth, site of Richard III's final encounter with destiny, a substantive makeover just before the whole location was called very seriously into question.

It is said of the statue of Vercingetorix in Alise-Saint-Reine, that beneath the drooping Gallic moustaches (though he was more probably clean shaven), the noble hero bears a distinct likeness to the young Napoleon III. We can safely conclude this was not accidental. Vercingetorix wasn't the only ruler seeking validation. It was Napoleon Bonaparte's nephew who, in 1864, issued a definitive decree that Alise-Sainte-Reine was indeed the undisputed site of classical Alesia. This wasn't open to debate. Vercingetorix had become a card in the game of

19th-century nationalism. Not unlike William Wallace or James IV in the Scots assertion of nationhood, (though the Gaul has managed so far to escape the full Hollywood treatment. There has been a French film version (2001) with Christopher Lambert, suitably virile as the hero and Klaus Maria Brandauer, suitably shifty as Caesar.)[4]

Napoleon's assertion was based on significant archaeological evidence from the period, though the science was in its relative infancy and politicians have a tendency to mould the facts to suit their hypothesis. Nationalism mattered – France was facing a challenge from the unification of Germany directed by Bismarck's ruthless energy, a rise so inexorable it would sweep Napoleon III aside and rub France's collective nose in the dirt. New empires were on the rise.

Bismarck also had Arminius, the Germanic warlord who had so thoroughly trashed the inept Roman general Publius Qunictilius Varus and his four legions at the Teutoburger Wald in 9 AD. His grand monument, 170 feet in height, wasn't completed until 1875 (begun thirty years earlier). He was a winner not a loser. Bismarck preferred winners.

Despite controversy, Alise-Sainte-Reine does have some powerful arguments ranged in its favour. There is a long history of identification, going back to the medieval period. It does broadly fit Caesar's description and he is writing a story rather than a geographical essay. It has been suggested that Mont Auxois is too small to have held an army of (say) 80,000. As Peter Inker points out, the whole force would never have been billeted in the town.[5] As at Gergovia, they'd have been in cantonments, spreading over the whole plateau, particularly to the west, Caesar even tells us this – that the garrison was encamped outside the walls and had constructed temporary defences, trenches and a six-foot-high stone barrier.[6]

There are inconsistencies between the archaeological traces and Caesar's description of his own siege lines but again, his written version was intended to give a general impression rather than provide a detailed survey – he was writing primarily for his current audience, not just posterity.[7] There are some inconsistencies among the classical writers generally but that is inevitable given that these were writing later and had not visited the location. Although the archaeological remains on Mont Auxois are Gallo-Roman, there is every reason to suppose they're built on top of the earlier *oppidum*.

Nineteenth-century excavations did harvest a rich crop of coins both Roman and Gallic, including those of Vercingetorix and the Arverni which, together with some from other Gaulish allied nations, does lend weight to the argument. More recently, the find of a single Roman slingshot marked with the name of Labienus suggests very strongly that this is the right place. Some, inevitably, see this is a conspiracy. No historic location was ever adversely affected by a decent conspiracy theory.

In the 1960s, French archaeologist Andre Berthier had doubts about the place. He didn't think the hill fitted Caesar's description. It wasn't high enough, the plain was too wide and the rivers unimpressive.[8] It was Berthier, after painstakingly checking out all possibilities, who decided in favour of Chaux-les-Crotenay, which is about 50 kilometres from Geneva in the Jura Mountains. Berthier's successor in this view is Professor Danielle Porte of the Sorbonne:

> The archaeological establishment has never paid the slightest heed to our doubts. They are too wrapped up in their own reputations, and now there are the economic interests at stake as well, with the museum. 'No-one dares question the orthodox thesis. Lethargy, careerism and money are all taking precedence over historical truth, and that is something I cannot put up with'.[9]

It has become pretty lively with very distinct battle lines being drawn between these dissidents or 'Jurassics' as they're labelled and the conventional champions of Alise-Sainte-Reine. With seventy-five million Euros of investment at stake, you can see why. Whilst the 'Jurassic' site has yet to be fully dug, Berthier did find traces of a Gallic *oppidum* there with suggestions of Roman works nearby. One of the more passionate Jurassics, historian and broadcaster Franck Ferrand, is adamant:

> We believe this is the most important unexcavated archaeological site in Europe, and yet the French state refuses to authorize excavations here. Why? Because it might jeopardize the official theory; it's the only case in history of an excavation being banned for cultural reasons.[10]

Laurent de Froberville, director of the Alesia centre (naturally not one to lend credence to the Jurassics), discounts their claims entirely:

> So much evidence has been found in the ground here. Just one example: There were three types of horses in the battle, from the Roman, Gaulish and Germanic cavalries. And we have found bones here from all three breeds. The Jurassic people rely far too heavily on one element: Caesar's texts. But we cannot be sure how accurate these writings are. Most experts rely on an accumulation of different evidence. There comes a point – like in an detective enquiry – when everything points in one direction, and you have to say: It's here.[11]

Professor Porte is confident that one day *the truth will out*. Presumably and, as ever, it is out there somewhere. What Berthier does not seem to have taken into account is the main purpose of Caesar's description. He relied on a literal interpretation, but what conquering general ever ran down the strength of an enemy position? Certainly not Julius Caesar. He was as much a storyteller as an historian. It was his own trumpet he was blowing. If he had admitted it wasn't much of a place, then it wouldn't be that much of a story.

So the real Alesia doesn't have to be as strong as the account suggests, what Caesar was conveying is that this would be a very tough nut to crack and from his account, it was. Vercingetorix did not intend to make a stand at Alesia. This wasn't some form of national redoubt, identified like the ridge of Mont St. Jean, as a place to fight from. It was a last-minute expedient. If he'd had the leisure the Arvernian would probably not have allowed himself to be bottled up there. At the time, such decisions are dictated in the fog of war. It's not always tidy.

For our purposes we intend to stick with Alise-Sainte-Reine. It 'feels' right, especially to one who has walked numerous battlefields in the role of historical guide. Broadly the place conforms to Caesar's description and it fits the military facts. Sometimes Colonel Burne's 'inherent military probability'[12] makes sense even if it is no longer in favour. It seems very reasonable to rely heavily on reading the ground where the literary and archaeological evidence falters. The terrain there does broadly conform to Caesar's description, the distance lines from the fight at Mont Reux, the assembly and deployment of the relief force all fit the ground.

Vercingetorix is portrayed today as a great popular hero, a freedom fighter and populist. It is not a picture that would have been recognised or even approved of in his own time. It is pretty pointless sticking modern labels on historical characters. Caesar was a ruthless, self-seeking opportunist and his intervention was cynical and exploitive. On the other hand, his conquest did stick, and ushered in five centuries of relative unity and prosperity. Little of our modern intermeddling could claim the same result.

CHAPTER 2

DE REI MILITARII

With armies consisting overwhelmingly of fully-armed infantry, battles could be adequately conducted against any commander who was not of exceptional calibre by satisfying the few basic conditions – courage, supplies and training. Any good drill master, therefore, was a fairly good general. Caesar was an excellent drill master, with continual awareness of the importance of knowing and mastering details and subordinating means to end.

Michael Grant, Julius Caesar.

Si vis pacem, para bellum...[1]

'If you seek peace, prepare for war'. Vegetius, writing in the 4th or 5th century AD pretty much sums it up. Over a century after Caesar confronted Vercingetorix, another notable Roman general, G. Suetonius Paulinus, campaigning in Britain, was facing desperate odds against Boudicca in 61 AD. His biographer Tacitus, who got his core narrative almost directly from the horse's mouth, his future father-in-law Julius Agricola was tribune, essentially aide-de-camp, to the general, records this pithy battlefield oratory. Suetonius was very much a soldier's soldier. He didn't waste words or prettify the task ahead. But as descriptions of Celtic armies go, this one can't be far off the mark. After all, his men could see all too clearly what they were up against:

> Disregard the clamours and empty threats of the natives! In their ranks, there are more women than fighting men. Unwarlike, unarmed, when they see the arms and courage of the conquerors who have routed them so often, they will break

immediately. Even when a force contains many divisions, few among them win the battles – what special glory for your small numbers to win the renown of a whole army! Just keep in close order. Throw your javelins, and then carry on: use shield bosses to fell them, swords to kill them.[2]

Part of what Suetonius was doing was remind his men that they were the professionals, the Britons were a mob, a rabble of boasters. By the time of Boudicca, Rome had amassed generations of fighting experience across all terrain and against an impressive range of adversaries. Popular during the age of chivalry, Vegetius' *Epitome of Military Science* distils these centuries of experience and tactical doctrine into a single user's guide and manual. Though writing long after Caesar's campaigns, he draws on the accumulated wisdom of the Republican and Imperial heritage.

> Next, the manner in which the battle array should be drawn up for imminent battle may be demonstrated from the example of one legion. This could be extended to more if need demands. The cavalry are stationed on the wings. The infantry line begins to be ordered from the First cohort on the right wing. It is joined by the Second cohort. The Third cohort is placed in the middle of the line. The Fourth is placed next to it. The Fifth cohort holds the left wing... [3]

The moment that Vercingetorix put his army into Alesia, he was effectively defeated. History would show time and again that 'putting your faith in fortresses' was generally, if not invariably, a prelude to disaster – Masada, Krak des Chevaliers through to Sedan in 1871, Fort Douaumont at Verdun and the Maginot Line. History provides us with a comprehensive catalogue of dire reminders. The Gallic leader had surrendered the initiative and allowed Caesar a second chance. Furthermore, in opting to endure a siege, he allowed the professionalism of the Roman army to dominate the action. He surrendered the initiative.

And the Romans were professional. Even Josephus, that wily survivor of the First Jewish Revolt (66–73 AD), Rome's former enemy turned enthusiastic collaborator and latterly historian, was forced to respect his adversary's capacity:

> This vast empire of theirs has come to them as the prize of valour, and not as a gift of fortune. For their nation does not wait for the outbreak of war to give men their first lesson in arms. They do not sit with folded hands in peace-time

only to put them in motion in the hour of need. On the contrary, as though they had been born with weapons in hand, they never have a truce from training; never wait for emergencies to arise. Moreover their peace manoeuvres are no less strenuous than veritable warfare...[4]

On paper, recruitment to the Roman army was open to those aged 17–46, though most recruits were in their late teens or twenties. City boys certainly joined up but the majority tended to be from the country-side, that hardy peasant stock that traditionally provided citizen warriors for the early hoplite and manipular armies (see below). Vegetius has no doubts that the country lad makes for a better soldier:

> On this subject I think it could never have been doubted that the rural populace is better suited for arms. They are nurtured under the open sky in a life of work, enduring the sun, careless of shade, unacquainted with bath houses, ignorant of luxury, simple souls, content with a little, with limbs toughened to endure every kind of toil, and for whom wielding iron, digging a fosse and carrying a burden is what they are used to from the country.[5]

This does rather sound like a townsman's condescending view of his rustic contemporaries, though Tacitus certainly agrees; when speaking of Augustus' time, he refers to the pernicious influence of townie recruits. Physically, most legionaries tended to be stocky and well built, not par-ticularly tall, as there are constant references to the impressive height and physique of those fair-haired Gauls who appear alien by comparison. They had to possess strength and stamina. The legion was no place for those who couldn't make the grade. Training was tough and discipline harsh. Normally, in Caesar's day, the recruit would serve for six years and he'd be paid his annual wage in three tranches with a substantial bonus on discharge. He suffered deductions for kit, food, burial club and a compulsory savings scheme.

He swore an oath of loyalty, the *sacramentum*, in an age when these things mattered. By Vegetius' time the Church had hijacked the oath: the recruit was now bound to God as well as the state. Though he was a cog in the corporate machine, the individual soldier could expect medals and commendations for bravery. Napoleon wasn't the first to recognise that men respond to praise and that decorations bolster unit pride. And there was the prospect of loot. Expansion meant opportunities for pillage and pilferage. At Alesia, Caesar promises his men slaves from among the haul of captives – cash on legs.

Then as now, some relied on parcels from home. They didn't always arrive, so not all grousing was aimed at officers:

My dear Mother,

I hope that this finds you well. When you get this letter I shall be much obliged if you will send me some money. I haven't got a penny left, because I have bought a donkey cart and spent all my money on it. Do send me a riding-coat, some oil and above all my monthly allowance. When I was last home you promised not to leave me penniless, and now you treat me like a dog .... Valerius' mother sent him a pair of pants, a measure of oil, a box of food and some money. Do send me money and don't leave me like this.[6]

If this whining note had been penned by a 20th-century soldier, we wouldn't have been at all surprised. The lot of the new recruit was never an easy one.

Michael Grant[7] describes the army as a *corporate force*. Rome possessed a standing army; the sword of the state, which from a tradition rooted in the hoplites of Greek city states, would grow and develop into the anvil of empire. The original legionary was a citizen, a man of property and position who could afford to turn out with his own kit. He had a personal stake in the survival and expansion of the state but he only expected to serve for the duration of hostilities. Essentially, he was a small farmer who went to war when called upon. Nonetheless, he was tough, resourceful and competent. What he didn't like were long periods of service at a distance. He was never a regular in that sense. As the empire began to expand, his limitations (notably in relation to length of service) became more pronounced.

Under the Republic two consuls were elected by the people every year. Power would never vest in the hands of one man. At least not until Caesar challenged the tottering Republic, ushering in the move to hereditary emperors. The new appointees would in turn select their officer cadre, the tribunes, whose job was to keep the legions up to strength. All citizens within the age bands of 17–46 had to muster on the Capitoline Hill where they were shaken out by age and physique. Then, in fours, they paraded before the tribunes who chose their men by rotation. Hopefully, this ensured an even distribution of effective manpower.[8] The early legion (from the Latin *legere* – 'to gather together'), was comprised of ten *maniples* (literally 'handfuls'), each made up of three main troop types; *principles, hastate* and *triarii* with a fourth category of lightly armed skirmishers or *velites*.

On 22 June 168 BC Aemilius Paullus brought three exhausting years of war with the rump of Alexander's Macedon to a successful denouement at the battle of Pydna in Greece when the legions utterly thrashed the mighty phalanx. Rome had finally arrived as a global superpower. She had previously tamed her rivals on the Italian peninsula, won the long, bloody and costly wars with Carthage and was set to expand. Yet for half a century after Pydna she would mostly consolidate, cementing her grip on Spain, Tunisia and Greece.

Further expansion would demand a new type of army, led by a new type of general. The adventurer Julius Caesar was the greatest of these, a consummate gambler and opportunist. His restless genius, not to mention personal economic necessity, would lead to the conquest of Gaul (58–51 BC), the boldest and most ambitious of Rome's imperial gambits, one of the boldest of all time and one that would shape world history. It would lead directly to the confrontation at Alesia.

Caesar's campaigns would not have been possible without the giant shadow cast by his predecessor (and uncle by marriage), Gaius Marius (157–86 BC), a formidable, brilliant bruiser who transformed the Roman Army. Marius came to prominence during the long-drawn-out war with Jugurtha in what is now Algeria. A bitter, sapping campaign fought at a considerable distance: It wasn't a job for Saturday Night soldiers and recruits were very hard to come by. Out of necessity, Marius changed the whole social mix by throwing enlistment open to all, to any citizen, regardless of status. The old, traditional link between property qualification and service went out of the window. Not surprisingly, volunteers came forward in large numbers. War is always popular when you are poor. Regular wages, regular feeding and the prospect of loot are very persuasive when you have no work or are stuck in a backbreaking job with no prospects beyond an early and impecunious death.

Marius' legions weren't disbanded at the close of a campaign. They stayed on the books as permanent formations – a regular army. Poor recruits couldn't be expected to provide their own – inherently expensive – gear. So they got better wages and the state supplied their kit, mass produced and not necessarily top quality, but at least it came with the job. As all the men were equipped similarly, the distinction between heavier hoplite-type infantry and lighter armed skirmishers, those *velites*, was abolished.

During the early days of the Republic, the army generally consisted of four citizen legions. This number could of course be expanded if the threat level increased. Normal ration strength was 4,200, divided into thirty *maniples*, each of which was comprised of *hastati* (front rank) and *principes* (second rank). Both types were drawn from experienced men: strong, fit, armoured, equipped with both light and heavy javelins plus stabbing swords. The *triarii* – the third line, all veterans, were primarily spearmen and formed a tactical reserve. If things went according to plan they wouldn't be committed. If the fight 'came to the *triarii*' that meant things were getting pretty desperate.[9]

Another casualty of Marius' reforms was the old manipular system. Distinctions between the three ranks of *triarii*, *hastati* and *principes* were abandoned and all ranks now carried a short, thrusting blade – the *gladius* (see below) and the javelin or *pilum*. This reorganisation meant that the legion would consist of ten cohorts rather than thirty maniples. Command and control of the new legions was still exercised through half a dozen military tribunes. These were young gentlemen of good family but not necessarily with any fighting experience – their appointments were essentially steps up the political ladder. Clearly such a system had major drawbacks and the legion as a unit was commanded by a senior officer, the *legatus* or legate.[10]

Once Italian natives domiciled south of the Po were accepted as citizens, the other archaic distinction between true Roman and allied formations could also be consigned to history. In Caesar's day these *socii* or allies performed the functions of later Imperial auxiliaries. The other element that disappeared was the cumbersome baggage train that dragged and straggled behind earlier Republican armies. Citizen soldiers don't necessarily care for yomping and officers liked to travel in style. Marius did away with such comforts. His men were paid professionals and didn't need pampering. They carried their own kit – virtually all of it, armour, helmet, weapons, tools, personal gear and rations. This immensely speeded up the line of marching, though the men groaned under their mighty loads – 'Marius' mules'.

Vegetius, from the space of many decades, was in no doubt that such tough love paid dividends:

> In every battle it is not numbers and untaught bravery so much as skill and training that generally produce the victory. For we see no other explanation of the conquest of the world by the Roman People than their drill-at-arms, camp-discipline and military expertise. How else could small Roman forces have availed against hordes of Gauls? How could small stature have ventured to confront German tallness?[11]

This was a new type of soldier then, as much the armed extension of the body corporate as individual warrior. His loyalty was primarily to the state but all too often this transferred to the person of his commanding general who would lead him, hopefully, to victory and to riches. Charismatic and successful leaders like Marius, then Pompey and Caesar after him, were viewed as personalities rather than state appointees. Their style of leadership needed to be more personal, their armies were loyal to them. They would serve together for months or years. The fortunes of each individual soldier depended on the commander's success. This forged a strong personal bond but the legionary was still a tough independently minded and not infrequently cantankerous individual, ready and vociferous with grousing. The general might be in charge but he was no Olympian. Caesar had the great commander's gift of getting his men to love him, though this adulation might be expressed in unflattering terms:

> Home we bring our bald whoremonger;
> Romans, lock your wives away!
> All the bags of gold you lent him
> Went his Gallic tarts to pay.[12]

Publius Flavius Vegetius Renatus wrote his classic *Epitome of Military Science* probably in the late 4th or early 5th century AD.[13] Whilst this is very late in the Roman period, much of his canny, down to earth tactical advice would be equally applicable to the legions of the late Republic:

> When the general is ready to draw up his line, he should first attend to three things, sun, dust and wind. When the sun is in front of your face, it deprives you of sight. Head winds deflect and depress your missiles while aiding the enemy's. Dust thrown up in front of you fills and closes your eyes …. 'Line' means the army drawn up for battle. The 'front' is the part that looks toward the enemy … The rule of drawing up an array is to place in the first line the experienced and seasoned soldiers, formerly called 'principes', and to rank in the second line archers protected with cataphracts[14] and crack soldiers armed with javelins and light spears, formerly called 'hastati'. Individual infantrymen regularly occupy 3 ft. each. Therefore in a mile 1,666 infantrymen are ranked abreast…[15]

Caesar, in drawing up his legions, typically used a 4-3-3 deployment – four cohorts in the first line, three each in the support and reserve lines behind: 'He himself drew up in a triple battle line'.[16] This first line would engage the enemy head on, usually deluging the attackers in a hail of javelins: 'At the signal our men attacked the enemy so fiercely, and the enemy rushed forward so suddenly and swiftly, that there was no room for throwing javelins at the foe. These weapons were cast aside as a sword fight ensued.'[17] Such a sudden advance to contact was rare, the cohorts relied on thinning the enemy ranks with their javelins before drawing swords. The support line was ready to add weight to the attack or depth to the defence whilst the third brigade could extend on the flanks or be used to exploit any opportunities that might arise. The key to Roman success was the combination of several key factors, discipline, cohesion, flexibility, command and control, superior equipment and well-honed skill at arms.

Training and tactical drills allowed the cohort to form up to a depth of four, six or more ranks to meet any immediate need. When in close order the men likely fought in files made up of individual eight-man squads or *contubernia*.[18] The squad was the most basic tactical unit, where close comradeship became the cement of daily function.

In combat, in fighting order, the men likely adopted a kind of 'chessboard' stance. Vegetius gives each soldier three feet of fighting space,

Polybius suggests rather more. Clearly this might vary according to training. This formation meant that the javelin or *pilum* could be thrown without the risk of injuring a comrade in front. Relentless training implied the men would be able to adopt whichever fighting order best suited the ground and the nature of the threat as it emerged. Good soldiers aren't automata, they respond through training and instinct. We talk about 'a soldiers' battle' and many of Caesar's fights were just that. In close country in the whirling scuffle of ambush or sudden contact, the general can't actually control the melée; he has to rely on the capacities of his men.

This is the essence of war, something that Caesar understood. Successful command is not all about tactics: these may be regarded as a given. Victory is brought about through logistics and the ability to concentrate, what Rupert Smith calls 'the utility of force'. The general who can ensure he has his forces in the right place and the right time and that they are fed, watered, supplied, supported and motivated, has already come a long way towards success. The legionary instinctively understands this. He knows all about hard marching and the hollowness of an empty belly. He won't tolerate fools and isn't shy about voicing an opinion. Officers are to be obeyed, even feared and sometimes revered but never God-like or unchallengeable.

When it came to manoeuvring for battle open ground was always to be preferred, bare of cover or impediment, ideally sloping to add momentum to the charge when it came:

> This is judged the more advantageous, the higher the ground occupied. For weapons descend with more violence onto men on a lower level, and the side which is higher dislodges those opposing them in greater force. He who struggles uphill enters a double contest with the ground and with the enemy.[19]

This changes if the infantry are facing cavalry where broken ground that can disorder the enemy charge is preferred, naturally for your own cavalry a clear run is preferable.

Trees were not liked. The astonishingly incompetent Quinctilius Varus danced to the tune of his nimble foe Arminius in the forests of Germany in 9 AD and led his legions to annihilation at the hands of enemies who, on open ground, they would have trounced in an hour. Command and control, essential tools for victory, could not be properly exercised out of sight. Controlling a classical-era battle once the troops were committed was no easy matter at the best of times. The commanding general needed to see how his units were performing and be able to adapt his plan to circumstances. Once that function became obscured it was lost.

Caesar is clear in a number of instances that battle lines were not continuous, gaps existed between formations, deliberately created.[20] This makes sound tactical sense; the commander needs to be able to shift units without destroying overall cohesion. These gaps were quite significant, possibly the width of a *maniple* allowing fresh men to come up.

Cavalry were generally deployed on the flanks:

> When the infantry line has been formed up, the cavalry are posted on the wings ... For the heavy cavalry should be used to protect the infantry's flanks, while the swift, light cavalry are for overwhelming and throwing into disorder the enemy's wings.[21]

Roman cavalry, the old equestrian order, had traditionally been drawn from the ranks of the better off – minor gentry or *equites*, only one rung down from senators. One suspects Caesar might have agreed with the Duke of Wellington on the worth of his own cavalry. Around three hundred horsemen were attached to each of the legions. Squadrons (*alae*) were split into troops or *turmae* divided again into core tactical units of decurions (*decuriae*). He didn't have a very high opinion of his cavalry's overall reliability. In Gaul he relied quite often and heavily on Germanic mercenaries, easily able to intimidate their Gallic enemies with their superior élan and who mixed mounted warriors with fast-moving infantry, an effective combination. The horses of the day were small, perhaps 13–14 hands at most. The Romans had hijacked the Gaulish saddle, which, in an age before stirrups, gave the rider a far more secure seat.

Junior battalion officers, the centurions, always fought and led from the front, often deploying on the extreme right of the first rank, the post of honour and maximum risk. Casualties could be high yet these officers were the army's vital cement. Effective leadership at this level was essential, always has been and always will. Any army thrives on the character of its NCOs and junior leaders. Centurions were a kind of hybrid version of the two. They often came from the same class as legionaries, though not always; some were of the middling sort, same as the cavalry, the *equestrian* order. Nonetheless, they spoke the same language as the legionaries yet enjoyed significant status and power. Where they were seen as brutal and corrupt (and they could be both) discipline and *esprit de corps* would suffer in consequence.

There was a mutiny amongst the legions stationed in Pannonia (modern-day western Hungary and Croatia) in 14 AD. At Emona (near Ljubljana), one particularly savage officer Lucilius – known as 'fetch another', after his brutish habit of breaking vine staffs over men's backs – was killed outright. A more senior officer, the camp prefect, a former ranker who loaded his legionaries up like Marius' mules was ritually humiliated by being burdened with the weight of kit he inflicted on others![22] In contrast, brave and inspiring officers, as Caesar confirms, could work miracles:

> In this legion there were two centurions, both men of great courage, and close to reaching senior rank. Their names were Titus Pullo and Lucius Vorenus.[23] There was always a dispute going on as to which had precedence over the other, and every year they clashed in fierce rivalry over the most important posts.[24]

During the protracted, hard-fought struggle against the Nervii, superb warriors all, Pullo shouts a challenge to Vorenus and charges the enemy. Not one to shirk, Vorenus leads his men out as well. Pullo gets stuck in, driving his javelin clean through one unlucky Gaul.

The man's comrades launched a counter-barrage of their own against Pullo, well out in front, splintering his shield and dislodging his sword belt. Now surrounded, the centurion was in real trouble. Until Lucius Vorenus barged into the melée and 'fought at close quarters, he killed one man and drove the rest off a short way'.[25] It was his turn to be surrounded, tripped and sprawling. Pullo, recovering his breath and his *gladius* weighed in, took the heat off Vorenus, giving him breath to get back on his feet. Fighting together, they accounted for a number of the Nervii. Both got back alive, 'It was impossible to decide which should be considered the braver of the two'.[26]

Such Henty-esque moments sound just like the Celts but it is actually very different. The Romans compete within the corporate sphere – they are soldiers, not individual warriors. They vie fiercely, they are ambitious for renown, but that will reflect on the unit as a whole as much as them as individuals. The Celts compete with each other for purely personal acclaim. What they achieve marks them out as great champions, a Hector or Achilles. The Roman soldier shares his tent with the rest of his eight-man section, living, messing, training, marching, fighting together all engenders the corporate spirit, a collective pride in being part of the elite. Soldiers refer to each other as 'brothers' – comrades. Juvenal, albeit in a satirical vein, sums up some of the values of army life:

> Who can count up the rewards of a successful army career? If you do well during your service, thy sky's the limit, there's nothing you can't hope for. Find me a lucky star to watch over my enlistment and I'd join up myself, walk through those barrack-gates as a humble recruit ... [27]

He goes on to list the benefits of a military career; civilians are wary of you, show you respect, don't take liberties. Anyone who does will find he's picked a fight with an entire regiment – those who mess together, live together and stick together.

In all, the legion would field sixty centurions, six per cohort. The officer who commanded the first century of the first cohort enjoyed the rank of *primus pilus*. This 'First Spear' would be a soldier of vast experience with outstanding leadership skills. Such men, though drawn at best from the middling sort, would sit in on the general's council and well-born young gentlemen would be expected to listen and act on their advice. As Dr. Fields points out, these tough professionals were the backbone of the army. Caesar conquered Gaul but his centurions fought the battles.

Standard bearers were seriously important, the totemic badge-holders of the unit. Yet they too fought in front. It was Marius who gave his legions their eagles (*aquila*), while each individual cohort had its own banner (*signa*). These standards, emblems of pride and tradition, were sacred. To lose the legion's eagle was an unimaginable disgrace and the rank of standard bearer – *aquilifer* or *signifier* – was a badge of trust. Men follow the banner, they inspire courage. They provide rallying points and their presence can shame the faint-hearted, as Caesar describes when his legionaries prepared to come ashore in Britain:

> Meanwhile our soldiers were hesitating, chiefly because the sea was so deep; then the man who carried the Eagle of the tenth legion appealed to the gods to see that his action turned out well for the legion, and said; 'Jump down, soldiers, unless you want to betray our Eagle to the enemy – I at least shall have done my duty to the Republic and my commander'.[28]

With that the standard bearer leapt into the surf and waded towards the enemy. Everyone followed, with a loud hurrah from every schoolboy who's learned the story ever since!

If the centurion was the lion of his unit, the NCO or *optio* was the policeman. His job was at the back rather than the front. That's where the rot starts. The soldier in the front line can't run, he's already hemmed in all round and very likely fighting for his life. The *optio* was stationed behind the line and funerary monuments show him equipped with a weighted staff,[29] literally to put some stick about. Even the best men can waver at times. Morale is never a fixed resource. Celtic armies were visually terrifying, very loud and adept at the psychology of battle. The trick was to stand firm, to hold the line and soak up the fury of the charge. Once that adrenalin-fuelled rush was played out, once the deadly *pila* and stabbing points had thinned out the ranks, then the wave would abate, and fury rapidly give way to despair.

Then they were beaten. And all that was left was the killing. Big casualties were sustained when one side broke and ran; abandoning their weapons and kit and generally you can't run in a helmet. Cavalry would swoop down in pursuit hacking down tired and demoralised survivors. Roman soldiers were good at killing, it was their trade. The short, workmanlike *gladius* could deprive an enemy of life with a single economical thrust, a surgical incision that pierced vital organs. Wounded left on the field had rather poor prospects. Findings from a mass grave from the English field of Towton, fought on Palm Sunday in 1461, revealed the majority of victims seem to have died from head wounds, often a terrible flurry of blows. Clearly none had helmets, suggesting these men had been fleeing, helmet-less, for their lives.

There is no learning curve like experience. Caesar was several times rescued by the readiness of his troops, men who understand what the situation demands without specifically needing to be told. Such experience saves the general's bacon during the desperate fight on the Sambre in 57 BC when the Gauls, using tree cover and their own astonishing speed of manoeuvre, attacked Caesar's legionaries labouring on their fortified camp:

> Two factors counter-balanced these difficulties. The first was the knowledge and experience of Caesar's men. Their training in previous battles had taught them what needed to be done, so they could just as easily devise their own orders as receive them from others. Secondly, Caesar had forbidden any of his officers to abandon either the defence-works or their individual legions before the fortification of the camp was complete. And in fact the enemy was so close at hand, and moving so swiftly, that those officers no longer thought of waiting for Caesar's orders but began to make dispositions of their own accord, as seemed necessary.[30]

Battle is always the ultimate test and no training or exercise can ever form a substitute. The Romans were very good at fighting battles. That was the purpose and objective behind campaigning – to bring the enemy to bay as quickly as possible. Rome, especially generals of the calibre of Marius and then Caesar, transformed classical warfare. It was to them an industrial process, linked to acquisition of territory, merely commercial expansion carried on by more direct means. Glory was worth having, it bought political capital but filling the Republic's (and the general's) coffers almost mattered more. Then as now, political patronage was an expensive business. Successful wars promoted the commander's status and his bank balance in equal measure. This was never risk free, Crassus came dramatically unstuck in Persia as later did Mark Anthony. Varus, had he lived, could have written his own treatise on the subject.

Once battle was joined, having flung their javelins, the legionaries would advance to meet the enemy charge. No jubilant rush this but a steady and inexorable movement to contact:

Then the heavy armament [infantry] took up the battle, and stood so to speak like a wall of iron, fighting it out with javelins and at close quarters with swords. Even if they routed the enemy, the heavy armament did not pursue, lest they disturb their own line and battle order, and the enemy charge back on them while dispersed and overwhelm them when disordered, but the light armament, with slingers, archers and cavalry pursued the fleeing foes. By adopting this disposition and these precautions, the legion would win without incurring danger, or if overcome was preserved intact; for the rule of the legion is neither to flee nor pursue easily.[31]

Normally, javelins wouldn't be thrown till the enemy was say, 30 metres away. Then the front rank moved smartly forward with swords drawn to exploit casualties and confusion caused by the volleys. This wasn't sophisticated elegant swordsmanship. Heavy shield bosses were used to batter opponents, knock them off balance and open them up for a decisive thrust, a single purposeful lunge, pushing the victim, now dying, back into his own ranks, disordering them further.

Time for the next one, repeating the process of butchery till the enemy broke, rear ranks spilling outwards to escape the inexorable killing. As they stamped and hacked forwards, their shields, helmets and armour protected the legionaries from the deluge of missiles zipping across the fight. Generally, Celtic forces would have their best-equipped fighters in the front line. When they went down, those further back were less protected and so more vulnerable. There was nothing vaguely romantic or chivalric in this business, the legionary's work. Personal honour and reputation had no part in the enterprise of slaughter.

As the Roman line punched forward, giving their deafening war-shout or *barritus*, the rear closed up, adding their *pila* to the barrage. Wounded legionaries could be carried clear and any gaps instantly filled so those coming into the fight were fresh. If the contest was drawn out, the second rank could shift their javelins, normally intended for throwing, to stab between the lines of swordsmen. Momentum and cohesion were preserved. The enemy was offered no chance to recover. Discipline, training and comradeship all combined to create a battle-winning formation. Wounded enemies still breathing would be swiftly dealt with and trampled.

Once the initial shock of collision had occurred, the fight, if the opposition had any fight left in them, would break down into series of smaller actions. Tactical flexibility meant the legionaries could function at squad level and above. Their enemies probably could not, certainly not with the same level of confidence and élan. As ever in war, victory went to the side that offers the other no respite, piles on the pressure and does not relax till they've taken the field.

Vegetius offers handy advice on deploying for battle. He stresses how important morale is. Soldiers shouldn't fight on empty stomachs nor should they be worn out by long approach marches. Traditionally the commander in chief 'usually stands between the infantry and cavalry on the right flank. This is the position from which the whole line is commanded, and from which there is direct and unobstructed forward movement. He stands between the two arms so as to be able to direct with his advice and exhort by his authority both cavalry and infantry'.[32] His second-in-command takes a central position among the infantry, having a strong reserve under his personal command to use as shock troops, either to form a *wedge* to splinter the enemy line or to form a pincer and pinch out any similar attempt by the opposition.[33]

The inexorable disintegration of Varus' force is a classic example of an irreversible decline in fighting capabilities brought on by bad leadership. In this earlier, late Republican age of the adventurers, the charisma of the commander in chief was paramount. Caesar embarked on the most ambitious adventure of all and tested his men to the limit. He was invariably outnumbered and occasionally, as by the Nervii, caught off balance. Until the climax of the 52 BC campaign, he was virtually out-smarted by Vercingetorix, yet he kept his army intact, turned the tables and won a dazzling victory that effectively completed his unparalleled conquest.

Pragmatism marched alongside the eagles. Each legionary's kit was pretty much standardised and while, in many ways, Romans weren't great innovators, they picked up on others' designs and applied their genius for mass production. The usual form of body armour was mail, *lorica hamata*, ironically and almost certainly, a Celtic invention. The mail shirt was reinforced over the shoulders by a further short cape secured with a double hook fastener. This harness came down to the wearer's hips and could weigh 12–13 kilos. Each contained around 40,000 separate rings.[34] Mail is flexible and the added shoulder guards would protect against a downward slashing blow of the sort favoured by Gallic swordsmen.

Helmet construction again was a Celtic derivative, often described as the 'jockey cap'. More exactly known as the 'Montefortino' pattern on account of a discovery of several bronze and iron survivors dating from the 4th century BC and found in a Celtic cemetery at Montefortino near Ancona. For four centuries this pattern was used by Roman legionaries and, as Peter Connolly estimates, in total over a million of them may have been manufactured.[35] The rounded bowl is raised or cast as a single piece with a distinctive jutting neck guard and attached ear pieces. It's secured under the chin and may, certainly at times, have sported a horsehair crest, possibly even feathers.

Only one example of a Republican-era shield or *scutum* (plural *scuta*) survives and that comes from El Faiyum on the Nile. The carcass is of birch, three-ply laminate, with opposing grain for extra strength. The wood is thicker in the middle and covered in lamb's-wool felt, doubled at the rim and stitched in place through the timber. The vulnerable rim was edged in protective bronze piping and the wooden boss also reinforced with additional bronze. It is a body shield, covering the soldier from shin to throat. When he crouched in his fighting stance it offered full protection. It was intended to be held stiffly in front rather than swung for parrying as one might with a handier buckler; at 8 kg, it is too heavy. The curve not only conforms to the body but provides deflection against hacking strokes. It came with a leather cover for all-weather protection on the march.[36]

His sword, the famously utilitarian *gladius hispaniensis*, was another piece of kit the legionary filched from Celtic adversaries sometime in the 3rd or 4th century BC. The blade was short and broad, no longer than 50 cm, with a long tapering point, intended for the surgical thrust. Combined with the curving *scutum*, the *gladius* formed a battle-winning duo. Even against physically larger opponents with a correspondingly extended reach, good sword drill would prevail, using the shield as a ram to counter the enemy's swing then lunging in with the point. To add deadliness to the thrust, blades were slightly thinner below the ricasso, 'waisted' to facilitate a deeper penetration.[37]

There's an old fighting dictum that asserts correctly that the point will always defeat the edge. Proper use of the gladius would reinforce this maxim across a hundred battlefields. Slashing strokes look good and can inflict fearful wounds but overall they're less likely to be fatal than a well-aimed thrust. The latter will puncture vital organs, leading to trauma, catastrophic tissue damage and a rapid bleeding out of the victim. A number of well-preserved swords were found near Mainz on the Rhine, associating the pattern with that city. Handles, with their distinctively contoured grips and rounded pommels, can be made from bone or wood, sometimes, if rarely, from metal. Scabbards, again true to their Iberian ancestry, were wood framed with bronze furniture and slung on the right side.[38] This seems an unnatural draw for a right-handed swordsman but was probably necessary with the bulky shield being carried on the left. It's a knack but not too hard to master with practice.

Marius', or latterly Caesar's, mules didn't just carry their arms and armour, they humped their personal kit, their bronze mess kit, cooking pot and canteen, plus rations and whatever additional tools they were burdened with. Beneath the chafing mail, which was normally only donned either for the fight or exposed marches in enemy country, the legionary wore a reinforced woollen utility tunic and studded leather marching sandals or *caligae*. On his left hip he carried a short, thick-bladed all-purpose fighting knife. He was very much a warrior for the working day, his looks pretty hard boiled and his kit distinctly lived in, though well maintained. After all he was paying for it.

As a missile weapon he hefted the fearsome javelin or *pilum*. This was a specialised yet universal piece of kit. It was typically over two metres in length with a long iron shank, topped by a pyramidal or barbed point. It was anti-personnel and anti-protection. The shank was fixed in place, tanged or socketed so it would bend on impact, weighing down an enemy's shield. That made it almost impossible to dislodge in the heat of the charge so rendering the shield useless. Easier to discard the shield even if this left the attacker exposed. The javelin volley was the essential opening move in the legionary's fight, the necessary precursor before the move to contact.[39]

Archers (*sagittarii*) and slingers (*funditores*) were specialists, recruited from the allies (auxiliary troops are a feature of the later Empire), or hired in as mercenaries – Cretan archers or Balearic slingers. The humble sling was a pretty effective instrument in skilled hands, as David demonstrated to Goliath. Slings were used in Ancient Egypt and were still appearing on battlefields as recently as the Spanish Civil War (1936–1939) when, rather than lead shot, they hurled grenades, adding considerably to the distance and accuracy of the throw. As ever, Vegetius is on the case:

> The inhabitants of the Balearic Islands [Majorca, Minorca, Ibiza et al] are said to have been the first to discover the use of slings and have practised with such expertise that mothers did not allow their small sons to touch any food unless they had hit it with a stone shot from a sling.[40]

He goes on to observe that, in the right hands, the sling is deadlier than the bow and that a man protected by helmet and cuirass is still vulnerable. It is easy to run out of arrows but small stones are usually in plentiful supply and the cohorts would cast their own lead shot. Recent archaeological work in Scotland has demonstrated that the sling shot might well have been pierced to ensure a loud whistling noise when it was released. Noise as a method of inducing terror is nothing new.

Archers were still important. The Cretans may have been the acknowledged masters but training with bows formed an integral aspect of the Roman system:

> Instructors should be chosen for this training who are experts, and greater care should be taken that (recruits) hold the bow scientifically, string it smartly, keep the left hand firm, draw the right with calculation, let the eye and mind concentrate together on the target to be hit, and learn to shoot straight whether from horseback or on foot.[41]

Both sieges and operations in the field were supported by artillery. As ever, the Romans borrowed their ideas for these heavier weapons from the Greeks. Stone-throwing *ballista* and arrow-shooting *catapulta* could be deployed in battle to support the legionary infantry. Some lighter, handier pieces look like large crossbows, standing around two metres in height and effective at ranges way beyond the reach of bows or slingshot. Called 'scorpions', the legion carried around three score of these and perhaps a few heavier weapons. The scorpion could pick a man from the rampart at several hundred metres in a sniping role, or could launch a barrage of suppressive fire, forcing defenders to keep their heads down.

An essential element in the universal soldier that was the Roman legionary lay in the fact he wasn't just a fighter; he was also a skilled tradesmen. He could build fortifications as well as he could knock them down – and the roads and bridges that led to them. He could be a surveyor, a mason, a carpenter, joiner, smith, road-builder, wheelwright, farrier or armourer. This was the essence of the Roman genius for warfare. All those hardy traits Vegetius cited came together in the legionary.

He was the complete professional and, in his own way, has never been surpassed. He held centre stage for the best part of a thousand years and whilst he suffered some dreadful hammerings – Cannae, Carrhae, the Teutoburger Wald – he showed enormous resilience and a constant ability to learn from his, or more often his commander's, mistakes. A recent commentator suggested that the army that emerges victorious is that which 'can best absorb its own cock-ups' as the British military maxim runs. As a one-sentence summary of the military art, that's pretty much spot on.

Where the legionary marched he built roads, that vast umbilical network that linked all outposts of empire. They could build over swamp and marsh, up dizzying gradients, bore through solid rock and stamp Rome's seal wherever they went. Roads didn't just facilitate marching troops and lines of supply; they brought trade and commerce, the arteries of *Pax Romana*. The old roads across Europe continued in use long after the demise of the eagles: when Rome and *Romanitas* were just mythical memories of a lost golden age. The legions built those roads, solid, sound, well drained and immensely durable.

They didn't necessarily enjoy it. Such laborious, back-breaking work was the source of much grousing. Civilian contractors weren't held in very high esteem: 'If you want a decent job done, get the army to do it'.[42] The psychological effect of these engineering feats could be as effective as winning a battle:

> After the battle he [Caesar] had a bridge built over the Saone and led his army across it to pursue the Helvetii. They were thrown into confusion by his unexpected arrival, and when they learned that he had taken only a day to cross the river, a task which had taken them twenty days – and then with extreme difficulty – they sent envoys to him.[43]

Impassable rivers and wet gap barriers were overcome by building bridges. Caesar crossed the great expanse of the Rhine, a feat beyond the imagining of the Celts. Probably near Coblenz, his engineers flung a timber trestle bridge clear across the mighty river, perhaps 500 metres wide and a good 8 m deep.[44] As with the Helvetii, the Germans were as impressed as they would have been by a major defeat. Superior technology equates to a victory often more lasting than one secured just by killing.

Siege warfare had existed since the time of the Trojan War. Alexander the Great and his successors had excelled at it. As ever, the Romans copied and expanded, taking the art to new heights. In essence the legions had two standard methods of approach. The first was to prepare for storming. Habitually (as at Avaricum – today's Bourges, in 52 BC), a series of ramps were constructed to provide a viable base for assault. Towers were constructed and dragged close to the walls so that infantry, covered by missiles, could fight their way in. Hazardous and strenuous as these operations were, such meticulous planning invariably paid off. Even the seemingly impregnable fortress of Masada would be breached by use of ramps, a truly Sisyphean feat.

As Joshua ably demonstrated, mining was an important tactic, as was the psychology of the siege. 'Shock and awe' have always been effective in sapping an enemy's will to resist:

> For the side wishing to enter the walls doubles the sense of panic in hopes of forcing a surrender by parading its forces equipped with terrible apparatus in a confused uproar of trumpets and men. Then because fear is more devastating to the inexperienced, while the townspeople are stupefied by the first assault if unfamiliar with the experience of danger, ladders are put up and the city invaded.

> But if the first attack is repelled by men of courage or by soldiers, the boldness
> of the besieged grows at once and the war is fought no longer by terror but by
> energy and skill.[45]

If it seemed that the strength of the defences and advantages of ground
(as at Alesia), were such that a direct escalade was out of the question
then the army would resort to blockade: surrounding the enemy citadel
with a ring of walls, forts and forward operational bases. This steel-tipped
ring would interdict any re-supply, frustrate any attempts at relief and
ultimately serve to starve the defenders into submission.

For the legionary, pioneering is a daily task. Every night he digs a
fortified encampment, surrounded by ditch and palisade, and puts up
heavy leather tents, one for each section, laid out in precisely the same
order. The camp resembled a permanent fort, gates facing north, south,
east and west; the main thoroughfare (*via principalis*) linked the left (*porta
principalis sinistra*) and right (*porta principalis dextra*). The commander's
tent was always pitched centrally with his officers ranged on both sides;
legionaries, cavalry and allies/auxiliaries knew their places. Uniformity
made for efficiency, cohesion and constant readiness.

At reveille, tents are struck, then loaded onto baggage animals and
finally, as the army is about to move off, the camp is levelled. The men
shout out in response to the herald's call that they are ready to march.
Three times the call to arms is repeated and the column steps forward.
At the front, the vanguard comprises auxiliary infantry and mounted
skirmishers. Behind them comes at least one legion with more cavalry.
Pioneers march near the front to clear obstacles and ensure smooth
passage for the army. The officers' baggage, precious as ever, comes next
followed by the commander in chief with his personal escort. Next
rides the rest of the cavalry, followed by the mule train. Behind them
the rest of the senior officers with their bodyguards and then the bulk of
legionary forces, each led by the standard-bearer, all marching six abreast.
Allied units, if any are serving, form the rear with a tail of cavalry and
probably some infantry. Above all the army fears being attacked when
deployed in column and the order of march can be varied to reflect the
nature and likely direction of the perceived threat.[46]

In the close, wooded terrain of Gaul, ambush was always a strong possibility. The Nervii, some of Caesar's toughest adversaries, used the sudden rush as a tactic. Caesar ordered his line of march to counter this possibility,

> ... sent his cavalry on ahead, and then followed with all his forces. But he employed a different order and strategy of march from the one the Belgae had reported to the Nervii. Because he was approaching an enemy Caesar was, as usual, leading the six legions carrying only light kit. He had put the whole army's baggage behind these legions, while the two legions most recently enlisted brought up the rear of the whole column and acted as rearguard for the baggage.[47]

At the same time he deployed his mounted and missile troops as aggressive skirmishers, keeping the screen of Gallic cavalry at a respectful distance. The Gauls used the encroaching woods as cover, the Romans dared not pursue too far. Gallic infantry massing under the blanket of trees waited till they could pounce on the baggage train before actually attacking. Caesar's cavalry halted the charge but the Celtic warriors pelted down the slope towards the river, using speed and manoeuvre to very good effect, got across and laid into the legionaries who were busy digging ditches for their camp. It became a very close-run thing indeed.[48]

Rome invested heavily in its soldiers, their training, subsistence and kit. It also looked after them. Medical services normally came under the aegis of a senior regular officer, the camp prefect (*praefectus castrorum*). The legion had its own medical staff and military surgeons such as the Greek Claudius Galenus (129–*c*. 200 AD), anglicised as Galen. Galen became highly adept in the treatment of wounds, leaving behind a series of medical texts that would form the basis of care across Europe well into the 17th century.

If, like one of us, you grew up in the shadow of Hadrian's great wall, it would be hard not to have conceived a respect for the legionaries. In seven summers, less time than would be required now to get planning permission, they built one of the greatest military monuments in history. They constructed a wall that stretched across the neck of Britain, studded with cohort-sized garrison forts, section outposts, milecastles and inter-vening turrets. Imagine what it would have looked like from the wrong side, leaping from crag to crag along the high escarpment of the Whin Sill in its most breathtaking stretch, possibly finished in dazzling white-wash: more than enough to overawe any locals or northern interlopers. The power and majesty of Rome proclaimed in sandstone, the northern flank of an empire whose southern border rested on the Euphrates.

Well-preserved forts such as Housesteads or Vindolanda (a survivor from the Agricolan frontier, the Stanegate), provide a wonderful insight into everyday life for the auxiliary units, both infantry and (in the case of Chesters and others), cavalry. You can visualise the forts as they were with a bustling settlement or *vicus*, sprawling beyond the south gate. Add a romantic temperament and a fondness for swords and you have the perfect playground. It was impossible for a small boy not to develop a liking for Rome – the *Aeneid* and *Gallic War* just added to the appeal. That this was foreign rule imposed on an often-unwilling local populace, that the wall imposed a false frontier where none had existed (and this certainly had consequences), didn't really count.

Some find it difficult to identify or sympathise with the Celts, we see them as vain, disorganised, shallow and untrustworthy but then we only have, as have generations of equally unwilling scholars before, Caesar's word on that. For some reason everyone thinks they would have been the Romans! The Celts were the *impi* at Rorke's Drift and Romans were the redcoats. *Zulu* with Stanley Baker and Michael Caine has a lot to answer for.

It was that 'article' as Wellington might have described him, the Roman legionary soldier, the distillation of half a millennium of experience and adaptation that empowered Caesar to conquer Gaul and allowed him, despite the difficulties and reverses of the 52 BC campaign, to finally get the better of Vercingetorix and bring him to bay and corral him at Alesia.

CHAPTER 3

WAY OF THE GAUL

The whole of Gaul is divided into three parts.... [1]

Many of a certain age will remember that famous opening line as their introduction to Latin. In Britain we had our Vercingetorix, Boudicca, who like him, became something of a nationalist icon in the 19th century. Unsurprisingly, she gets a poor write up from Tacitus: 'veterans were butchered, colonies burned to the ground, armies isolated'.[2] Boudicca's reign of terror and the relentless slaughter of her campaign were presented in the worst of terms whereas the Ladybird book, *Julius Caesar and Roman Britain*,[3] portrayed the future governor and his commander in chief as gilded and dashing Hollywood types and the Celts as gallant losers. And we didn't like losers. The tale of Boudicca could have come straight from the *Tain*, that collection of Celtic stories that depicted Irish warriors in all their violent glory, fractious, obsessed with honour whilst capable of astonishing duplicity.

Then you meet the Lady of Vix who died around 500 BC and was buried in the village of the same name in northern Burgundy. The most significant find amongst her splendid grave goods was the mighty *krater* or cauldron. These vessels were used for mixing wine and water. While the whole thing is made up of seven pieces, the vast bowl is raised from a single sheet of bronze. This Greek import stands 1.63 metres tall, weighs 200 kg and has a capacity of 1,100 litres – that's quite a hangover. You can tell it's Greek from the frieze of hoplites marching around the neck.

'Impressive' doesn't quite cover it. The thing is awesome – for once the adjective is deserved as the Vix Cauldron does indeed inspire awe. The sight of it opens a window into Celtic civilisation and shows it to be really very civilised. A culture endowed with enormous wealth and fascinating complexity.

Once we begin to look at 'Celtic' life we begin to see something quite remarkable and perhaps less alien than Caesar implies. Something very familiar. The great hillforts of southern England, Hod Hill or, most famously Maiden Castle, where Mortimer Wheeler's excavations revealed traces of the doomed, desperate last stand against Vespasian, are immense and thoroughly engineered structures. Those in Gaul, Avaricum, Bibracte, Gergovia and Alesia far more so, evidences of a highly sophisticated culture.

Caesar is pretty emphatic about his three regions but was writing for domestic consumption which recognised him (even his enemies) as the local expert: 'one of which the Belgae inhabit, the Aquetani another and the third a people who in their own language are called "Celts", but in ours "Gauls"'.[4]

The term Celts, as Dr. Fields points out,[5] is a constant source of controversy. Both Greek and Roman writers use the term sweepingly to refer to a broad swath of peoples living within a wide belt of territories north of the Mediterranean. They are generally perceived as barbarians, viewed with a mix of fear, grudging fascination and contempt. Nonetheless, it was these same unkempt savages who had occupied Rome in 390 BC and humiliated the Republic. This element of terror would colour relations. At no point were these peoples united, they shared cultural similarities but there was never any attempt at political cohesion, at least not until Vercingetorix.

Tacitus, writing of his father-in-law's time, the late 1st century AD, and about Britain rather than Gaul, is no more complimentary:

> On a general estimate, however, we may believe that it was Gauls who took possession of the neighbouring island. In both countries you will find the same ritual, the same religious beliefs. There is no great difference in language, and there is the same hardihood in challenging danger, the same subsequent cowardice in shirking it... Their strength is in their infantry.[6]

What we would broadly term 'Celtic' (and nobody can agree on the correct term, it's not a description the people themselves would ever have recognised) civilisation begins in the late Bronze Age, say 1300 BC, roughly around the time of Troy and in the Upper Danube region. Six centuries or so later iron had replaced bronze and the beginnings of the Celtic Iron Age are named after Hallstatt in Austria.

Celts, Gauls, and Galatians. As Alice Roberts points out, 'These three names sometimes seem to coincide in meaning. At other times they are used to differentiate between different levels of ethnic groupings: Celts within the larger territory of Gaul: Celts as a group of tribes in the West and Galations as a group of tribes in the East. Celts and Galations are essentially the same and referring to anyone living across a huge territory, maximally defined as stretching from Iberia to Central Europe'.[7] How this grouping spread across Europe is still under investigation. The old theories which showed them spreading through what would become Gaul, into the Iberian peninsula and across the Channel into southern England have been challenged by the work of archaeologists like Barry Cunliffe. A new focus on the Atlantic Fringe is bringing to light the challenging complexities of these remarkable people. A people with differing languages, customs and social organisation. They had as much to distinguish them as they had in common.

Quite what factors drove these groups to settle over such a wide area in wave after wave is open to debate. Overpopulation and the need for land certainly played a role in the move of the Helveti in the 1st century BC. Classical writers asserted it was simply a love of brawling, pillaging and wine! In some ways, that would fit with what were regarded as virtues by these communities.

Hallstatt culture fused with the subsequent La Tène culture (from the region around Lake Neuchatel in Switzerland), in around 500 BC. The earlier traditions were overlaid with Mediterranean influences to create a vibrant and distinctive hybrid. Note the use of the term culture: it seems to be a spread of ideas, artefacts and art rather than of people or languages. This awakening spurred the Celts to successfully take on both Rome and Greece whilst also spilling across into Anatolia.

> The River Garonne divides the Gauls from the Aquitani, and the Marne and Seine rivers separate them from the Belgae. Of these three, the Belgae are the bravest, for they are furthest away, for they are the furthest away from the civilisation and culture of the Province.[8]

Caesar equates boisterous vigour with remoteness from civilising influences. Tacitus later picks up on this same thread,

> the peoples nearest to the Gauls are correspondingly like them. Perhaps the original strain persists; perhaps it is climatic conditions that determine physical type in lands that converge from opposite directions on a single point. But the Britons show more spirit; they have not yet been softened by protracted peace. The Gauls, too, we have been told, had their hour of military glory; but then came decadence with peace and valour went the way of lost liberty…[9]

Collectively these 'free' areas of Gaul were referred to as *Gallia Comata* (literally 'long-haired' or 'hairy' Gaul), a derogatory term similar to that later adopted for the British – *Britunculi* i.e. 'wretched Britons'. The 'Province' to which Caesar refers was the southern part of Gaul, *Gallia Transalpina* 'over the Alps' as opposed to *Gallia Cisaplina* 'this side of the Alps'. The province was already integrated into the empire, consolidated by Marius' victories half a century beforehand. Caesar's predecessor had fortified Aix-en-Provence (*Aquae Sextiae*) as a border post and the port of Marseilles, originally a Greek colony, was a booming entrepôt.

In Rome, the security of the province mattered very much. It was the land bridge/balcony between the Republic, Spain and the interior of Gaul, a vital trading umbilical. Cicero boasted, correctly no doubt, that the province was full of Romans and Gaul full of Latin merchants, fuelled by the wine trade.[10]

Any threat to the province would be taken very seriously indeed and it would be just such a perceived threat that would provide Caesar with his pretext for war in 58 BC.

'They live, moreover, in close proximity to the Germans who inhabit the land across the Rhine, and they are continually at war with them'.[11] To a Roman reader of the 1st century BC, the Rhine was the edge of the world and the Germans the last word in barbarism. In reality, the boundaries between Celt and German were far more blurred and fluid.

What we'd now call northern France, past the Seine and the ground on both sides of the Rhine, was far more shaded than divided, constantly being refreshed by the shifting sands of migration and cross-fertilisation. Caesar liked clear definitions, it was easier for his readers and what he was really writing about was Caesar and his accomplishments, the natives were just wallpaper.

If the hairy Gauls were uncouth, then the Germans, living east of the Rhine, were proper savages: 'The Suebi are by far the greatest and most aggressive of all the German peoples. It is said they possess a hundred villages, from each of which they take a thousand armed men every year for waging war outside their own territory.' He goes on to report that the Germans don't have any form of private land tenure, they are essentially semi-nomadic. They're immeasurably tough and disciplined, inured to hardship 'which nourishes their strength and produces men of enormous physical stature. They have, moreover, trained themselves by constant practice, so that however cold the region they wear no other clothing than skins, which are so small that most of the body is left uncovered; and they bathe in the rivers.'[12] Anyone who has ever tried wild swimming will appreciate just how cold that can be and how tough that makes the Germans.

Though the Celts, if we can call them that, dominated Gaul, they were not necessarily the only inhabitants. The older strains still lingered. In Armorica (Brittany), Nora Chadwick clearly identifies some of the tribal names as being pre-Gallic.[13] It may be that Caesar rather misidentifies the inhabitants of Aquitania as being Gauls. Strabo informs us that the people were closer in character to the Iberians. Pride and independence of spirit were seen as Celtic traits. Dio Cassius tells us the story of a Caledonian gentlewoman, on being teased by Septimius Severus' wife, Julia Augusta, on the subject of what we might now call 'free love'. The Pict haughtily replied; 'we fulfill the demands of nature in a much better way than do you Roman women; for we consort openly with the best men, whereas you let yourselves be debauched in secret by the vilest'.[14]

The Celts' occupation of Gaul occurred piecemeal, not the result of any planned or centrally directed strategy – very different to Caesar's conquest. The early settlers probably moved in over an extended period, individual war bands filtered into the valleys, staked out their turf, gradually extending and consolidating over time. Various clans or tribes coalesced into loose alliances and very frequently fought among themselves. Early collisions occurred with Rome's interests when, as the Gauls penetrated southwards, they linked up with the indigenous Ligurians of Provence and used their combined strength to have a crack at the temptingly rich prize of Marseilles. Twice in succeeding generations Rome was obliged to intervene, in 154 and 125 BC. It was the second relief that resulted in the establishment of the province.[15]

It was probably during the 3rd century BC that Celtic expansion peaked. From then on they would be under pressure from Germanic peoples to the north and east and from the spreading influence of Rome to the south. In 225 BC the Celts in what became Cisalpine Gaul were well and truly hammered at the battle of Telamon, leading to Rome's takeover of the region. The reduction of Carthage cleared the field, facilitating the conquest of Iberia. The acquisition of the province created the springboard for further Roman expansion. The emergence of a conqueror such as Caesar became inevitable.

In the dark and distant north, the formidable Belgae, including Caesar's inveterate and formidable adversaries the Nervii and Bellovaci, were relative newcomers, displaced by upheavals east of the Rhine in the 3rd and 4th centuries BC. The Bellovaci were great fortress builders though the Belgae as a whole tended to be more rural without much urbanisation.[16] It was the Belgae who'd colonised much of southern England, finally pushing up to what would become the border-lands. In the decades preceding Caesar, the Gallic polity comprised sixteen larger confederations (*civitates*), themselves agglomerations of sub-units or *pagi*. Caesar tells us of four such groupings within the Helvetii and half a dozen for the powerful Aedui, centred on their grand stronghold of Bibracte.

He is equally terse on the structure of Gallic society: 'In the whole of Gaul two types of men are counted as being of worth and distinction. The ordinary people are considered almost as slaves; they dare do nothing on their own account and are not called to councils.'[17] Caesar is enormously valuable as the only written source on the Gauls. But he views them from a Roman perspective and that severely limits his understanding. Gallic society was not based on principles he could recognise. Or rather, the many Gallic societies were not.

Any description of the politics and society of Celtic Gaul has to deal with one fundamental problem: the inhabitants did not leave a written record, theirs was an oral society. What they have left us are physical remains: their art, their artefacts and the landscapes they inhabited. Archaeology offers many clues, as does anthropology. By studying other communities for which we have a firmer record we can infer a great deal. In Ireland, for example, ancient stories were handed down for generations. Changed by the passage of time, they still have recognisable and persistent themes e.g. the responsibilities of kingship. Those stories were codified in the Middle Ages so are still available. Obviously, care needs to be exercised in the use of what is, at best, semi-fictional material. However, taken in conjunction with the physical evidence and the historical record left by the Celts' neighbours in Greece and Rome, we have a significant body of material. It is necessary to take the accounts of those neighbours with a pinch of salt: after all Caesar did have his own agenda when writing about Gaul in *Bello Gallico*. Caesar, like many another writer also had difficulty in seeing alien cultural norms in their own terms. His description of *oppida* reflects this – he appears to regard them as the direct equivalent of a large Roman town or city. The story is a bit more complicated.

Oppida were large fortified (usually urban) settlements. We find them in many Celtic areas, regardless of the relationships between the tribes or communities. Gaul, Danubia and the right bank of the Rhine all have them. There are rural structures too, mostly open air like the *nemeta*, which seem to have had a ritual function. The Romans took a dim view of these sacred groves (they often utilised trees and natural space) reflecting their horror and suspicion of Druids. Here is Lucan on the subject:

> No bird nested in the *nemeton*, nor did any animal lurk nearby; the leaves constantly shivered though no breeze stirred. Altars stood in its midst, and the

images of the gods. Every tree was stained with sacrificial blood. The very earth groaned, dead yews revived; unconsumed trees were surrounded with flame, and huge serpents twined round the oaks. The people feared to approach the grove, and even the priest would not walk there at midday or midnight lest he should then meet its divine guardian.[18]

The *nemeta* appear to have been extensive but mostly survive now as inscriptions and place names. There are one or two that still offer some remains, Nemetobriga in Portugal for example. Those place names give us interesting clues to the size of the rural population. Areas with many (e.g. south Germany) suggest it was substantial.

Oppida are a late arrival in the Celtic world (2nd–3rd century BC) and appear to represent a bit of a transition. By this time the hillfort of the late Bronze Age has been influenced by contact with southern Europe. The *oppida* have a Mediterranean feel to them. Massive external walls typically enclose a spacious layout with a commanding view of the surrounding area. Caesar came up with the term, although today it is routinely used to describe major circular earth works dating from the Late Iron Age. It has been suggested that the large central enclosures were intended to act as a refuge in time of conflict. If this is correct the space available suggests a sizeable local population, possibly from the rural hinterland as well as the more urbanised settlements nearby. Archaeology is giving us evidence of increasing numbers of unwalled farming communities and of manufacturing sites.

Caesar categorises Gaulish settlements as *oppida* (fortified towns), *vici* (villages), or *aedificia* (farmsteads). It's a pattern of settlement confirmed by modern excavation that suggests that the *oppida* had a function rather akin to the developing cities of England in the 17th century. Too large to be self sufficient, they functioned as storage and trading points. Animals and crops from the surrounding countryside would make their way here to be traded for processed raw materials or shipped on to be swapped for objects of desire (such as wine). A marketplace such as this requires a medium of exchange and it is no coincidence that we see small bronze (and increasingly gold) coins appearing in the 2nd century.

The number of mints, and a reduction in the amount of precious metal in coinage increased as circulation grew. At some point coins become the norm as a means of payment and provide a useful clue to the scale of trade: the greater the rate of exchange, the larger the number and types of coin. Terracotta dies used in the minting process have been found on many sites alongside artefacts of increasing quality and far-flung points of origin. Trading contacts with Rome led to the establishment of Roman trading posts in the *oppida*. Ceasar highlights the importance of a number of large *oppida* in areas outside Roman control as well as those within Rome's sphere of influence. *Urbs* he calls them, referring to sites like Alesia and Gergovia. He is well aware of the *oppida* as key locations in Gaulish political, economic and cultural life that also makes them ideal for use as a fortified Roman outpost. He lists sites for 29 different tribes, sometimes with more than one *oppida* per group. The Helveti, for example, had twelve.

Oppida were not the only trading or production points. The excavation of numerous unfortified sites that show evidence of pottery or metal workshops, often close to navigable waterways or crossing points, suggests significant trading potential as well as a population base. Archaeology has also given us a number of smaller urban settlements, possibly the loci of small territories (e.g. a *pagus*). Unsurprisingly, given the varied nature of Celtic society, these settlements all vary. Location and importance have an impact on layout and function, though there are many common features.

The variety of activities in these towns was immense. There is evidence of mining and metallurgy, including the forging of weapons and ornaments, woodworking, tool making for a wide variety of activities from fishing to medical instruments and, of course, a vast number of production processes needed to equip horses and wagons for domestic and other uses.

Perhaps the largest *oppidum* we know of is that of Manching in Bavaria. Occupied from the 3rd to the 1st centuries BC, estimates place its population in the range of 5,000–10,000. At its height (2nd century BC) it covered 380 hectares. Like so many of the *oppida*, large plots were left uncluttered for grazing livestock. Alice Roberts in her excellent book, *The Celts*, offers a personal experience of another *oppida*, Heuneberg in southern Germany. Located between Hallstatt and La Tène, the site appears to have been extensively occupied from the middle Bronze Age. It was at its height during the 7th–5th centuries BC when it traded extensively with the Mediterranean, taking on board some exotic building styles and construction techniques. Alice Roberts reports handling pottery that appeared to be Greek and Etruscan in origin.

The citadel itself, 'encircled by its whitewashed mud-brick wall'[19] was big enough to house around 2,000 people. But continuing research, using LIDAR technology, has revealed a major surprise outside the fortified area. What had been thought to be a respectable lower town proved far more complex. Two substantial sub towns, a network of palisaded and banked farms that may have housed individual extended families, have increased the potential population for the upper settlement alone to 5,000–10,000 in the 7th–5th centuries BC. The lower settlement may have housed as many again. Like so many important *oppida*, Heuneberg sits just north of the Alps on important trade routes from Italy and southern France. Its position on the Danube gave it a potential river connection to the Balkans and the Black Sea. The evidence of grave goods, many of them luxury items, speaks to the wealth of the town and suggests an equally large hinterland. Archaeologists have calculated that the citadel and its sub towns could not have fed themselves and would have required substantial supplies from elsewhere.

They were also very well defended – excavation often reveals a complex and detailed pattern of extremely well-constructed ramparts and oblique gateways.

Even Caesar was impressed:

> All Gallic walls follow virtually the same pattern. At right angles to the wall, along its entire length, beams are placed in the ground at equal intervals, two feet apart. These are secured firmly from the inside, and then covered with large amounts of rubble; the intervals between them are filled with large rocks at the front. Once the beams are laid and joined, another level is added on top; the length and the gaps remain the same, but the second set of beams does not touch the first. Rather, because the spaces in-between the beams are the same, each one is kept firmly separate by single stones. The whole construction is built in this manner until the wall reaches the appropriate height.[20]

The rubble core is faced off with finely dressed stones, leaving the heads of the beams, averaging forty feet in length, exposed, 'the finished edifice is not unattractive', Caesar somewhat grudgingly conceded. He also noted the practical benefits; the stones are proof against fire while the timbers make battering almost totally ineffective. The beams are secured by long iron spikes or nails. Caesar christens this work as *murus Gallicus* – literally 'Gallic wall' and the description has stuck.

One of the most impressive, if not the most impressive, of all these great cities is Mont Beuvray, ancient Bibracte, the Aeduan capital. It was here Vercingetorix held his great council and where Caesar, pointedly, over-wintered in 52–51 BC. The site stands around 20 kilometres west of Autun. It's very big. The inner ramparts alone extend for 5.25 kilometres and the sweeping summits encompassed by the walls rise to 800 metres. It's an astonishing site, vast in area and offers an insight into just how grand a major town or *oppidum* might have been and would have appeared.

Much excavation has been undertaken since the mid-19th century with sections of the wall and the north-east gate, Porte du Rebout, superbly reconstructed. The internal space measures 135 hectares. This isn't a mere village, it is a massive enclosure by any standards and the careful rebuilding shows just how formidable these Gallic walls must have been.[21] With any defended space, the point of access and egress (usually the gateways) are the point of maximum vulnerability. Many forts had strong gatehouses or *torhaus* – one of the most impressive is at Manching, with twin access ways for vehicles flanked by separate pedestrian footways. The gates were hung and housed within a defended timber-framed *torhaus*.

Bibracte, on the other hand appears to have been different. There's no real archaeological evidence to support the idea of a large timber structure and the gap at Porte du Rebout is very wide at 19 metres and may have been undefended.[22] This seems very odd given the massive construction of the walls but it may be that the space was left open to allow for the heavy volume of traffic and some form of wooden palisade thrown across the gap if it had to be defended. The angle of the two flanking bastions would have left any direct assault exposed to shooting from the walls.

Nico Roymans[23] took on the subject of the organisation of Gaulish society in the 1990s using a combination of historical and archaeological evidence to compare northern and southern Gaul. He focused on the area bounded by the Channel, the Rhine, the Seine and the Marne rivers, studying the ways in which the political and social structures of what would become Germany through the Low Country mirrored or contrasted with the area of the Aisne and Somme basins. In so doing he gives us a useful summation, confirming many of the views of this society taken from other sources. He incorporates an anthropological approach, particularly those theories relating to the organisation of tribal societies to provide a general framework of reference and ethnographic comparisons derived from later historical data on the Irish Celts and north Germanic societies.

Roymans concludes, 'these pre-Roman societies had a segmentary structure; they consisted of a number of subgroups or segments, which, in turn, consisted of smaller segments. Within the tribal formations three political levels can be distinguished, i.e. the local groups, the pagi, and the tribes, or civitates'. The term *pagus* (plural *pagi*) refers to a sub territory within a small regional polity, typically pre-urban. *Civitates* refers to the body of citizens or tribe (although we need to be careful not to confer citizen status on the Gauls, they were a profoundly hierarchical society).

The basic unit of society was the kinship group (*sub pagus*) based on family or affinity and incorporating friends, clients and slaves. Kinship groups formed local communities (Caesar calls the unit a *domus*), typically with a local leader who exercised authority as a kind of *paterfamilias*. This local leader would often also be the head of a prominent local family, with several wives, many servants/slaves and clients. The Germanic version formed their own units of infantry and cavalry, which also operated as separate units in military actions. The *domus* collectively provided hostages and received compensation for ending feuds, which were endemic. Rivalries, disputes, competition and feud were rife in Celtic society, requiring a complex system of law and code to resolve. Inevitably these groups acquired names, some of them derived from founding individuals, others from geographical locations.

Groups occupied a hierarchical structure – differences in group size, status, wealth, degree of nobility, and, above all, power and political influence marked them out. At the top stood, if one existed, a royal family, followed by the important families of the nobility. At the bottom were the groups with the least status and power. Any council of nobles may well have incorporated the heads of those groups.

Subtribes (the *pagus*) appears to have formed their own armies, which came into action as separate combat units during military operations. That a *pagus* operated as a military unit implies that it enjoyed a certain political autonomy. An extreme case arc the Morini, who, in 55 BC, made a treaty with Caesar with the exception of those *pagi* who were opposed to negotiating with the Romans.[24] *Pagi*, certainly in the case of the Irish, often had a petty king. This figure, like more important kings above him could well have derived his position through the tanistry system which required a suitable candidate to be effectively elected by a select group drawn from his affinity.

Irish society offers an interesting insight into the potential powers and limitation of kingship. We are told that the *tuath* (the equivalent of the *pagus*) was 'a group of people sufficiently large to be ruled by a king, and conscious of their otherness from neighbouring groups'.[25] A number of *tuatha* constituted a larger tribal entity, which was comparable to the Gallic *civitas* in size and dominated by a high king. The *tuath* had an *oenach*, or public assembly institution, where important political issues were discussed, athletic games played, and, presumably a lot of drinking was done. A king could make a treaty with another king, but this only had binding force after proclamation at the *oenach*.

A picture emerges of the tribes: large units who bear their own names, make decisions about war and peace, have their own political and military leaders, and their own political structures – be it a public assembly, a council of nobles, and/or (in some tribes) a system of kingship. At inter-tribal level, we only find loose alliances and fluid dependencies. Nor were the tribes necessarily stable. Fissiparous tendencies were as endemic as feuding and drinking: shifting loyalties and alliances could see new groupings emerge as tribes split and reworked themselves.

Women enjoyed a complex status in Gallic society. On the one hand they had a place on the battlefield and enjoyed a high social status, particularly as marriage partners cementing relationships between the various groupings. Most marriages were endogamous, that is individual members sought a marriage partner within their own tribe. An exception, however, was the members of the leading aristocratic families, who for political reasons kept up an intertribal marriage network. On the other hand polygamy – a marriage form in which one male was legally married to two or more females at the same time and not a practice that suggests anything approaching gender equality – was also practised in aristocratic circles. Women played a key role in the formation of alliances between tribes.

Once married, the husband was expected to contribute a sum equal to his wife's dowry and maintain this as the family pot of capital, to be invested and the profits shared evenly; ownership of the pot passed by survivorship. Nonetheless, the man or rank had power of life and death over both spouse and offspring. If such a man died in suspicious circumstances, his wives could be interrogated, if necessary under torture.[26]

The power of a leader was determined by a number of factors, including his alliances with other leaders from within his own community and with neighbouring tribes. Such alliances could include long-lasting treaties as well as short-lived military agreements. Typically accompanied by an exchange of gifts, the giving of women in marriage sealed the deal. The woman was a token of alliance; she created a political tie between the group who gave her away and the group who received her, reinforced by the system of dowry and bride price. Caesar tells us of Dumnorix, a man of great power. He had married his mother to the noblest and most powerful man of the Bituriges, he had taken himself a wife from the Helvetii, and had married his half-sister and his female relations to men of other clans. A marriage tie, however, did not always guarantee a lasting alliance, as is illustrated by the bitter power fight between the Treverian Indutiomarus and his son-in-law Cingetorix.

In a society in which kinship played such an important role, descent mattered. Important political ties were established by marriage between members of leading aristocratic families and, above all, by sacred genealogies, in which entire peoples, subgroups or individual families traced their descent from mythical ancestors, usually gods or demigods. This belief in the sacred origin of a social group was a deeply rooted. Indeed, it still holds: It is nothing short of amazing how many Irish claim to be descended from Brian Boru. Fostering, the placing of a child in the household of another member of the affinity group, was another method of creating a shared descent. The old tales are full of fosterlings whose conflict in later life has all the resonance of a conflict between blood relatives. To some degree those tales reflect another factor holding communities together. Co-residence, sharing territory or home could also create affinity between clans with little blood relationship. The inclusion of servants, slaves and clients in a household was not uncommon. Whilst they may have been of low status, they were viewed as members of the group rather than outsiders.

There is common agreement that Celtic societies were extremely warlike. 'It seems that it was important to Celtic warriors, and probably to their status and identity to have something warlike to do and this need appears to have been satisfied by raiding or by fighting as mercenaries'.[27] Roman commentators noted a tendency to quarrel and fight at the drop of a hat, viewing it as a sign of weakness. Ironically, this quarrelsome propensity is something that was probably a matter of pride to the participants.

Tacitus tells us how important to young men was the public initiation rite carried out on reaching the age required for becoming a warrior. He says of the Germans,

> ... yet the custom is ... no one takes arms until the tribe has endorsed his future competence: then in the assembly itself one of the chiefs or his father or his relatives equip the young man with shield and spear; this ... is youth's first public distinction; hitherto he seems a member of the community. Among the Chatti, the newly initiated youths let their beard and hair grow until they had killed their first enemy; the most valiant also wore an iron ring, a symbol of self-humiliation, which they took off only after the death of an adversary.[28]

Caesar refers to similar practices among the Gauls:

> They do not allow their own sons to approach them openly until they have grown to an age when they can bear the burden of military service, and they count it a disgrace for a son who is still in his boyhood to take place publicly in the presence of his father.[29]

Caesar may well have been referring to the practice of fostering that, as well as providing the equivalent of a medieval squire's training, also helped to cement relationships and alliances. Indeed there is some evidence that young men may have been sent to something like a military school. The Irish oral tradition in particular has numerous references to such educational 'establishments'. Because of its strongly military character, the *iuventus* (the group of young men who had most recently taken their place as warriors) probably had a political influence. Roymans cites Dobesch[30] on north Italian tribes in the 2nd century BC. The *iuventus* rebelled against the elders of the tribe, meeting in assembly to form their own army and begin a war.

Oddly, one characteristic shared by Roman and Celtic societies was a system of clientship, albeit in rather different forms. Caesar notes that the lower orders of Gallic society were treated little better than slaves. While this undoubtedly has an element of truth to it, it is also a gross simplification and highlights Caesar's failure to recognise a society more complex than it first appeared. Clientship permeated Gallic relationships, politics, culture and art. The great cauldrons used for feasting found in higher-status tombs reflect the need for a leader to be seen publicly display-ing generosity, creating and cementing relationships and emphasising their own status by the quality of their provision, taking the opportunity for period reward. Membership of the tribal elite required the largest possible collection of clients, the tool of power as well as the expression of it. By its very nature, clientship is hierarchical; the patron provides protection, influence and material goods while the client offers services (including military ones) and recognition of the difference in social standing.

For the Gauls, clientship cut across all networks. Asymmetrical obli-gations existed not only between tribal leaders and lower social groups, but also among the tribal elite. The nobility recruited clients first from their own local group or within the wider circle of their *pagus* but it did not stop there. Members of other subtribes or even tribes could become linked in this way, sometimes creating obligations that cut across those of kinship. At its simplest the system dictated a sort of social contract between nobles and their own lower orders (free and unfree). These 'base clients' were occupied primarily with subsistence activities, yet could also furnish military services. Networks of clients also existed within the nobility, appearing to be factions from the outside but actually reflecting a more complex reality. For example, Caesar tells us of two factions within the Treveri. One, led by Cingetorix could be seen as sympathetic to Rome. The second, under Indutiomarus (markedly opposed to Rome), staged a successful grab for power in 54 BC, ousting their opposition and confiscating the possessions of Cingetorix.

Powerful tribes would take other lesser tribes as clients offering protection in exchange for tribute and military service. Sometimes the arrangement was consensual but it could also be imposed, with hostages required to stand surety for their clans. Ties such as this could exist at a number of different social levels leading to what Roymans calls clientage 'pyramids', complex networks of vertical relations among individuals and groups of people which cross-cut tribal boundaries and were headed by powerful paramount leaders.

Ironically, a society of warriors may find it difficult to recruit a standing army. An emphasis on personal glory and prowess makes taking orders a tad difficult. Clientship offered a way round this. By the 1st century BC tribal nobles had sufficient wealth to permanently surround themselves with a body of horsemen, an elite force. The material rewards offered to them by their patron were seen in relationship, rather than employee, terms. Caesar quotes numerous examples of war leaders supported by groups of followers who show more than the obligations of duty. Of course, there was also a larger substrate, people of lower status discharging a more basic obligation.

Forming and running a client network required wealth, a large and continuous investment of wealth, publicly displayed to reinforce the status of its possessor. Most potent are those goods that are hard to obtain, have value in their own right (e.g. gold) or represent a long trading arm. Archaeology reveals them in quantity, drawn from graves, rivers and settlements. Amongst the elite we find the insignia of high status. e.g. golden ornaments (especially torcs) ornamented chariots, costly horse harnesses, and bronze vessels imported from Italy. Lower down the social ladder we find less valuable but still prizeworthy items, such as iron weapons, bronze ornaments, gold coins, and that beloved object of all Celts, the horse.

We learn a great deal about lower-level clientship from early Irish society. Free or unfree, they still had a connection, but the former could break off the relation with their leader, whereas the latter could not. The clients received a holding from their lord and promised to make a yearly payment in goods, usually cattle and to provide a number of services including military service. The lord would reciprocate by loaning cattle, seldom land. The archaeological records tells us a great deal about the importance of cattle raising and the use of cattle as a 'primitive money', suggesting that conditions were similar in Gaul. Indeed, Caesar implies that the connections were expanding. He notes that those at the bottom of the pile faced increasing economic pressure. So many free farmers were weighed down by heavy burdens of debt that they were forced to give up their free status and to enter into a dependent relationship with the nobility. That had major benefits for the elite – a substantial agrarian surplus had to be available if they were to sustain a retinue, give feasts and redistribute produce to clients, which were all activities necessary for the effective pursuit of power, allowing the patron to strengthen the bonds of clientage and foster alliances.

It was not simply the lowest-level Gauls who provided access to agricultural surpluses. More or less obligatory tribute payments by free families to heads of local groups could be modest but it would reinforce the bonds of connection. 'It is the custom in their civitates to bestow upon the principes unasked and man by man some portion of one's cattle or crops; it is accepted as a compliment, but also serves his needs'.[31] Whilst high-level Gaulish society would become more and more dependent on produce extracted from the base, it would continue to have elements of agricultural tribute redistributed at a higher level. Lesser leaders and tribes would formally send grain and cattle higher up the chain whilst in Ireland lesser kings made tribute payments to high kings.

How did the nobility acquire the wider material goods of clientship? Many items could be produced in the tightly controlled environment of the *oppida*, or acquired in the form of payments from clients. Agricultural material and services would help to sustain the craftsmen of the *oppida*.

Raiding and warfare would account for more. Successful warfare furnished booty and slaves and put the warrior elite in a position to reward and maintain itself. External trade, particularly with the Mediterranean, allowed for the exchange of loot and prisoners for Italian bronze vessels and especially for wine.

This is the period when wine had become a highly desired luxury item. Barry Cunliffe estimates that Gaul was taking about 100,000 hectolitres (one hundred litres) of Italian wine per year by the early 1st century BC.[32] Of course, the Celts had much to offer in return: Cunliffe suggests that there were 300,000 Gaulish slaves in Italy. That number would require to be topped up over time, a process estimated at a further 15,000 per year. Diodorus sets the price of an amphora at one slave, a bit of a bargain when you consider that same trader could expect to get six amphorae of wine back home for a healthy Gaul. Archaeology allows us to track the wine trade by looking at the distribution of amphorae over time. We first find them in significant numbers in southern Gaul in about 200 BC and the numbers increase over the rest of the century. It is possible to trace the path of the wine along the major rivers, moving deeper and deeper into the interior and up to the ports of Brittany, reversing the route along which tin had traditionally come. Finds peak at around mid-1st century BC when it looks as though both the Gauls and Caesar's men were fuelling demand. By then the amphorae are reaching Britain – archaeologists working at Hengisbury Head in Dorset have found evidence of them coming through in substantial quantities. Plus figs, raw glass and metal vessels, all evidence of major trade routes.

Public assemblies in one form or another are a feature of the Celts regardless of whether it was a tribe (or tribes) who recognised kingship or those with an aristocratic leadership. Meetings were attended by the king or tribal leaders, noble weapon-bearing free men of the tribe. The assembly made important decisions, particularly those concerning war and peace, election of military leaders, legislation, and justice in weighty cases. It would be a mistake to assume some element of democracy about this kind of structure. It was a necessity in a society characterised by fissiparous instincts, interlocking kinship and client networks and a social structure based on tribe rather than state. If the elite were to retain influence they had to demonstrate a willingness to continuously take the opinion of the public into account.

Representatives of the most important families among the nobility (supported by their followers) pulled the strings, with the right to speak reserved for leading members of the aristocracy, as Tacitus explained:

> Then the king or chiefs are listened to, in order of age, birth, glory in war, or eloquence, with the prestige which belongs to their counsel rather than with any prescriptive right to command. If the advice tendered be displeasing, they reject it with groans; if it please them, they clash their spears; the most complimentary expression of assent is this martial approbation.[33]

The meetings, particularly in times of crisis, seemed more like a military rally – Caesar tell us the Treveri men appeared fully armed at their assemblies.

An assembly seems to have gone hand in hand with the performance of rituals and ceremonies, a bit like the prayers offered up at the start of Parliament each day. Of course, the latter are voluntary – it's hard to imagine Gallic society showing tolerance for those who dissented.

Tacitus describes the role of priests or religious functionaries in the public assembly of the Germans: acting to maintain order with the right to inflict penalties on dissenters. Regular meetings might well be convened according to a religious calendar. The initiation of young men who had reached martial age or rituals associated with the agricultural cycle may have been performed as part of the gathering. A mechanism existed for calling special meetings to consider the selection of a new king, the creation of a military leader in response to war or a peace conference.

Organisation of the meetings tells us much about the personal characteristics of the wider Celts and the Gauls in particular. Some of it has a modern resonance. The phrase 'herding cats' springs to mind. It could take some time for a regular meeting to get down to business. Tacitus offers an insight into the German model: 'It is a foible of their freedom that they do not meet at once, and as if commanded, but two or three days are wasted by dilatoriness in assembling'.[34] One can imagine the state of those who had been sitting around waiting for the rest of the tribe to turn up. Presumably some mechanism existed to allow a quick assembly in times of crisis but you get the impression that the voice of experience dictated the rules. Here is Caesar commenting on a crisis meeting called by the Treveri:

> This in the practice of the Gauls marks the beginning of a war; and by general law all grown men are accustomed to assemble at it in arms, while the one who comes last to the assembly is put to death with every kind of torture in sight of the host.[35]

The Gauls (like most Celtic groups) also had a smaller, more aristocratic assembly, a council of nobles. By the 1st century BC this formed the most important political body, especially in those tribes without kings. They were substantial bodies – the Galatians, a federation of three Gallic tribes, had a council of 300. This suggests they were recruited from both higher and lower nobility; perhaps with the addition of chiefs of the local groups. Sometimes referred to as councils of elders, they do not seem to have been exclusively aged since there are records of substantial numbers of council members killed in battle. All but three of the Nervii council died fighting Caesar.

The power of both public assembly and the council of nobles faced severe challenges in the period leading up to the conquest, particularly in southern Gaul. The hardening of hierarchy as social competition increased amongst the nobles diminished their power. We have already seen how free-born Gauls of the lowest level were becoming debt ridden and dependent on patrons. The power expansion of the aristocracy was based primarily on their ability to form a strong clientage, acquiring a greater grasp on wider society as dependency grew. This was reflected in the elite's political utilisation of its clients in both assembly and council – leading to the formation of large political factions. Plus, of course, the influence of the public assembly was reduced by the deteriorated economic and social position of the common people, a process that at the time of the conquest was in full swing and was closely connected with the increasing power of the nobility.

The institution of kingship had gone through a long development, with its character changing over the course of time. In its oldest form kingship is closely connected with tribal political systems. Kings occupied a central position in comparison to other nobles but their power was often limited. Nor was there a single form of kingship. There were tribes with one or two kings, those with an aristocratic leadership, and those who combined such a leadership with a royal family. Plus those who had moved or were transitioning from one form of government to another. The Suessiones for example, had a strong kingship, built under Diviciacus, and which at the time of the conquest was occupied by Galba.

The Eburones had a dual kingship in the persons of Ambiorix and Cativolcus. The former (quoted by Caesar) was wont to complain that the people had as much authority over him as he had over them (although he is likely to have been talking about nobles rather than the base level). There were tribes that had an aristocratic leadership – that is, they were led by groups of nobles. We often see these referred to as elected magistrates but you have to forget democracy when it comes to the Gauls. The 'elections' were more likely the result of a balancing act between factions, client groups, noble families and in some cases the remains of royal families. Caesar tells us that *principes* occupied the position of leadership among the Bellovaci, the Remi, the Nervii and the Treveri just as they did among the Tencteri, Usipetes, and Ubii on the right side of the Rhine. These were tribes led by an aristocracy but which had a royal family – an indication that the institution of kingship had existed in the recent past. What is equally interesting are those tribes for whom we can find no explicit statement of kingship or rule by *principes*. For example, the Morini, Menapii, Arnbiani and Aduatuci. In the case of the Morini at least, we know Ceasar had to carry on negotiations with the delegates of individual *pagi*.

Kingship was complex – both political and sacral. The person of the king was not divine although he might well trace his descent from gods or demi gods. Rather, his status brought him into intimate contact with the supernatural giving him a liminal place between the everyday and the supernatural. Kings had a cult function with an active role to play in rituals. Thus, kingship was frequently associated with the fertility of men, land, and animals. In Ireland this was made explicit in the inauguration rite of a new king, which consisted of symbolic sexual intercourse with the mother goddess of the people. Through this ritual marriage with the goddess, the king gave fertility and prosperity to the people. A bad king (one who did not stick to the norms) brought famine and defeat to his people; his relation with the supernatural was regarded as disturbed and he could be banished or killed. In Irish mythology King Bres was deposed by his people because of his avarice and the infertility of the land.

Caesar reports that the Eburones King Cativolcus killed himself with poison from the yew tree after he saw the adversity his tribe experienced following the failure of the rebellion against the Romans. Although Caesar states that Cativolcus committed suicide because he was too old to bear the tensions of war, it is also possible that his death was a ritual suicide, connected with the responsibility of the ruler for the well-being of his people.

The political position of tribal kings can be characterised as one of *primus inter pares*. At tribal level their power was often limited and unstable. We see kings repeatedly appearing as war leaders of a tribe or group of tribes in combat against external enemies (e.g. Ambiorix leading the Eburones, Maelo the Sugambri, and Galba the Suessiones), but the function of army commander did not convey absolute power to the king. There was near constant tension between the king and other families of the nobility who tried to limit their influence. Even a strong king had no monopoly on economic resources or, indeed, the use of violence. Other families among the nobility also had their own base of economic power and a client group that could be used for military purposes: typically those families who dominated alternative *pagi*. Most likely they would be his most important rivals. The king, whilst central, found himself participating in the competition for power and prestige. He required personal wealth to consolidate client networks and alliances. Hence the famous potlatches of the Arvernian King Louernius (2nd century BC) designed to expand prestige and influence by the giving of lavish gifts at feasts. A tradition made all the more important by the nature of regal succession. For many tribes the decision on who would be king was not a matter of primogeniture but of a combination of heredity and choice.

The power of tribal kings should not be underestimated. In tribes that retained kingship, the royal family was usually the most influential group and its prominent position would have been recognised by most of the nobility. The king probably attempted to control other leaders through political alliances and connections of clientship. Establishing relations through marriage and the taking of hostages from noble families as a pledge for their loyalty would also play an important role. Both mechanisms appear to have been highly significant in early Irish and pre-Roman societies.

Tacitus confirms that among the Germans the king's successor was not predetermined, but elected. It is assumed that the choice was among a limited number of candidates who were all 'king worthy', that is belonging to the royal family.[36] For the Irish, claims to the throne could only be made by the male line of an already royal family. Individual members who were potential candidates could not claim automatic succession. Factors such as personal capacity, physical qualities, and the number of clients they had determined the final choice.[37]

What led some tribes to move from leadership by a king to rule by an aristocratic elite? It is generally accepted that the political tensions between king and aristocracy which created the phenomena owed much to the increasing importance of the *oppida* from the 2nd century BC and the opportunity to take advantage of this change offered by the client system. We have already discussed the rise of the *oppida* as centres of craft production and trade. The archaeological record and historical data suggest that control of these economic centres provided the elite of the *pagus* with a new source of wealth that they could and did use for political expansion. Clientship allowed aristocratic groups to concentrate power and invest it in political competition.

Of course, royal families would have had a head start in this process. Some kings had the opportunity to transform their role from *primus inter pares* to that of a new and strengthened leadership. In so doing, however, they ran up against the leading aristocracy of other subtribes, also bent on furthering their position. Whenever the prominent groups among the elite worked together, they were able to depose a king who was striving for centralisation. The Treverian kingship seems to have disappeared before the conquest and the internal conflict between Indutiomarus and Cingetorix testifies to intensive competition for clients. The Suessiones kingship did not collapse under the pressure of a rival aristocracy, but instead was able to strengthen itself. This was primarily the result of King Diviciacus' successful policy of expansion, which probably brought various tribal groups in northern Gaul and Britain into dependency.

CHAPTER 4

WAY OF THE WARRIOR

The Greeks are pugnacious enough, and start fights on the spur of the moment without sense or judgment to justify them. When they declare war on each other, they go off together to the smoothest and flattest piece of ground they can find, and have their battle on it.

Herodotus 7.9. B.1.

Herodotus is speaking of the Greeks here, but this bullish aggression could have been equally ascribed to the Celts. Warriors were the cream, the fêted elite. But the priesthood, the druids, were also a very important class: part judge, part healer, part custodian of tradition. They were the cement that held Gallic society loosely together, the common thread that bound the tribes.

If not technically of the most elevated rank, priests or druids still enjoyed very high status. Their role as 'men of art' – a distinction they shared with bards and skilled craftsmen, extended to more than religious observance:

> The druids are involved in matters of religion. They manage public and private sacrifices and interpret religious customs and ceremonies. Young men flock to them in large numbers to gain instruction and they hold the druids in great esteem. For they decide almost all disputes, both public and private. If some crime has been committed, if there has been murder done, if there is a dispute over an inheritance or over territory, they decide the issue and settle the rewards or penalties.[1]

They had power akin to excommunication, banning sinners from ritual practice – a most severe penalty. Those excommunicates were denied recourse to law – being shunned put you effectively beyond the pale of society: such was the weight of priestly sanction. The chief priest held office for life, his successor being chosen by vote or, if necessary by duelling.[2]

Annually they convened a part-religious, part-civic assembly in the territory of the Carnutes – the very heart of Gaul. In theory they didn't fight and were certainly exempt from all local taxes (this seemed to have the magical effect of boosting recruitment).[3]

Druidical law and traditions were passed on orally. There was no written code of belief or practice – to the immense frustration of later historians. They certainly believed in the immortality of the soul, which passed on death to another. So death was never the end and this conviction fuelled courage in battle; 'because the fear of death is thereby put aside, they consider this a strong inducement to physical courage'.[4] Religion was important and universally so and human sacrifice was, if we follow Caesar and other Roman writers, a regular occurrence: 'For they believe that unless one human life is offered for another the power and presence of the immortal gods cannot be propitiated'.[5]

Certainly, there is one site in France that raises some interesting questions about the nature of Gallic rituals. A temple dating from the Roman period has been excavated at Ribemont sur Ancre. Celtic remains from beneath the temple layer revealed at least three ritual enclosures that between them have so far produced over 700 bodies. Most are the bones of young men almost all showing signs of violent injury, suggesting that they were killed in battle. The bones have been moved around and rearranged in different areas of the location. There is no indication that they were dismembered shortly after death: the absence of cut marks suggests disarticulation after the corpses had decomposed. One group of bones had been stacked like a logpile, criss-crossed to form a square solid stack 1.6 metres across. This stack also contained the bones of 40 horses. There is some evidence of decapitation. Archaeologists are not really sure what the bones represent. A vanquished enemy sent into the other world? Human sacrifice? The bones of their own community carefully conserved and arranged for some reason? A ritual to honour dead warriors? The jury is still out.

Druids have become popular in modern culture, starting with the 19th-century quasi-mystical romantic revival and boosted again by the interest in alternative religions that was a feature of Western society in the 1960s and 1970s. We merely have to witness the annual solstice at Stonehenge, which has little to do with Iron Age druids: a confection and conflation of myth and wishful thinking divorced from historical realities. Rome seems to have felt a collective frisson of horror whenever the subject of the druids came up and took steps to eradicate them when given the opportunity. This may have also been a wish to disambulate a unifying factor in the Celtic society Rome was trying to annex. At the time Boudicca's rebellion flared in East Anglia, governor Paulinus was druid-bashing on Anglesey.

Mercury was chief in the pantheon of their gods, closely followed by figures reminiscent of Apollo, Mars, Jupiter and Minerva. Though these are very similar to classical belief, they were rather more demanding in terms of blood. Caesar refers to the 'Wicker man' ritual where tall statues of the gods were constructed out of a wicker framework, filled with victims who were immolated when the edifice was set on fire. It was apparently better when these sacrificial victims were drawn from the ranks of convicted criminals but if there was a dearth of criminality, the innocent would do just as well.[6]

As god of war, Mars was inevitably popular given the Gauls expended much of their restless energy in his service. Loot, valued though it was as a lubricant of clientage was also used to venerate the god. Great heaps of captured treasures were left piled as tribal installation art, dedicated to him. And the penalties were severe for anyone who helped himself:

> When victorious, they sacrifice the animals they have captured and gather all the rest of the spoils in one place. In many states one may see mounds made out of such objects in holy places, and rarely does it happen that anyone defies the bounds of religion and dares to hide away his spoils at home, or steal them away once they are placed on the mound. The most serious penalty, including torture, is set down for such behaviour.[7]

Amassing loot was seen as an expression of glorious achievement rather than individual enrichment.

Society funerals, as might be imagined, were lavish affairs, the warrior could always be assured of a decent send off in best Homeric style. Homer is writing of the Bronze Age, yet the heroic society he depicts would have been recognised by the later Celts. The deceased's valuables frequently went onto the fire. This could, in the era before Caesar, certainly have included livestock and possibly slaves, maybe even dependants![8]

> Agamemnon accordingly dismissed the people, while the mourners remained, and piled up the wood, and made a pyre of a hundred feet each way and upon it they laid the body. They killed flocks of sheep and herds of cattle in front of the pyre, skinned them and cut them up; Achilles took away all the fat, and covered the dead with it from head to foot, and heaped the flayed bodies about him. Jars of honey and oil he placed leaning against the bier. Four horses he laid carefully on the pyre ... Nine dogs the prince had, that fed from his table; two of these Achilles took and cut their throats and laid beside him. The twelve noble young Trojans he slew without mercy.[9]

Caesar does acknowledge that the more enlightened tribes, those that had adopted the magistracy/consular system, also ensured news from abroad was to be reported first to elected officers rather than being more widely disseminated as idle rumour. The magistrates would then decide what and how much was to be cascaded among the people. It's a brand of state censorship of which Caesar, not unsurprisingly, approved.[10] Caesar commented on the fickle nature of the Gauls, their switches of loyalties, which he found a constant irritation – Rome did things differently.

Warriors then were the real cream, the *beau sabreurs* of tribal society; gaudy, vainglorious, quixotic, prickly and cantankerous. This was the clay Vercingetorix would have to mould into an effective army. Ultimately he failed but he still achieved remarkable successes:

> When necessity arises and some war flares up – which before Caesar's arrival used to happen almost every year, so that they were either on the offensive themselves or fending off attacks – they are all involved in the campaign. Each man has as many retainers and dependants about him as are appropriate to his status in terms of his birth and resources. This is the sole form of power and influence they know.[11]

Much, much later, lowland English and Scottish writers were describing the affinity of highland chiefs, as representing the last survivors of Celtic warrior society whose window in history would close so completely in the sleet and screaming of Culloden on 16th April 1746. The chief, mounted on his sturdy garron, was resplendent in blazing, ostentatious plaid, his sheer trews showing a fine calf and befitting his rank. Behind him trailed his piper, bard, senior tenants or *tacksmen* and a troop of warriors. To the eye of the Age of Reason, these appeared as creatures from a different time. Their lowland contemporaries were ashamed of them, though partly fearful. Eighteenth-century travellers wrote about highlanders with the same tone of condescension Caesar adopted toward the Gauls. After the infamous massacre of Glencoe in 1692, the recusant highlanders knew what it cost to be different. Later, it was Cumberland who would play Caesar.

Having your tail of warriors was all about status, it defined your significance. To be a famous warrior: to have the bards, during those long, cold winter nights, extol your triumphs, your individual feats of arms was what it was all about. Warfare was, for these paladins, never a collective undertaking for the weal of the state. It was all about the individual. This was wonderfully hubristic but it only worked against those like-minded. Against a superior state, geared for war as a matter of policy, trained, equipped and superbly led, the warrior elite were redundant, an archaic survival, out of kilter with the new reality.

We know that Vercingetorix led a collection of war-bands, young blades seeking adventure, patronage and fame. The noble youth was probably dispatched to his foster home at the age of seven. His apprenticeship lasted another seven years, so he would be classed as adult by 14. Girls came of age at the same time. The number seven was of itself significant in mythology and custom. By 14 the lad had to either attract a following of his own or, more likely, attach himself to the banner of some established leader and grow his reputation in the great man's shadow and under his patronage.

Battles were personal, a series of combats rather than a cohesive tactical blow:

There were a number of scattered combats here and there. First Patroclos pierced the thigh of Areilycos at the moment he turned to fly; the spear broke the bone, and he fell flat on his face. Next Menelaos wounded Thoas where his chest showed over the side of the shield and he collapsed. Phyleides watched his moment as Amphiclos ran at him, and lunged at him first – hit the bulging thigh where the muscle is thickest and cut through the sinews and darkness came over his eyes.[12]

Homer is recounting heroic combat on the Plain of Troy, in around the 13th century BC with the warriors clad in bronze and sparring with bronze, but even so the Celts of Caesar's time would have recognised in this description the individual nature of the combats where warrior sought out warrior and craved the kudos of the hero-kill. To kill an opposing champion was to assume his strength and reputation. Like a gladiator, the more duels the hero won, so his prestige soared, every swashbuckling blade wanted to make it into the premier league.

Feasting and raiding were the warp and weft of warrior culture. Boasting and bardic panegyrics went with honing skills and winning reputation. Physical appearance, too gaudy and too loaded with bling for censorious Roman eyes, was important, the manifestation of status. War has always been about dressing up and the Romans were far from immune – the medieval knight in his polished harness, winged Polish hussars, the Napoleonic cavalryman in gorgeous dolmen and pelisse – there are numerous examples of the phenomena. Classical writers stress the imposing stature of their barbarian contacts, tall and well muscled. The height of the average Roman in the 1st century BC was about 5ft 5 inches, the average Gaul about 5ft 6 inches. So, although the average male was not nearly as tall as their modern counterparts, they were still built on a larger scale than their stocky Mediterranean adversaries.[13]

Washing the hair with lime water, which gave an ethereal spiked effect, was popular, particularly since it added to the effect of height. Depending on the era, some wore beards and gentry tended to sport extravagant moustaches. Partly this was for effect but also linked to shamanic practices and good luck emblems. The Celt lived in a world that revolved and breathed around him. He was in touch with nature to an extent we can barely imagine in an age where the natural world is seen only as a heritage attraction. There was life in the trees, in the flora and fauna and in the dark, deep waters that opened a passage into the next world. Death was commonplace. It did not quite hold the terror we might feel today. Celts believed in the migration of souls, so that death was never the end. Physical courage, endurance and a heroic sangfroid in the face of mortality were the normal currency of this warrior elite.

Well-made colourful clothing often, in the case of high-status garments, fabricated from fine wool, linen and even silks, distinguished the nobles, who were badged indelibly as such by a decorated neck ring or *torc*. Visitors to the 'Celts' exhibition at the British Museum and latterly on show at the National Museum of Scotland in 2015/16 would have marvelled at the intricacy and art of these. Many were of gold, others bronze and iron, clearly an expression of rank. High-status weapons such as swords, mail armour and bronze or iron helmets were the preserve of the nobility. Most workaday warriors went to battle armed with spear and shield, generally without body or head protection.

Warriors ranged up behind their individual leader, the size of his war band depending on his status, kinship and clientage. This made for small-unit tactical cohesion but did not promote any sense or concept of universal discipline. Tacitus confirms that 'once they owed obedience to kings; now they are distracted between the jarring factions of rival chiefs. Indeed, nothing has helped us more in war with their strongest nations than their inability to cooperate. It is but seldom that two or three states unite to repel a common danger; fighting in detail they are conquered wholesale.'[14]

Rome was both fascinated and repelled by these Celts. The two nations had form. In 390 BC a chief of the Senones, Brennos burst out of Cisalpine Gaul and defeated a Roman army at the battle of the Allia. His victorious forces occupied and sacked the city, only the redoubt of the Capitoline Hill held out – famously saved by patriotic geese. Rome had to pay an enormous indemity to be rid of their uncouth and uninvited guests. Finally, the timely arrival of the hero Camillus saved the day, driving the occupiers from the streets then decimating their army. But it was too close a shave altogether and a massive humiliation, one that Rome would never forget. In nearly a millennium no other enemies would breach Rome's gates. Not till 410 AD would the city experience such abject suffering.

This event left a mark. Rome might sneer at these Gallic peacocks, arrogant, strutting and anarchic but her citizens would never forget that these same barbarians had held their city to ransom and made the Republic grovel in the dust of its own streets. It would always be to a degree personal. Rome had to be safe from any threat of it happening again and Caesar's brand of conquest, often immeasurably harsh, would be seasoned in the light of necessity.

Not all of the Celtic army would be made up of gentry; most would be free men, but mainly without wealth or ostentation. Rank-and-file Celtic warriors would be dressed in homespun leggings and lacked helmets, armour or swords. They'd more likely carry two types of spear, one intended for close combat and the thrust, the other, considerably lighter, intended primarily for throwing. Most shields recovered from archaeological sites or dredged up as votive offerings are, like the very fine Witham Shield, intended purely for ceremonial use. They are beautifully fashioned but far too flimsy for the fight. Still the elliptical shape with distinctive rounded corners gives a good impression of the more practical model. These were long enough to provide adequate bodily defence but handy enough to be used for parrying and even for punching blows.

Swords were precious, not mass-produced like the legionary's *gladius*. They broadcast status and many of those that have survived are beautifully crafted and richly decorated. They had long slashing blades of excellent temper, flexible and capable of taking a very sharp edge. Many had highly ornate hilts and from surviving examples it seems the rather sneering comments of Roman authors on the quality of their opponents' blades are wholly misplaced. These were primarily slashing weapons, the favoured cut being a sharp downward blow aimed at the neck or shoulder, intended to sever main arteries, leading instantly to loss of function quickly followed by exsanguination. As late as 1746, observers touring the field of battle at Falkirk noted how many of the Hanoverian dead had been cut down by highland broadswords in just this manner.

The Romans, as we noted earlier, weren't above stealing ideas from their despised Gallic enemies – It was the Gauls who probably invented mail and adopted the Montefortino type of helmet. Some examples are largely functional and others more decorated. It was an unfair and unduly pejorative observation that the Celts 'decorated everything and built nothing'. The levels of artisanal and artistic skill displayed in the manufacture of weapons equal anything seen in the classical world. Prestige was personal rather than civic. Society in Gaul at the time of Caesar was going through a period of adjustment whilst Roman politics of the era were as murderously robust as anything seen on the far side of the Alps. Brawling and murder were commonplace; Caesar knew this and would find out just how violent on 15th March in 44 BC.

The Gallic tribes certainly possessed missile weapons though bows may not have been used extensively.[15] Slings certainly were, caches of shot have been discovered within hill forts and it is possible the construction of gateway defences was intended to maximise their deadly effect.[16] Clearly, these were essentially 'peasant' weapons and didn't excite the high-status appeal of hand-to-hand combat:

> Nestor's two sons each brought down his man. Antilochos drove his spear into the flank of Atymnios; his brother Maris ran in front of the body and made a thrust at Antilochos; but Thrasymedes got in first before he could strike, and tore the upper arm from the muscles, breaking the bone, and killing the man. So the two sons of Nestor sent down to Erebos the two valiant sons of Amisodaros...[17]

On the field of battle Gallic armies likely deployed by affinity, each group of fighters standing around and with their lord. That is not to say they were a disorderly mob as so often portrayed. The idea of affinity regiments persisted until World War One: men fight better alongside their mates: it's them you don't want to let down, it's their opprobrium you risk everything to avoid. A good commander in chief would allow his units to deploy in a known and tried manner. At the battle of Flodden in 1513, some of Sir Edward Stanley's men – forced to gather on the English right under Edmund Howard, a commander unknown to them, and denied the chance to stand beneath their traditional eagle's claw banner – bolted at the first clash. This was down to disaffection rather than cowardice. In Celtic armies such niceties really mattered.

Such small-unit tactics could be highly effective. Even experienced legionaries could be disconcerted when hit and run was used to good effect, as Caesar found out in Britain during his second expedition of 54 BC:

> Throughout this unusual combat, when the fighting took place and in front of the camp, it was evident that because of their heavy weaponry our men were ill-equipped for such an enemy, for they could not pursue when the enemy ran, and dared not abandon their close formation. The cavalry fought at great risk too, because the enemy frequently drove away from the fighting on purpose, so when our horsemen had gone some little distance from the legions they could jump down from their chariots and fight on foot with an unfair advantage.[18]

Getting your kit off was another Gaulish specialty. More 'civilised' armies were astounded when faced with troops of nude warriors. Quite why some units fought naked is unclear. Possibly, this was a kind of badge of elite status or, more practically, the fighters were aware of the risk of infection carried by scraps of fabric into wounds. There is another theory: battle can be arousing – fear has its effect on the body as well as the psyche. There have been those who suggest that the spectacle of another male, quite clearly erect, can be a trifle disconcerting. Especially in large numbers... Polybius (in *The Histories*) tells us,

> The Gaesati, who were in the forefront of the Celtic army, stripped naked for the fight, and the sight of these warriors, with their great stature and their fair skins, on which glittered the collars and bracelets of gold so loved as an adornment by all the Celts, filled the Roman legionaries with awe.

And there was noise; the din made by Celtic armies was deliberately fearful. Noise inspires fear in the listeners as it confers confidence in the maker. The great dragon-headed war trumpets or *carynx* added their blaring to the cacophony. Noise is a narcotic, the individual warrior or fighter is 'psyched up', adrenalin already pumping, fear and slack bowels banished. Recent evidence from Scotland suggests Rome was aware of this too. The number of slingshots adapted to whistle fearsomely as they flew evokes the image of the terror evoked by the medieval fire storms unleashed by longbowmen.

Battles frequently kicked off with the foreplay of single combats between champions. Here was an opportunity for the individual warrior to really show off his prowess and add to the lustre of his renown. Equally, he might of course, get killed. The loser's head would end up as a trophy for the victor; gruesome as this might seem, the head had a special status amongst the Gauls. Roman officers frequently found themselves challenged and, as often as not, proved the more skilful combatants. Like Hector and Achilles, or the Irish hero Cuchulainn, this involved a great deal of showmanship and, possibly, enough alcohol to impart a measure of added valour without scrambling the reflexes. Romans weren't immune to vainglory. Cassius Chaerea, one of Rome's more colourful champions and the assassin of Caligula, once leapt into the arena to confront a huge German gladiator who had seen off all the opposition and dared any Roman to take him on. Cassius won the fight.[19]

At some point the Celtic army had to advance, men (and some women) screwing themselves up to fighting pitch and then exploding in battle fury. This breed of courage among warriors is like an orchestra. It must begin when pitch perfect. Miss the moment and warrior ardour surely cools. The attack was probably not the mad rush Roman writers suggest but a controlled move to contact, cohesion of the warrior group more important than pure speed. A deluge of missiles was hurled by both armies; then the clash, a titanic roar like the ocean wave. Men heated white-hot smash into each other. Warriors, honed by training and experience seek targets, taking up any opportunities. The fight would have swiftly become a sprawling melée of loose combats until one side, depleted or demoralised, broke.

That key ascendancy in morale would have been established before contact. The rout would be fearful. It is when the lines break and men chuck aside their weapons to run that casualties mount. Caesar didn't value his cavalry but time and again we hear of the mounted arm chasing down a beaten enemy, killing at will. Courage in battle is a finite and oddly fickle commodity. Men who have fought like tigers can be reduced to panicked sheep almost in an instant when morale snaps. Celtic armies displayed this startling élan and seemingly unbounded ferocity, yet when that first furious rush was met, their enthusiasm ebbed away as quickly.

Warriors lacked the staying power of regular troops. Their command and control structures could bring them onto the field and deploy them for the attack but there were no mechanisms for rally and reform. It was the custom to place the best and strongest men in the front lines. This made sense as they were best equipped and probably had mail harness but inevitably they took the brunt of casualties so the qualitative element was rapidly thinned out. Centuries later, an English general, 'Hangman' Hawley, who led Hanoverian forces at Falkirk claimed that clan regiments put their best armed men 'those they call gentlemen' in the front ranks and that those at the back were, in his words, 'arrant scum'. The same scum, it has to be said, that won the day against him.

Although Caesar encountered British war chariots during his cross-Channel expeditions in 55 and 54 BC, these were already obsolescent in Gaul and do not feature in the Alesia campaign. Gallic armies relied far more on cavalry. The Gauls were great horse breeders and their mounts were as important to prestige as weapons and armour. The horse was the emblem of the sun god and so imbued with magical resonances. Of course, as ever, a cavalryman is only as good as his mount. Mounted Gallic warriors were the cream of their forces and of society. They, like the Germans, also combined the mobility of cavalry with the hitting power of infantry.[20] Gallic cavalry were not too proud to fight as mercenaries and were highly regarded as such. Both Hannibal and Caesar recruited them.[21]

Horses of the period, however well bred, were not tall; perhaps 13–14 hands and quite fine in build. Though spurs were in evidence, nobody was yet using stirrups. The invention of the four-pommel saddle, probably reaching Europe via the steppes, gave the rider a far more secure seat and the length of sword blades increases from the 3rd century BC onwards to afford a longer slashing blow from the saddle.[22] Gallic cavalry probably fought almost as dragoons later did – mounted infantry who fought on foot. This afforded opportunities for the warrior to demonstrate and increase his prowess. He could also get clear in a hurry if matters turned out badly.

There is evidence that the Gauls would adopt new battle mores. A leader of genius such as Vercingetorix took knowledge where he could and was willing to copy Roman tactics. The assaults from both within and without the *circumvallation* at Alesia showed that elite Gallic units could adopt complex defensive tactics such as the 'tortoise' (*testudo*), where soldiers formed a compact mobile column, locking shields to front and flanks as well as overhead, an armoured phalanx that could advance upon enemy defences, protected against most missiles.

Disunity – as Tacitus, echoing Caesar, condescendingly notes – was a fatal weakness. The Gauls could never put communal interest, however that might be defined, above local loyalties. Individual pride and kudos outweighed any corporate objectives. It was a power struggle between two noble brothers, leading men of the Aedui, Diviciacus and his younger sibling Dumnorix, which gave Caesar his opening. Diviciacus, the elder of the two, was quite prepared to turn collaborator to get the better of his charismatic brother. Three great tribal groups, the Aedui, Sequani and the Arverni (Vercingetorix' people), were sparring for dominance. It seemed that none of them realised that inviting Rome through the back door would ignite a conflagration that would ultimately consume them all. Caesar was coming and he would change history.

CHAPTER 5

DE BELLO GALLICO – THE GALLIC WARS 58–52 BC

He hath brought many captives home to Rome,
Whose ransoms did the general coffers fill:
Did this in Caesar seem ambitious?
When that the poor have cried, Caesar hath wept
Ambition should be made of sterner stuff.
Shakespeare: *Julius Caesar*, III, ii.

Of course, the main reason why Caesar conquered Gaul was because he was one of the greatest generals of ancient times and, indeed in the whole history of the world. Byron, Constant and Stendhal compared Caesar with Napoleon, and Napoleon himself, in the 'Precis des Guerres de Cesar' that he wrote at St. Helena, detected in the Roman an affinity almost amounting to identification.

Michael Grant, *Julius Caesar*.

Julius Caesar (*c*. 100–44 BC), famously refused the crown but Mark Anthony, in Shakespeare's gilded prose, is still wrong when he asserts his old commander was not ambitious. A story, possibly apocryphal and frequently told has Caesar, as his army crossed the Alps, riding with his staff officers through a pretty miserable local settlement, huddled bothies and general air of squalor. Somebody asks if, even among such wretched people, the same intrigues, the same contests for power and influence occur as do in Rome. The general replies, with feeling, that he'd rather be first amongst this lot than second in Rome. It's a neat tale but gets to the core of the man: he is driven entirely by ambition. A restless, ruthless drive to excel, to make his mark, which until he reaches Gaul in 58 BC, for all his brilliance, had led him nowhere.

Montaigne, writing in the late 16th century, the age of Machiavelli, was a great admirer of Caesar:

> 'Tis related of many great leaders that they have had certain books in particular esteem, as Alexander the Great, Homer; Scipio Africanus, Xenophon; Marcus Brutus, Polybius; Charles V, Philip de Comines; and 'tis said that, in our times, Machiavelli is elsewhere still in repute; but the late Marshal Strozzi, who had taken Caesar for his part, doubtless made the best choice, seeing that it indeed ought to be the breviary of every soldier, as being the true and sovereign pattern of the military art. And, moreover, God knows with what grace and beauty he has embellished that rich matter, with so pure, delicate, and perfect expression, that, in my opinion, there are no writings in the world comparable to his, as to that business.[1]

Caesar's fame rests upon his record as a soldier and it is a pretty impressive record. Napoleon Bonaparte fought seventy-two battles and was victorious in over three-score of these. Admittedly he lost the one that mattered. Caesar never did. He fought perhaps thirty major clashes in Gaul.[2] In all of these he never suffered a strategic defeat, no Waterloo, no Gettysburg. He certainly experienced tactical reverses, perhaps most notably at Gergovia in 52 BC. Having subdued Gaul, he went on to win the Civil War against his son-in-law Pompey, settling forever the argument as to who was the greatest general between them. Pompey got away but only as far as an assassin's knife off Egypt. Caesar, albeit briefly, was ruler of the world.

That Julius Caesar belongs in the front rank of history's great commanders is now a given. He may not have fought as often as Napoleon but he was probably in the field as often as the Corsican's nemesis Wellington. Marlborough and Montgomery fought far fewer battles by comparison. Longshanks fought in only three pitched battles, Henry V in just a couple. Caesar conquered the whole of Gaul, imposing Roman rule that would endure for half a millennium and leave an indelible mark on the subsequent history of France and so of Europe. He made history and what he created endured. Alexander's empire fractured on his death. Bonaparte ended his life as a sad exile, with only a few barren acres in the distant depths of the South Atlantic and arsenic in the wallpaper.

Caesar is called 'great', however that accolade may be defined. If it is that he was the leading man of his times, one who shaped and changed history and one who left his mark, then clearly the distinction is well earned. That doesn't make him a 'good' man or even a particularly nice one. He could be harsh, always ruthless and occasionally, vindictive. It has been suggested his conquest of Gaul cost the indigenous peoples over 1.5 million dead. That's probably an exaggeration but the toll was undoubtedly very high. The benefits (and there were many) of *Pax Romana* were acquired at a fearful price. His conduct towards Vercingetorix certainly appears purely vengeful. Partially, this was the inevitable consequence of Gallic atrocities such as the mass murder of Roman civilians at Orléans (Cenabum) at the outset of the rebellion. There is also a suggestion that Vercingetorix may have broken an earlier oath of loyalty. Besides, in 52 BC, the stakes were so high, there could only ever be one outright winner – and winner takes all.

Physically Caesar was imposing: said to have been tall, fair and well built, with a rather broad face and keen dark-brown eyes. His health was sound, apart from sudden comas and a tendency to nightmares that troubled him towards the end of his life; but he twice had epileptic fits while on campaign. He was something of a dandy, always keeping his head carefully trimmed and shaved; and has been accused of having certain other hairy parts of his body depilated with tweezers.[3] He was sensitive over his hair loss, combing forward the remaining thin strands to cover the bare crown. Wearing the laurel wreath, the conqueror's garnish, always appealed and had the added bonus of concealing his baldness, a source of mirth to his innumerable enemies in Rome.[4]

His physical courage and stamina were outstanding:

> But where necessary occasion required, never did any man venture his person more than he: so much so, that for my part, methinks I read in many of his exploits a determinate resolution to throw himself away to avoid the shame of being overcome. In his great battle with those of Tournay, he charged up to the head of the enemies without his shield, just as he was seeing the van of his

own army beginning to give ground; which also several other times befell him. Hearing that his people were besieged, he passed through the enemy's army in disguise to go and encourage them with his presence.[5]

He appears to have been very attractive to women and certainly never missed an opportunity for seduction: 'His affairs with women are commonly described as numerous and extravagant'. Suetonius goes on to append a list of his noble conquests.[6] Given the epithet of 'bald whore-monger' his soldiers applied to him (not necessarily disapprovingly), we can probably deduce that his appetites were not dulled by the rigours of campaigning.

As a soldier, he was bold, incisive, cool and (generally) lucky. Lucky is good in a commander, his men believe it rubs off onto them. He created, with his Gallic War legions, a superb field army; tough, experienced and loyal. 'It is a disputable point which was the more remarkable when he went to war; his caution or his daring. He never exposed his army to ambushes, but made careful reconnaissance ... '[7] Caesar the soldier was always in control or certainly appears to be as, generally, we have to rely solely upon his account.

Sixteen hundred years later and his reputation remains undiminished:

> He always carried a stricter and tighter hand over his soldiers when near an enemy. When the ancient Greeks would accuse any one of extreme insufficiency, they would say, in common proverb, that he could neither read nor swim; he was of the same opinion, that swimming was of great use in war, and himself found it so; for when he had to use diligence, he commonly swam across the rivers in his way; for he loved to march on foot, as also did Alexander the Great. Being in Egypt forced, to save himself, to go into a little boat, and so many people leaping in with him that it was in danger of sinking, he chose rather to commit himself to the sea, and swam to his fleet, which lay two hundred paces off, holding in his left hand his tablets, and drawing his coat-armour in his teeth, that it might not fall into the enemy's hand, and at this time he was of a pretty advanced age.[8]

He was adept at exploiting the chronic weaknesses of his Gallic adversaries and taking advantage of their endless internecine feuds. In Gaul, he had the inestimable advantage of being absolute commander in chief. He was of course answerable in Rome but that was a very long way away and even his most vitriolic opponent had to rely on Caesar's own account. The nature of Gaul, of the campaigning and Caesar's pivotal position, combine to form the perfect platform for a spot of opportunistic imperialism and self-aggrandisement on a truly epic scale.

'Empire' – the idea of imperialism is none too popular in the 21st century, it is unfashionable to be seen to be oppressing your fellow men. This concern would have found no currency in Rome. Empire was good. It meant increasing revenue, loot, slaves and prestige. Like British adventurers in the 18th and 19th centuries, Roman conquerors would claim they were in fact bringing the benefits of civilisation to the barbarian fringes.

'What did the Romans ever do for us...?' The Monty Python script continues to conclude that it was in fact quite a lot, and the same is true of Gaul. Caesar's campaigns were bloody, destructive and invariably self-seeking, but they did lead to the establishment of a prosperous Gallo-Roman society that endured for five hundred years. One that subsequent ages looked back on with desperate longing. Rome, *Romanitas*, was the holy grail of Charlemagne, the strong man who could lead the people back into that golden age of secure and comfortable civilisation. We will never know what the country would have looked like had Caesar lost.

Caesar understood his soldiers. It's the mark of a great commander that he made them love him. He always gave praise where it was due. After the successful relief of Quintus Cicero's camp in 54 BC, the end of a terrible and desperately fought siege 'he praised both Quintus Cicero and his legion as they deserved; then, one by one, he addressed the centurions and military tribunes, of whose outstanding bravery he had heard from Quintus Cicero'.[9] One can almost see the men glowing beneath these tributes.

He also understood the psychology of his soldiers and how to inspire the cult of leadership, this extract is from his campaign in Africa of 46 BC:

> His army, being in some consternation upon the rumour that was spread of the great forces that King Juba was leading against him, instead of abating the apprehension which his soldiers had conceived at the news and of lessening to them the forces of the enemy, having called them all together to encourage and reassure them, he took a quite contrary way to what we are used to do, for he told them that they need no more trouble themselves with inquiring after the enemy's forces, for that he was certainly informed thereof, and then

told them of a number much surpassing both the truth and the report that was current in his army; following the advice of Cyrus in Xenophon, forasmuch as the deception is not of so great importance to find an enemy weaker than we expected, than to find him really very strong, after having been made to believe that he was weak.[10]

He often needed money – politics in Rome was expensive. Hefty bribes, costly shows and usually a cadre of paid fighting men require wealth. Caesar was frequently and massively in debt. He compensated by being totally unscrupulous:

> He was not particularly honest in money matters; either while a provincial governor or while holding office at Rome. Several memoirs record that as Governor-General of Western Spain he not only begged his allies for money to settle his debts, but wantonly sacked several Lusitanian towns, though they had accepted his terms and opened their gates to welcome him.[11]

Caesar was also a writer, a great one. His output was considerable but all that survives are the seven commentaries or accounts of the Gallic Wars (the last was written up by Aulus Hirtius after his death) and three more on the subsequent Civil War. There was, certainly according to Suetonius and others, far more but only these few have survived. Caesar comes across as the professional objective historian, writing always in the third person and never succumbing to flights of obvious vainglory. This makes him all the more credible and his terse, authoritative style is at all times fluid and compelling. The man was a gifted storyteller and enjoyed the marvellous advantage of there being no competition. He is the only real contemporary source we have.

It is easy to be seduced, generations have been. He was a raconteur yet always the consummate politician. His descriptions are a popular rendition for a mass audience back home. We merely have to turn to some of the more turgid and laboured memoirs of some modern statesmen to appreciate what a really fine job he does. Two millennia on and we still read him. This slavishness obscures caution.

To offer a more modern 20th-century parallel, look at General Bernard Montgomery's memoirs. His version of *Overlord* – the D-Day invasion of Hitler's 'Fortress Europe' – and of the subsequent grinding battle of attrition to finally win through in Normandy suggests Monty was always in control. He planned to draw the German reserves onto the British and Canadian front in the east to allow the Americans to build up and then break out from the west. That did happen but the reality is the campaign in the east floundered through several dismal failures to break through. Attempts at *Blitzkrieg* in Operations *Epsom* and *Goodwood* foundered completely. Monty did win through in the end but it was far from a flawless textbook victory.

There's more than an echo of this in Book VII of *the Gallic War*. The campaign of 52 BC was a very close-run thing indeed. Caesar emerged victorious but only because Vercingetorix blundered and left the back door open. Almost until the climatic stages, the Gallic commander was marginally ahead on points. Once he had stumbled, Caesar never gave him a chance to get back on his feet. He seized the proffered initiative and never let it go.

Montaigne for one applauded:

> Having undertaken that furious siege of Alexia, where there were fourscore thousand men in garrison, all Gaul being in arms to raise the siege and having set an army on foot of a hundred and nine thousand horse, and of two hundred and forty thousand foot, what a boldness and vehement confidence was it in him that he would not give over his attempt, but resolved upon two so great difficulties? – which nevertheless he overcame; and, after having won that great battle against those without, soon reduced those within to his mercy.[12]

Gaius Julius Caesar, the outstanding figure of the Late Republic and the one who finally brought it down, was born into a senatorial family of impeccably patrician credentials, rich in blood but otherwise asset poor. Roman children were not supposed to enjoy themselves, their upbringing was strict, even harsh and Caesar lost his father when he was only 15. He was related by marriage to the formidable Marius, whose army reforms made Caesar's career as a successful soldier possible. Unfortunately it was the old general's archrival Lucius Cornelius Sulla who held power. In 80 BC, the young Caesar dared to offend the dictator, one whose commandments were normally writ in blood, by refusing to divorce his first wife Cornelia.

This was a brave if impolitic gesture. Stripped of whatever dignity he had inherited; the young Julius lived like a fugitive. Powerful relatives interceded and the fear was lifted. It was said that Sulla, finally bowing to pressure, issued a dire warning that 'the man… will one day prove the ruin of the party which you and I have so long defended. There are many Marius' in this fellow Caesar'.[13] The future conqueror's military career kicked off with a term in Asia where he was suspected of a liaison with King Nicomedes. He came back with a top gallantry medal for saving a legionary's life during the storming of Mytilene.[14]

Next he campaigned in Cilicia but returned to Rome when Sulla stepped down from office. Remarkably, despite all the bloodletting, the latter died of natural causes. Caesar found the political climate in the *Urbs* rather less promising than he might have hoped. Travelling to Rhodes his ship was captured by pirates; at this time the eastern Mediterranean was totally infested with them. It took forty days for his ransom to arrive and that had to be borrowed. Though affable towards his captors, Caesar didn't bear humiliation and no sooner was he at liberty than he was on their trail in sleek war galleys. He caught and crucified the lot of them.[15] While he was in the vicinity, he discovered that Mithridates[16] was laying waste the coastal areas of Rome's territories in Asia Minor (now Turkey) and he raised an ad hoc force of militia to disperse the attackers.

On his return to Rome, the citizens voted him into high office and he actively assisted in dismantling Sulla's repressive legislation. Whilst he was serving as *quaestor,*[17] he lost his wife Cornelia and acquired another, Quintus Pompey's daughter Pompeia, a grand-daughter of Sulla himself. Later, he divorced her on the fairly flimsy pretext she might have entertained the outrageous Publius Clodius.[18] Caesar's wife had to be above suspicion even if Caesar did not.

As *quaestor* he served in Western Spain where the famous story concerning Alexander's statue in the temple at Cadiz arises. Caesar, then forty, was said to have wept that he was such an under-achiever. His hero, dead at 32, had conquered the world. He seems to have been driven by restlessness to get mixed up in some murkier regions of Republican politics and was accused of variously plotting to overthrow the state and

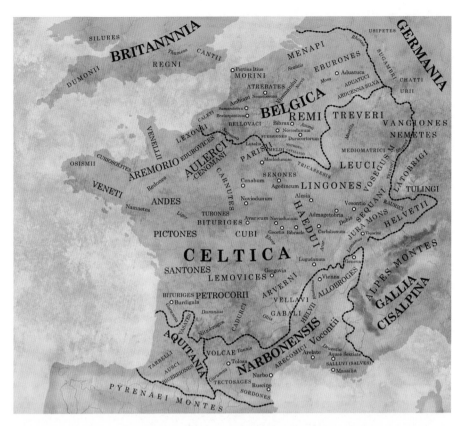

Map 1: The tribes of Gaul in 58 BC.

Right: An idealised portrait of Vercingetorix, gold stater held at the Cabinet des Médailles, Bibliothèque nationale de France, Paris. *(Siren-Com, Wikimedia Commons)*

Opposite: Commemorative statue of Vercingetorix by Aimé Millet. It was commissioned by Emperor Napoleon III, and installed on Mont Auxois, Alise-Sainte-Reine in 1865. *(Myrabella, Wikimedia Commons)*

Left: Tusculum bust of Julius Caesar, white marble, which dates from 50–40 BC. Here shown in an exhibition in Paris in 2014. *(Gautier Poupeau, Wikimedia Commons)*

Below: Gallic helmet found at Amfreville-sous-les-Monts (4th century BC) now in the National Archaeological Museum of Saint-Germain-en-Laye (Yvelines). *(Siren-Com, Wikimedia Commons)*

A *carynx* (Celtic war trumpet) found in the Gallic sanctuary of Tintignac, Corrèze, France. *(Claude Valette, Wikimedia Commons)*

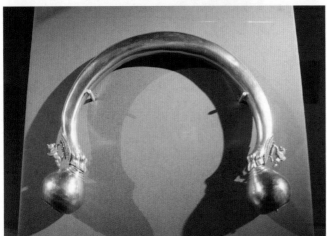

Torc found in the grave of the Lady of Vix, Côte-d'Or, France, *c.* 530 BC. It is made from over 40 different parts. *(Rosemania, Wikimedia Commons)*

Statue of Vercingetorix by Frédéric Bartholdi, on Place de Jaude, in Clermont-Ferrand, France. *(Fabien1309, Wikimedia Commons)*

Poster advertising the 1909 French film Vercingetorix (unknown director, produced by Pathé Frères). *(Cândido Aragonez de Faria, EYE Film Institute Netherlands, Public Domain, Wikimedia Commons)*

Below: Modern recreation of the type of clothing worn by a Celtic warrior, in Kelten-Keller Museum, Rodheim-Bieber, Germany. *(Gorinin, Wikimedia Commons)*

Right: Gaulish sword and scabbard *c.* 60 BC. *(PHGCOM, photographed at Metropolitan Museum of Art, Wikimedia Commons)*

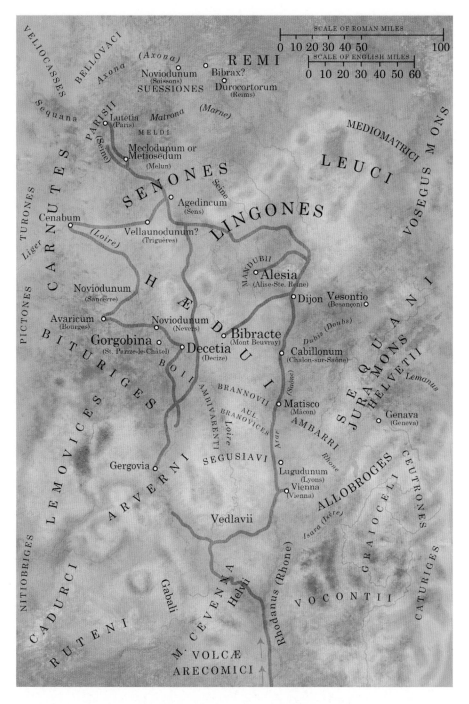

Map 2: The campaign of 52 BC.

Recreated Roman camp scene at Museo-Parc Alesia, typical of the accommodation within the lines. Note the soldiers' shields, '*scuta*' and javelins, '*pila*'. *(Museo-Parc Alesia)*

Reconstruction of a section of the lines at Alesia, with tents pitched in between. *(Museo-Parc Alesia)*

Closer view of the reconstructed lines, showing the height of the rampart and battlement. *(Museo-Parc Alesia)*

View of reconstructed lines of circumvallation. *(Museo-Parc Alesia)*

Roman legionaries. Note the montefortino style helmets and mail shirts. *(Museo-Parc Alesia)*

A Roman legionary squad. The contubernium was the core tactical unit. *(Museo-Parc Alesia)*

Close up of legionary in light marching order, note style of helmet and gladius. *(Museo-Parc Alesia)*

Legionary wearing mail shirt and shoulder cape for additional protection. *(Museo-Parc Alesia)*

Combat drill. *(Museo-Parc Alesia)*

Celtic warriors. *(Museo-Parc Alesia)*

Overleaf: Celtic warriors *(Museo-Parc Alesia)*

Celtic warriors. *(Museo-Parc Alesia)*

Celtic warriors. *(Museo-Parc Alesia)*

Celtic warriors. *(Museo-Parc Alesia)*

Celtic warriors. Note with all these photos the kit, clothing and equipment of the warriors, montefortino style helmets, oval shields and long slashing swords, very different to the short stabbing blades of their Roman adversaries. *(Museo-Parc Alesia)*

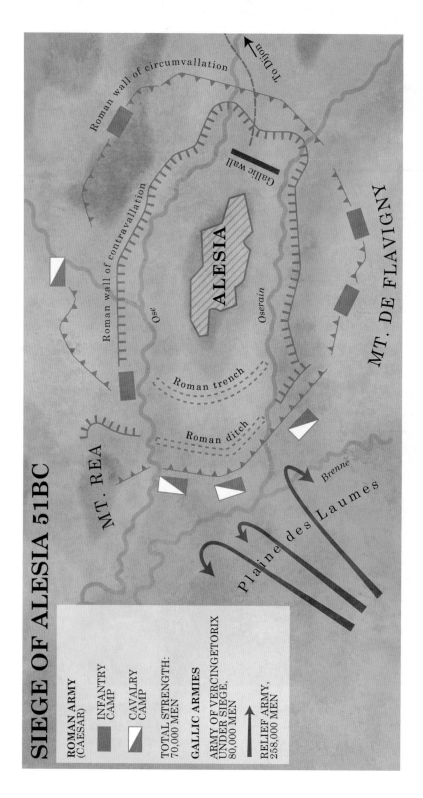

Map 3: The siege lines at Alesia 52 BC.

set up a dictatorship.[19] During all of his public service Caesar sought to buy popular favour with ostentatious show. Not that this was unique, it was just that he couldn't afford it. The number of combatants he scraped together for gladiatorial fights so alarmed his opponents that they instigated emergency legislation to restrict numbers.[20] To boost his finances he sought to wangle a plum job as governor-general in Egypt but that foundered on the rocks of patrician hostility.

Next he stood for election as Chief Pontiff.[21] Though he won, he had laid out a fortune in bribes and inducements. When the Catiline conspiracy burst onto centre stage, Caesar was suspected of complicity though nothing was ever proven and his vehement denials won him the benefit of the doubt. Finally, he got his own province as governor of Western Spain; probably his enemies just wanted him out of the Senate. His creditors were less keen to see him go and his departure was more fugitive than decorous. Once there he did good service, putting some stick about, bashing the aggressors and then dashing back precipitately to demand a triumph and stand as consul. He lost out on the former but by careful manoeuvring and a vast outlay of bribes, secured the latter.[22]

Aristocratic opposition remained undiluted but Caesar made an agreement with both Pompey and the hugely rich Marcus Crassus to share power and influence – the triumvirate. He intimidated his less forceful fellow-consul and did pretty much as he pleased. He had finally 'arrived'. A joke, current at the time, recorded that fake legal papers were signed ironically as being sealed during the consulship of 'Julius and Caesar'.[23] His high-handedness, arrogance and self-obsession, even in a polity defined by such traits, won him few friends and a swelling chorus of enemies. Meanwhile he had married again, this time to Calpurnia, daughter of his consular successor Lucius Piso. At the same time Caesar betrothed his daughter to Pompey.

Having thus secured the goodwill of his father-in-law Piso and his son-in-law Pompey, Caesar surveyed the many provinces open to him and chose Gaul as being the most likely to supply him with wealth and triumphs. Proposed by Publius Vatinius, he was initially appointed governor-general only of Cisalpine Gaul and Illyria but afterwards the

Senate added Transalpine Gaul to his jurisdiction, fearing that if this were denied him, the enthusiastic commoners would insist that he should have it.[24] His opponents weren't minded to let him get away so easily and his consulship was already the subject of hostile enquiry – only the fact he was constrained to see to his new province got him off the hook, for now anyway.

Gaul wasn't just a plum, it was an opportunity. The area he controlled extended across both sides of the Alps and included the Dalmatian coast. It was a massive fief and the perfect springboard for expansion and personal enrichment. For Caesar, the Gallic wars were not just about conquering territory, they were a form of civil war whereby his successes confounded his enemies in the Senate. Though the wars ended in 51 BC, his political struggles would spark a renewed Civil War and ultimately lead him to his bloody *Gotterdammerung* on the Ides of March.

The Gaul Caesar was about to invade was not a homogenous state in any nationalist sense (refer to Map 1). No Gallic leaders would have viewed themselves as part of a distinct cultural and geographical entity. As Prince Metternich rather sneeringly observed of Italy prior to 19th-century unification, Gaul was merely a *geographical expression*. Gaul was a tribal society shading into more distinctly Germanic peoples to the east. The line, however, was very far from any modern notion of a frontier.

In the province, the settled tribes, such as the Allobroges were largely Romanised, certainly pacified. North, into what is now central and eastern France, the powerful Aedui and their neighbours were beginning to adopt Roman systems of governance. Those peoples to the west, in the fertile Aquitaine northwards as far as the sea-faring Veneti from what is now Brittany (Armorica), rather less so. Northwards toward Pas de Calais the Belgae were so far immune. To the east the Lingones and Sequani abutted Germany and the wild men of the east, most powerful and feared of whom were the Suebi.

In 58 BC he didn't have long to wait, opportunity knocked. A powerful tribe, the Helvetii, who inhabited what is now Switzerland, embarked on a mass migration, taking their affiliated peoples, the Raurici, Tulingi, Latobrigi and Boii, with them. They intended an invasion of western Gaul, pushing aside those who lived there. There were numerous precedents for such wholesale transhumance and attempted Roman interventions had cost the state dearly. The Helvetii, hemmed in by their own mountains, were also under pressure from Germanic tribes moving west.

Their leader Orgetorix had prepared his ground thoroughly. Aside from massive logistical preparations, he'd formed an alliance with Casticua of the Sequani[25] and the influential Aeduan[26] noble Dumnorix. The Aedui, from their mighty capital at Bibracte and through Dumnorix' brother Diviciacus, had established links to the province and thus to Rome. The objectives of this coalition were, as it appears, to divide up supreme power in Gaul between themselves and repel German intruders under their king Ariovistus who had established a foothold on the west flank of the Rhine. It turned out Orgetorix' posturing had overstepped the mark with his own people who, fearful of his dynastic ambitions curtailed these for good by obliging him to kill himself.

This didn't halt the proposed migration. To Caesar this was intolerable. The potential damage to Roman security and interests was incalculable. Something had to be done. Unwittingly, Orgetorix and the Helvetii had provided Caesar with the *casus belli* he needed and the perfect stage to strut upon. He was still in Rome when he received news the tribes were moving. He dashed to the province, sending the single legion stationed there to break the vital bridge across the Rhone. Playing for time, he pretended to negotiate while building up linear frontier defences that would channel the invaders away from Roman territory.

One legion wasn't going to be enough so he raised two more hurriedly in Italy and swept up another three veteran formations from garrison duty. Showing the lightning touch that would become his trademark, Caesar marched his army over the Alps and caught the Helvetii spread out on both banks of the Saone. Though most had already crossed, he beat up those who hadn't, threw a pontoon over the river and gave chase to the rest. A game of cat and mouse followed – he wouldn't listen to peace overtures or be drawn into a fight precipitately. He was still heavily outnumbered. When the decisive clash came, Caesar deployed in his classic *triplex acies* formation.

It was no pushover but, despite the fact the Helvetii and their allies demonstrated an element of tactical flexibility, Roman discipline added to their commander's genius won the day. The enemy had unwisely hemmed in their battle line with baggage and dependants; the latter suffered particularly:

> Tablets were found in the Helvetii's camp, written in Greek characters, and were taken to Caesar. They contained a complete record under several headings – the numbers which had set out from the homeland, those capable of bearing arms, and a separate list of the boys, the old men and the women. The sum total of all these categories came to 263,000 of the Helvetii: of the Tulingi there was 36,000, of the Latovici 14,000, of the Raurici 23,000, and of the Boii 32,000. About 92,000 of these were capable of bearing arms, the total number was about 368,000. When a census was taken of those who returned home, in accordance with Caesar's orders, the number came to 110,000.[27]

As ever, we have only Caesar's tally of numbers to rely on. Did his soldiers really kill 250,000 enemies, even allowing for slaughter of non-combatants? It is a suspiciously high total, 25,000 dead seems rather more likely. In 57 BC he utterly hammered the Nervii, a pretty tough bunch who, in the final battle, were reduced from 60,000 warriors to a mere 500. Yet a couple of years later, besieging Cicero, their numbers are miraculously restored just in time to lose another 60,000.

This whirlwind campaign to chastise the intruders had all been entirely legal. Caesar had a duty to protect the province and the Helvetii were clearly a significant threat. But now it came to the Germans' turn. True, Ariovistus had bullied his way into Gaul but he also claimed to be an ally of Rome and it was harder to see how his actions constituted a direct threat. Caesar, on the pretext that the Gallic tribes had begged his intervention, nonetheless moved against him, occupying the key bastion of Vesontio (Besançon). Here a tremor of panic spread amongst the soldiers, fearful of the formidable reputation of their adversaries. Caesar dealt with these murmurings and confronted Ariovistus. It is doubtful the German actually wanted a fight; there was nothing in it for him. But Caesar would have his battle. Again, this was no walkover but he won another resounding victory and drove the Germans back to the Rhine.

Ariovistus escaped across the broad river: 'He found a small boat moored to the bank'.[28] Both of his wives and one of his daughters were less fortunate, all three were killed and another captured. One wonders which had the better fate. Caesar does not leave a note of enemy casualties but these were clearly considerable. In his first year of office he had fought two major campaigns and won. Caesar might have been – and his enemies would cheerfully brand him as – vainglorious, preferring battle to talk. In part this may have been true, conquerors need to conquer and a good, bloody thrashing always reads better than a negotiated truce.

Appeasement generally wins few friends. Yet, in all of his marches, Caesar constantly experienced supply problems. His men could only fight if they were fed – his Gallic allies, unreliable at best and notoriously fickle, provided the vital corn supply. Besides, battle was what Roman legions did. They were heavy assault infantry. Any commander worth his salt would seek to bring the enemy to a decisive clash as soon as possible. Long drawn-out asymmetric, guerrilla-style campaigns were to be avoided at all costs.

Caesar warms to the theme in terms of Gallic duplicity. He portrayed the Gauls as a body of delinquent bullies with the statesmanship of the schoolyard; easily swayed and led like children, naïve yet also cruel and spiteful. These descriptions remind us that Caesar was writing self-promoting propaganda intended for home consumption. From 57 BC onwards his campaigns in Gaul were aimed at pure conquest. The balcony of legitimacy that had allowed him to intervene had long since disappeared. This was a war of conquest – of aggrandisement. His innumerable enemies, particularly silver-tongued, waspish Cicero, were quick to pounce, accusing him at one point of near-genocide. Self-justification is a major theme throughout the *Gallic War*. Caesar was operating way beyond his remit, pushing out the borders of empire as a private venture.

Not that most Romans minded this. Enlarging the empire was a worthy objective and Caesar added more territory than even the great Marius:

> Briefly, his nine years governorship produced the following results. He reduced to the form of a province the whole of Gaul enclosed by the Pyrenees, the Alps, the Cevennes, the Rhine, and the Rhone – about 640,000 square miles – except for certain allied states which had given him useful support; and exacted an annual tribute of 400,000 gold pieces.[29]

In cashflow terms this was a vast boost to Rome's finances. In personal terms, Caesar was transformed from hounded debtor to a man of great wealth. Very few in Rome would lose any sleep over the deaths of mere barbarians, in whatever numbers. Memories of 390 BC still stuck deep.

In the theoretically more enlightened society of the 21st century, the bungled invasion of Iraq – both the short campaign and its extended death throes – may have cost the lives of up to half a million casualties. No official statistics appear to have been compiled. Some in the West protested against the war but most did not and the popular press will always find the off-screen indiscretions of mindless minor 'celebrities' will sell more newspapers than unpleasant realities from far-off places. As with the Romans in Rome, Western society generally did not feel any affinity with the population and were, with exceptions, indifferent to their fate.

In his second year of campaigning Caesar moved north. This was pure acquisition, almost impossible to justify. Defeating the Helvetii and ejecting Ariovistus could clearly be said to have served Rome's strategic interests. But now, lacking obvious good cause, he still needed to justify his action, which he dressed up as a pre-emptive strike: 'Caesar was in Nearer Gaul; there he heard a host of rumours, confirmed by a letter from Labienus, that all of the Belgae ... were hatching a plot against the Roman people and exchanging hostages.'[30]

His reasons were a bit woolly. He claimed the Belgae feared just his kind of blow, the tribes had been 'stirred up' by disaffected Gauls, some just liked trouble for its own sake and others feared the imposition of universal law would be a brake on personal ambition.[31] Caesar continued to show favour to the still-powerful Aedui, who acted as a bulwark in the centre. From amongst the northern peoples the canny Remi decided to throw in their lot with Rome. The rest could field a powerful coalition and, he claims, all of 200,000 warriors. As he had already explained to his audience, these northerners were fiercer and hardier, proper 'hairies' – far less exposed to civilising, sybaritic Mediterranean influences.

This was a lot farther north than Roman armies were used to. It was a different kind of country, colder, harder and free from the veneer or taint of classical influences. Broad river valleys, dense belts of virgin forest, rolling hills, marsh and bog, towns were fewer, the warriors tougher, forged steel-hard in the dark forests. This was alien country.

Having added another two legions to his order of battle to make a total of eight, perhaps 35,000 effectives, he marched north. He intended both to deal with the Belgae and cut them off from any German reinforcements coming across the Rhine. His allies the Remi saw off an attack on their capital near Bibrax and a confrontation between the two field armies followed. Logistical problems frustrated any chance of a decisive battle. Caesar next marched against the capital of the Suessiones at Noviodunum (Soissons) on the Aisne. Shock and awe did the job and the startled tribesmen surrendered or fled.

The Nervii, whose courage and tenacity were renowned, were made of far sterner stuff and, with their remaining allies, planned to ambush the Roman army while it was strung out on the line of march: a sound and potentially devastating tactic. It very nearly worked, Caesar had a hard fight on his hands by the wooded banks of the Sambre but Roman pluck and Caesar's luck both held.

Beaten but fighting on doggedly to the end, the Nervii lost vast numbers. When the battle was over the name and fighting strength of the Nervii were almost wiped out. When news of the battle reached the elders, who were gathered in inlets and marshes along with the women and children, they assumed that nothing stood in the way of the victors, and that for the vanquished nothing was secure. So all the survivors agreed to send envoys to Caesar and surrender to him. Describing the disaster that had befallen them, the Nervian envoys declared that they had been reduced from 600 senators to three, from 60,000 fighting men capable of active service to a mere 500.[32]

It was very nearly game, set and match for 57 BC, only the recalcitrant Aduatuci remained to be dealt with. The tribe had prepared a strong defensive position but agreed to submit once they appreciated they couldn't hope to withstand a siege. They agreed terms, but this was simply a ruse to lower Roman watchfulness so they could then attempt a night attack on the lines. This assault was seen off and no clemency shown. Four thousand Aduatuci died in the failed breakout, the rest, some 53,000 of them, were sold off as a job lot into slavery.[33] According to the rules of war, this response was perfectly acceptable. It also brought Caesar an enormous profit. All in all, things weren't going too badly.

On the rugged coasts of Armorica (now Brittany), maritime states such as the Veneti had become master ship-builders and mariners. Truculent over the defeat of so many other tribes, they offered resistance in the following year, 56 BC. A very tough nut to crack, these hardy, experienced seafarers posed a significant tactical problem. As ever, Caesar reacted quickly. He found sailors, he built ships and he beat the Veneti at their own game. His subordinate Publius Crassus (son of the triumvir), carried the eagles south and west into what would become the Aquitaine. Quintus Titurius Sabinus successfully campaigned in Normandy. By the end of the summer Caesar was mopping up pockets of resistance (the Morini and Menapii from the Channel coast region). Wisely, these tribes had avoided a pitched battle. It had proved to be another successful campaigning season.

Caesar could report that Gaul was quiet. He needed to. His armies had won a number of significant victories without suffering any serious reverses. Profits from these actions flowed back to the centre but war is an expensive business. Field armies are very expensive, a huge upkeep in wages, equipment, supplies and materiel. Besides, Romans didn't like their generals enjoying too much power. They might develop a taste for it. Caesar, already unpopular with many, was effectively a law to himself. He was campaigning beyond any remit he might have enjoyed at the outset. The longer the war dragged on, the more his enemies would focus. Caesar was fighting on two fronts, only one in Gaul, the other, just as deadly, in Rome. A constant string of victories and rewards were needed from one to keep the other quiescent.

This New Year, 55 BC, promised to be strenuous. Crassus and Pompey were consuls in Rome, at the very heart of the world. They could use all the tools at their disposal; bribery, patronage, intimidation, propaganda to strengthen their own position. Caesar needed some spectacular PR of his own. Bashing more Gauls wouldn't do it, so he decided on a double-pronged spectacular. He'd bridge the Rhine in the east and cross the Channel to the west. He'd turn Germany and Britain into his stage and *deus ex machina*, he'd deliver the goods.

Once again the course of events obliged. Two Germanic nations, the Usipetes and Tencteri had swarmed across the Rhine, citing pressure from their all-powerful neighbours, the Suebi. Caesar was having none of it but the unit of allied cavalry he sent out to recce the invaders' camps was caught and badly mauled by a far inferior force. Retaliation was swift and sure, the invaders were savagely ejected despite the fact 'the enemy numbered 430,000'.[34] This does seem an improbably high figure but, as ever, we only have Caesar's account.

Just to ram his point home, Caesar then had a bridge built across the river, a feat the Gauls and Germans would have considered totally impossible. This huge undertaking was completed in only ten days, shock and awe indeed. Caesar marched into Germany, beat up a few local quarters then marched back again, dismantling the bridge. He hadn't conquered Germany, hadn't scratched the surface, but he'd beaten the obsessively warlike Germans again and crossed the symbolic wet gap. Caesar understood the value of showmanship.

Plus, while there was no real tactical or strategic gain, he had demonstrated the superiority of Roman arms and engineering. Moreover, he'd hammered and stunned the Germans sufficiently to free up resources for his second project of the season, a reconnaissance in force over the Channel. The pretext was that Britons had been lending military assistance to their Gallic neighbours and such temerity merited a riposte. By now it was late in the summer and his expedition suffered more from adverse weather than local opposition. With only two legions (and those deprived of cavalry whose transports never made it over), this could be no more than a gesture. There was extended skirmishing but without cavalry Caesar could not exploit any successes. Storms battered his ships and he was lucky to get back without serious loss.

The whole show, rather pointless as it was in strategic terms, did remarkably well at the box office. His expedition really caught imaginations in Rome and he was awarded twenty days of thanksgiving.[35] He might not have conquered Britain but he had neatly trumped his fellow triumvirs. Moreover, he intended to return. If Caesar had achieved little of permanence in his first cross-Channel jaunt, he was aiming to make a lasting impression with a much bigger foray in 54 BC. This would involve four legions and 2,000 cavalry, leaving three legions and the same number of mounted troops to hold down Gaul. This time he was far better prepared and the British campaign, fought primarily against Cassivellaunus of the Catuvellauni, was brought to a successful conclusion. Hostages and the payment of an annual tribute were secured. In the long term it made very little difference to anything, but it won plaudits in Rome, the main battleground.

It did seem that 54 BC might be a vintage year for Julius Caesar but any such hopes turned sour in the autumn. Harvests had been poor, grain was in short supply. The tribes groaned under the burden of supplying the legions. Scarcity meant Caesar had to disperse his men widely in winter quarters, probably more widely than he might have preferred. Still, all Gaul seemed quiet. It wasn't. Ambiorix of the Eburones targeted the easternmost forward base, a single rookie legion commanded by Lucius Aurunculeius Cotta and some additional cohorts under Sabinus. Ambiorix conned the officers with promises of safe conduct and they fell for it, leading to a general massacre. Only a few got out, some made it back to camp where they fell on their own swords rather than surrender. It was a total shambles.

If this was the 'Isandhlwana' of the Gallic wars, Quintus Cicero provided the 'Rorke's Drift', a brilliant defence against impossible odds. The Nervii did the attacking, having learnt from earlier mistakes they blockaded Cicero's camp with a complete *circumvallation*. There was no respite and no sign of relief. The legionaries fought for their lives and fought hard. Caesar, at length alerted, wasted no time in marching to the rescue. Only one man in ten of Cicero's garrison was uninjured.[36] He brought the Nervii to battle and thrashed them a second time (though with such large numbers of Nervii in action, this does rather suggest the tribe had not previously suffered the catastrophic loss recorded by Caesar).

The setbacks of the autumn and winter rather knocked the gloss off Caesar's successful raid on Britain. For 53 BC it was a question of re-asserting Roman control, weakened by the annihilation of Sabinus and Cotta. He had to recruit two new legions and get one on loan from Pompey to bring his army back up to full fighting strength. Before the campaigning season proper had opened, he had harried the Nervii into submission. Another lightning march as the snows receded caught the Senones unaware, forcing them to capitulate. Next Caesar marched to the vast plain of the Rhine Delta to confront the Menapii. They preferred Fabian tactics and melted into their marshlands. Caesar came after them, bridging wet gaps, burning and destroying. The Menapii too had soon had enough.

Meanwhile Labienus was encamped in the territory of the Treveri, who were restless and hopeful of German allies joining them before they raised their banners. Labienus was no Sabinus, however, rather a seasoned commander with 25 legionary cohorts and plenty of cavalry. He feigned retreat to draw his enemy out and they obliged. He savaged the Treveri in the ensuing battle. Then his cavalry conducted a murderous pursuit. The Germans would not be coming.

Caesar went to them, bridging the Rhine a second time and raiding into Germany. Supply problems again limited the scope of operations and he did not fight the Suebi. More flying columns penetrated the vast forests of the Ardennes, carrying fire and sword beyond. By the end of the season, no enemy remained in arms, even the Eburones, who had destroyed Sabinus and Cotta, threw in the towel … 'Caesar ruled over relative calm in Gaul'.[37]

Relative calm – Caesar might have thought the pacification of Gaul was at last complete but if he had, he would have been wrong. By far the greatest test of his leadership and the final battle for supremacy was about to begin. He had fought many enemies but never encountered a Gaul of equal stature and utter, unswerving determination. Caesar probably knew or had heard of a young Arvernian noble called Vercingetorix. He was about to hear a good deal more.

CHAPTER 6

TOTAL WAR 52 BC

This [Caesar's] uncanny quickness of movement went with an equal quickness of mind, ruefully recognised by Cicero: 'the wariness and energy of that bogeyman are terrifying!'

Michael Grant, *Julius Caesar.*

A united Gaul,
Formed into a single nation
Stirred by the same spirit
Can defy the world

This stirring invocation is a translation of the inscription on the base of the statue of Vercingetorix at Alesia. It tells us rather more about 19th-century French nationalism than it does about the 1st century BC. That in reality is its purpose. Viollet-le-Duc was commenting on the reign of his patron Napoleon III, the unintended irony being that the emperor would soon suffer the same total defeat and exile. Frenchmen in 1871 would come to appreciate how their Gallic forbears might have felt in 52 BC all too well. Napoleon's nemesis Bismarck was already mustering his legions, as effectively as Caesar marshalled his. History often tends towards cruel irony.

Vercingetorix might have struggled with some of his later hagiography, but it is impossible to tell as we hear nothing from him. We have to rely on his adversary Caesar. As ever, he tells us what he thinks his audience wants to hear and only that which ultimately shows him, Caesar, in a favourable light. He does not admit to knowing Vercingetorix or suggest they ever met until the very end. It is tempting to think he is being disingenuous and that they had certainly crossed paths. The impression he gives in Book VII of *the Gallic War* is that Vercingetorix erupts from virtual obscurity onto the stage as a major player in 52 BC: 'He was a son of Celtillus and his father had won dominion over the whole of Gaul; for this reason, namely, trying to gain a kingdom, Celtillus had been put to death by the state.'[1]

Caesar admits his opponent was a young man of considerable talent; in his abilities 'second to none'. He apparently launched a bid for individual power within his own tribe the Arverni relying on his personal affinity. Wary presumably because of family history, his uncle Gobannitio and other wise councillors drove the young hothead out of town, '... banished him from Gergovia'. Undeterred, Vercingetorix gathered a wider following; 'a levy of down and outs and desperadoes'. This may be unduly pejorative.

What Caesar was referring to was most likely a company of younger bucks, anxious to make a name and seduced by his undoubted charisma, young warriors tired of skulking in older men's shadows and chasing renown. Vercingetorix had created his own affinity and in typical Gallic style used his client group to overwhelm the other faction. With these restless blades at his back, Vercingetorix turned the tables, staging a lightning coup. The opposition were sent packing ... 'Vercingetorix was now proclaimed king by his supporters'.[2]

The present-day Auvergne derives its name from the Arverni, one of the most powerful of the Gallic tribes. In the 2nd and 3rd centuries BC they had held sway over not just their neighbours but most of Gaul. Their lands were fertile and they excelled at metal working with a wide trading network. Their king Luernios was head of a powerful alliance. His successor Bituitus clashed with Rome as the province was being established, losing out to Quintus and Gnaeus Ahenobarbus in 121 BC.

Although not brought under direct rule like the Allobroges, their wings were clipped, territory and prestige diminished and pre-eminence passed to the Aedui and Sequani. This reversal of fortune and Bituitus' defeat may have led them to reject the notion of kingship in favour of rule by aristocratic council (often referred as magistrates). Celtillus' bid to re-establish a strong centralised monarchy and revive tribal prestige clearly went down badly – he did not have a sufficiently strong clientage to pull it off. Vercingetorix, as the able son of a failed dictator, was bound to have been viewed with some suspicion.

As his dominance increased during 52 BC, Vercingetorix was always at pains to stress he was acting for the greater good rather than from personal ambition, an ostensible humility Caesar records. Nonetheless, the man who conquers the man who had conquered Gaul might expect some significant material reward. Caesar's campaigns had benefited Vercingetorix immensely. Without this compelling threat to the tribes' independence they would have been unlikely to offer any form of uni-fied command, local jealousies would have been far too prominent. And Caesar, the foreign invader, had exercised dominance over the whole of Gaul, an achievement none of his Celtic predecessors had ever been able to anticipate. We cannot say if Vercingetorix' revolt was a spontaneous decision based on opportunism, or the fruition of a carefully laid plan. What little we can tease out of his thinking, as demonstrated by his tactical genius, clearly shows him to be a young man of high intelligence, strategic nous and exceptional dynamism.

Possibly, he saw himself as Caesar's natural successor. By ruthless effi-ciency, strategic and tactical brilliance, the Roman interloper had made himself ruler of Gaul. He might have been accountable to the Senate in Rome but he was virtual dictator in Gaul. Vercingetorix understood that, but his fellow Gauls generally did not. Success is not about holding down territory or looking after individual interest. There is no personal glory or warrior renown. These are the very tools Caesar turns against the Gallic peacocks locked into their fissiparous worldview. Caesar is pure policy and decision. His main weapon, both scalpel and hammer, is his seemingly invincible professional field army.

Vercingetorix' rise in that spring was meteoric, which must lead us to ask whether this was not the working out of protracted patient diplomacy. No sooner had he made himself ruler of the Arverni than 'He sent out embassies in all directions, asking everyone to remain loyal, and soon formed alliances with the Senones, the Parisii, the Pictones, the Cadurci, the Turoni, the Aulerici, the Lemovices, the Andes and all the other Gallic peoples along the coast.'[3] These tribes along the western littoral were those over which his predecessors had exercised control and gained allegiance: so he was not building a new confederation rather re-activating an old one. His father probably had form for this as well, though the son intended to avoid the parent's mistakes.

He was both incisive and ruthless. Hostages were handed over and a levy of fighting men imposed. He wanted weapons, gear and horses. The cavalry would be even more important than previously. He saw mobility as key. There was no room for disagreement; 'he combined extreme conscientiousness with extreme severity'. He wouldn't brook dissenters or faint-hearts. Killing and torture were the main sanctions. For a minor infringement you might get lucky and just lose an eye or ear.[4] This wasn't a game for dilettantes, Gallic warfare had just come of age. Caesar would be facing the greatest challenge of his career. His six years of conquest and ostensible pacification were flung onto the scales. Both militarily and politically, neither man could afford to lose. The stakes in this particular 'Game of Thrones' had always been high and now they became even higher.

For all his star quality, Vercingetorix had not created the rebellion of 52 BC. He had in fact tapped into a rising discontent that was already beginning to bubble up. The tribes of the centre and south had grown wealthy on trade with the Mediterranean and had been influenced by its sophistication. Evolving systems of governance in Gallic society were fuelled by that wealth. It was to assist them, deliver them even from the threat of the Helvetii and to expel the German Ariovistus that Caesar had intervened in 58 BC. They had cause to thank him for their deliverance but he'd stayed and it was now pretty obvious, six years on, that he wasn't going home anytime soon. Rome was in Gaul to stay. Caesar understood diplomacy, he was a master. He wasn't ever heavy-handed with the allied tribes, more like a stern headmaster than conqueror. It had, however, dawned on the tribes that they were conquered nonetheless and the velvet glove didn't really disguise, as the more recalcitrant nations had discovered, the iron fist within.[5]

Plutarch, for one, was of the view that this was no brush-fire:

> Many years previously the seeds had secretly been sown and now the leading men of the region were spreading dissent amongst the most warlike tribes, whose confidence was increased by several factors: the considerable numbers of fighting men who had assembled there from all quarters, armed and ready; the huge amounts of money that had been accumulated; the strength of the cities; and the virtual impregnability of the territory.[6]

At the end of the previous campaigning season Caesar had executed Acco,[7] a ringleader of the earlier plot. And this killing seems to have served as the catalyst for rebellion. Caesar may also have taken his eye off the ball, distracted by goings on in Rome where tensions were boiling over, exacerbated by the killing of Clodius. The mercurial politician's death in a brawl and spectacular botched cremation (which resulted in the immolation of the Senate House) meant Caesar's eyes were fixed very much upon his own political future.[8] Besides, he probably thought Gaul was fully sorted. He had no reason to fear the more settled tribes who had caused him little or no bother to date. It was another calculated gamble and most often he won the wager. Not this time.

He'd underestimated the extent of the steadily boiling resentment and the finely attuned radar of the tribal leaders. With Caesar away and his legions spread out in winter quarters, individual subordinates could never react as rapidly as the conductor himself. Resentment over the beheading of Acco, and suspicions that a levy in the province could mean universal conscription all fed the simmering unrest. A secret meeting of the disaffected was convened 'in a remote forest location'. Speed was of the essence. Most vociferous were the Carnutes, one of the most powerful tribes of the centre, holding ground between the Seine and Loire, who swore they would strike the first blow. This pledge was underwritten by the putative rebels putting all their standards together, a declaration of joint intent.[9]

This pre-emptive strike was an attack on the Roman traders and officials based in Cenabum (Orléans). The ringleaders were Cotuatus and Conconnetodumnus and they murdered everyone, including Caesar's resident quartermaster Gaius Fufius Cita, an equestrian and thus a gentleman.[10] This act of butchery proclaimed the rebellion. Caesar commented on the rapidity of the Gaulish bush telegraph, how rapidly news was disseminated over great distances. Vercingetorix, 160 miles away in Gergovia, heard of it 'before the end of the first watch'.[11]

Once he'd received his cue Vercingetorix reacted but it seems clear he did not instigate the insurrection. Had he been one of those who had met earlier in the woodland location then surely Caesar would have said as much. Whether he was already primed is equally uncertain though the fact his first attempt bounced suggests not. Next Vercingetorix effectively hijacked the inchoate resistance and gave it a dynamic boost. Killing settlers and merchants achieves no military purpose other than to foster a hunger for revenge. It was, however, a signal that this was no ordinary war. Atrocity breeds atrocity, Caesar would not now show much in the way of clemency.

Vercingetorix wasn't an advocate of mercy either. He was preparing his followers for a new type of struggle *a outrance* – to the death. Plutarch was certainly convinced that Vercingetorix' own intelligence antennae were very firmly tuned: 'He wanted to use the opportunity created by the existence of an anti-Caesar coalition in Rome to arouse the whole of Gaul to war.'[12] This would certainly suggest that nothing here was entirely spontaneous. Even if he had not initially been directly involved, Vercingetorix would have been aware of the simmering pot.

His first targets were the collaborators, those peoples allied to Rome. Nobody would be allowed to sit on fences. Having sent a force to beat up the Remi, he moved with the main body against the Bituriges. With their capital at wealthy Avaricum (Bourges), the Bituriges were a powerful tribe, previously associated with the druidic cult. In Caesar's day the tribe had declined and had been relegated to client status. Under threat, the Bituriges appealed to their dominant allies, the Aedui.

This was at the suggestion of Caesar's own officers who appear, rather slow-wittedly, to have been very tardy in realising that this was not some mere tribal dispute. Adrian Goldsworthy considers, with justification, that the rest of his subordinates were pretty mediocre, with the exception of Labienus. Perhaps this was Caesar's choice: there is only ever room for one presiding genius.[13] The proper reaction for regular officers when faced with insurgency was to react rapidly and decisively – strike the snake before it begins to bite and the poison spreads.

Though the Aedui were Caesar's pet ally, they responded half-heartedly, their men advancing no further than the banks of the Loire, the traditional boundary. Citing fears about their own allies and their increased exposure if they advanced into the Bituriges' territory, they swiftly withdrew. Whether the Bituriges had already decided to defect or just jumped onto the bandwagon isn't clear. Finally Caesar's officers woke up and began, fumblingly, to react. Events in Rome now moved in their general's favour. Pompey, though appointed as sole consul, hadn't been made dictator but he had restored order. Caesar was free to re-cross the Alps to the province. He was back in Gaul but not yet reunited with his army. The impresario was back in the ring.

This was the strategic problem. With all of Gaul suddenly in flames, the old maxim, 'march divided, fight united' would be resonating. If he attempted to bring all his forces back into the redoubt of the province, he risked their being attacked and destroyed piecemeal on their various lines of marching. Yet concentration was vital. If he went to them, he risked ambush. Moreover, he perceived that he could not, with any degree of safety, trust his life even to those Gauls who still appeared friendly. Even the province wasn't safe.

The wonderfully named Lucterius the Cadurcan, presumably an agent of Vercingetorix, had stirred up the Ruteni and moved on to persuade the Nitiobriges and Gabali. His combined army (Caesar gives us no note of numbers) moved forward to have a crack at Narbo. Caesar could not ignore or bypass this threat so he rushed to stiffen the defences, brought up reserves from the province and scattered a ring of forward operational bases in the tribal lands around.

He had reinforcements available from Italy and concentrated his strength in the old Helvetii stamping grounds. Whatever was left of the Helvetii and their allies stayed quiet. They had had enough hammerings, too many to be seduced. This was enough to deter Lucterius, who had presumably been aiming at an easy and profitable raid. Caesar himself had to carry out a forced march over the snow-covered hills to join his troops. Now united with his forces, only the barrier of the Cevennes, still deep in winter ice, separated him from the Arverni.

They might have thought the winter still offered them protection but this was Julius Caesar with his back to the wall. He would never be' bolder or more daring or indeed more brilliant: 'with great exertion the soldiers cleared away the snow to a depth of six feet and opened up a way. Then Caesar made his way through into the territory of the Arverni. They were caught off guard and unawares – for they thought that the Cevennes protected them like a wall, and at that time of year the paths had never been passable before, not even for individual travellers.'[14] Once through the barrier, Caesar unleashed his cavalry to cry havoc.

Worrying as these raids might be for Vercingetorix, his army being a good hundred miles north, it is unlikely they caused major damage. That wasn't the point. The whole move was a ruse to draw the enemy south. After a couple of days of harrying, Caesar left Decimus Junius Brutus in command with orders to keep up the pressure. He gave out that he himself was retiring back to see to fresh recruiting. But instead, back across the hills, he headed for Vienne (Vienna in Latin) in the Rhone valley.

He had already arranged for cavalry reserves to muster there. With just these relatively few horsemen he spurred through the lands of the Aedui, not yet wavering, to join those two legions still in winter quarters amongst the Lingones. This was a risky gambit, but one which paid handsome dividends. He was poised to be reunited with his veterans and, at the same time, could put some stick about amongst the Aedui in case they were shaky. He sent gallopers to the remaining legions ordering a concentration at Agedincum near modern Sens.

Vercingetorix riposted by bringing his forces back to the country of the Bituriges. Though he had been wrong-footed, he was not fazed and began an attack on Gorgobina. This *oppidum* was a centre for the Boii, one of those nations who had joined with the Helvetii in their bid to migrate six years earlier. Though they had been beaten, Caesar had allowed them to set up under the wing of the Aedui. Vercingetorix was making no random gesture, he knew his actions presented Caesar with a difficult choice, something of a dichotomy.

Such a move could not go uncontested and inaction would not only hand Vercingetorix the initiative, it would equate to a sign of weakness and Caesar could not afford to allow the rot to spread any further, especially to the Aedui. On the other hand, if he took to the field now with his legions before spring, he would run into major supply problems. His legionaries would fight the battles but he needed his allies to ensure their bellies were kept full. Caesar did not fail the test. He summoned supplies from the Aedui, sent reassurances to the Boii and, leaving two legions as rearguard, set off to lift the blockade.[15]

His first target was Vellaunodunum, an *oppidum* of the Senones. After three days the defenders had had enough and opened their gates. Caesar took hostages, seeded a garrison and moved against Cenabum. The Carnutes, blood of Romans still fresh on the streets, can't have been in any doubt as to what was in store for them. They intended to fight for the place and were raising an army but the Senones' collapse wrong-footed them.

Within two days, he was in front of their walls. As it was late he deferred an assault until the next day but posted two full legions in case the defenders used darkness as a cloak while they debunked over the Loire. They tried and Caesar took the town without much of a fight. Very few of the panicked escapees made it over the jammed bridge. Caesar was not inclined to leniency, he sacked and burnt the place. Though it is not stated explicitly, the survivors presumably were sold off as slaves. The Bituriges were next for the axe.[16]

Caesar had clawed back the initiative. Next he targeted Noviodunum (literally 'New Fort', possibly Neung-sur-Beuvron). The equally panicked inhabitants attempted to negotiate. They had allowed a logistics team into the town to begin collecting weapons when they saw Vercingetorix' cavalry vanguard stirring dust in the distance. This produced a sudden stiffening of the sinews and the legionaries practically had to fight their way out. Caesar sent out his own mounted troops and a melée swirled in meadowland before the walls. The Roman cavalry were getting the worst of it until Caesar threw in his mounted reserve, those fearsome Germans. Vercingetorix' men were unable to withstand this fresh assault and fell back in disorder. The townspeople experienced another lightning change of heart. Ringleaders of the earlier volte-face were thrown to the wolves and handed over.

It was time to attack Avaricum (Bourges), the most important stronghold of the Bituriges. Today, delightful Bourges, the capital of the old medieval province of Berry, is noted for its fine Gothic cathedral and charming streets, rightly so. The citizens have cleared a walkway around the hilltop, which follows the lines of the old *Murus Gallicus* that Caesar now confronted. The site is formidable – even from among the far later streets, we get a clear impression of both size and strength. The Bituriges were famed as metalworkers and the considerable wealth of their capital reflected the success of their industry. These people would not expect to surrender their city without a fight.

Vercingetorix had different ideas. He convened a council and told his subordinates quite bluntly that it was time for a new form of warfare, probably what would now be called asymmetric. He understood that meeting the Romans head on would be disastrous. Victory could only be won by attrition, by attacking the legions where they were weakest, by denying Caesar the opportunity to demonstrate his brilliance as a field commander.

They would go for supply and logistics, cutting off and beating up small detachments wherever opportunities presented themselves. He argued that they had superior cavalry forces and this was the right time of year, with there being no fat harvests to sustain large infantry forces. Caesar's campaign would be strangled.[17] Later guerrilla fighters, T. E. Lawrence or Che Guevara, would have admired the thinking. It was a good plan. Vercingetorix was playing to the strengths of the Gauls, while minimising their many weaknesses.

In addition, from now on the Gauls would be engaging in total war, where all personal considerations were to be sacrificed for the common cause. Cutting off the umbilical supply meant scorched earth. Whatever the Gauls possessed would be burnt before their enemies could take possession. This was not just a reactive policy. Towns that could not be easily defended would be torched. There were no longer civilians; everyone was in the front line now: 'they must remember that it was far worse to have their children and wives dragged into slavery, and themselves be killed: and this was sure to be their fate if they were defeated.'[18]

From this point on, the campaign of 52 BC was very different in complexion to those fought before. There had been blood and tears enough but this was to be warfare on a scale and intensity Gaul had never witnessed. The tribes were not fighting their own corners any more. They were to be part of what amounted to a national effort. There would be no fences left standing for anybody to sit on. As President George W. Bush remarked about a far more recent struggle, 'You're either with us or against us'. That was how it was to be for the tribes. Their capacity for deceit and vacillation was as big a threat to Vercingetorix as it was to Caesar.

For Vercingetorix, this was a remarkable achievement and speaks volumes about his character and charisma. He was in deadly earnest. No sooner had the council unanimously agreed than flaming brands did the rounds: 'In a single day more than twenty cities of the Bituriges were set on fire. The same policy was carried out in the other states: fires were visible in every direction.'[19] The Bituriges drew the line at sacrificing Avaricum, which they considered the finest city in the country. Vercingetorix was not minded to listen but finally gave way, putting in a garrison but refusing to commit his field army. The townspeople could fight but they would be on their own.

In terms of both the natural obstacles and strength of their defences, Avaricum had grounds for hope. The town stood on a spur of high ground thrusting into surrounding wet marshland. The ridge isn't level;

it slopes away then rises to form a small hill or eminence. But in Caesar they had an attacker of genius and great experience. Like Vercingetorix he was playing to win and would do whatever was necessary. The Bituriges, in deciding to make their stand, had become the front line in the battle between these two utterly ruthless leaders.

Caesar seized on the spur, occupied the small hill and spent an industrious month dealing with the depression. The ramp, constructed in timber, was 100 metres across and 25 metres high. Writing of the later siege of Jerusalem (70 AD), Josephus noted that every tree within 18 kilometres had been cut down and the timber used up. The deforestation around Avaricum must have been on a similar scale. Once the ramp was in place, siege towers could be brought against the walls with the legionaries' approach screened by stout galleries.[20]

For Vercingetorix, defeat for the Bituriges, the fall of Avaricum, would only serve to vindicate his Fabian tactics. If Caesar could crack so tough a nut then clearly Vercingetorix was right. Meeting the Romans in battle, even from behind stout walls, was futile. Besides, Caesar's main problem, as his opponent had predicted, was supply. If we accept his available forces were somewhere between 20,000 and 25,000 soldiers, with cavalry and allied detachments,[21] he had a lot of mouths to feed. Both the Aedui and Boii were not keen to help with supplies, in fairness they wouldn't have had much to spare anyway. Supplies were running short. Vercingetorix, whose force was obviously very much larger, was experiencing similar difficulties but had moved his base camp to within striking distance.[22]

His tactical plan was to lure Roman foraging parties into prepared ambushes. Having got wind of this from deserters, Caesar decided to bait a trap of his own. Both sides got wind of each other and Vercingetorix withdrew all of his baggage and gear then took up a very strong defensive position on high ground, screened by a significant wet gap. It was more stalemate than confrontation. The Gauls would not be breaking into any wild rush – getting to grips if they held their ground was nigh on impossible. Caesar assures us his men were all for attacking, whatever the risks, but he wisely demurred and led them back to their lines. The siege went on.

For Vercingetorix there was significant fallout. Suspicions over his personal ambitions stuck deep. The Gauls were hoping for quick victory, they hadn't really understood that a war of attrition would be both hard and slow. Their instinct was to fight and yet they had not. Vercingetorix answered their charges and calmed their fears. It must have been galling for him to see how readily Caesar was obeyed, how well the legions, down to the dimmest of squaddies, understood what was expected. Furthermore, Caesar enjoyed one great advantage in that his political enemies were a long way away in Rome and could not effectively query or fetter his actions.

Both generals understood the value of what would now be called 'spin'. *Deus ex machina* Vercingetorix produced some suitably cowed prisoners, paraded as captive legionaries. Caesar maintains they were merely slaves, who'd been schooled to bemoan the dire situation the legions now found themselves in, starving and desperate. They obviously put on a good show, why would they not, their lives depended on it. His audience, as fickle as junior school, lapped it up and cheered him on.

Caesar would have us believe that morale amongst his own men remained high. We have only his word on this but, given the foul weather and hardships of the siege, it would have been remarkable if the men weren't grousing. On the other hand, the unrestricted nature of the campaign and a dearth of Caesar's traditional leniency meant there was more loot and more slaves to go round. Besides, it wasn't their fields and towns that were burning.

As the siege lines crept inexorably closer to Avaricum, as the beleaguered defenders, cut off from any hope of relief, realised they were definitely on their own, they 'used every kind of ingenuity to counter the extraordinary bravery of our soldiers'. They employed nooses to drag away or grab grappling irons. As miners, they knew all about tunnelling and put their knowledge into effect beneath the ramp. They built up their wall towers to match the height of Caesar's siege engines, cladding the timber structures with wet hides as proof against fire. They used fire and incendiaries to try to set the vast wooden structures alight. They blocked and countered the Romans' mines and cut loose with numerous sallies. It was a very active defence, Caesar was prepared to be impressed, 'they are an extremely resourceful people'.[23]

But the work went on. Caesar as ever, was up front, directing, leading, encouraging. The weather stayed abysmal, conditions for the besiegers and besieged alike deteriorated. The Gauls finally succeeded in sinking a viable mine beneath the ramp and fired the chamber. As smoke and flame rose steadily higher, beacons in the cool spring night, the defenders came out from two gates, threatening the siege towers. Those on the walls chucked every type of incendiary. Caesar had two legions on standby, in addition to those working their shift. It was a close-run thing but the towers were pulled clear, guttering flames extinguished and the sorties repelled.

The Bituriges didn't give up easily; the protective screens that had sheltered the legionaries as they moved up had been badly damaged by the fires. As quickly as the defending fighters became exhausted, they were replaced. These Gauls were fast learners. And, as Caesar almost applauds, they were certainly brave: 'A Gaul stood before the town gate, opposite our tower, and was throwing lumps of tallow and pitch – which were passed from hand to hand – into the fire...' One well-aimed bolt from a *scorpio* brought him down. As he fell another took his place, was shot down in turn and was immediately replaced by a third. He was killed as was the fourth.[24] It didn't affect the outcome, Caesar's lines stayed intact.

For the garrison, this failure was the cue for withdrawal, precisely as Vercingetorix had been urging, a local Alamo was of no value to him. His priority was to keep his field army intact. The men thought if they attempted to break out at night, slipping through the marshes, they might just get clear without too many casualties. This chase was to be a men-only affair, women would be left behind. Unsurprisingly, this caused consternation, wives and daughters, hysterical with fear, begged their menfolk not to desert them but 'at times of extreme danger, panic allows no place for pity'. Seeing their men remained unmoved, the townswomen shouted out to alert the Roman sentries. This did the trick. The warriors didn't want to run into a cavalry ambush. There'd be no escaping Avaricum.

Demoralised, the garrison returned to their posts in a day of driving rain. Not a good day for fighting and Caesar made sure his men gave just that impression. He massed his assault troops in the sheeting downpour, hard needles of the bitter wind driving into men's faces, fingers clumsy and half-frozen. At the signal though, they went forward in grand style. Bursting from the siege towers and taking the rim of walls almost without a blow. Disconcerted, the Gallic warriors regrouped in the central forum, forming a shield wall, ready for a last-ditch defence. But the legionaries did not oblige, they simply raced around the parapet, threatening to seal off any escape routes. That was enough. The defenders bolted, trampling each other in the narrow, confining gateways, vengeful *pila* finding many targets. Those who did get out were mopped up by cavalry.

The terrified women had dreaded this moment. Everyone knew what had happened at Cenabum. Caesar puts the death toll at Avaricum as around 40,000. Nobody was counting the corpses. He says only 800 got away.[25] Caesar made no attempt to rein in his men; the sack was their reward, more booty and more slaves. Vercingetorix cannily wouldn't allow the panicked refugees to flood into his camp. He knew too well how fickle his men's morale might prove. He split them up into small groups and spirited these away to their own people. Avaricum was a defeat but in reality only for the Bituriges. Vercingetorix had never wanted to hold the place. The slaughter only reinforced his point. This war would never be won by head-on confrontation.

Caesar could win any number of sieges but that would never equate to final victory, rather the opposite, the attrition would surely grind him down while Vercingetorix could keep his field army in being. That was the key to this campaign. Caesar had to destroy the Gallic army in battle. All too often in the past, they had given him the opportunity, always with the same inevitable result, total defeat. This time though he was facing an opponent with real strategic insight and a canny tactician. He'd only commit his army when the Romans were so enfeebled that their customary advantages of discipline and cohesion would be significantly degraded. Against a lesser adversary he might have succeeded.

After the fall of Avaricum, Vercingetorix pre-empted any hostile fallout by summoning a council and reinforcing the point this disaster was not his fault, he had warned the Bituriges they'd come a cropper. He claimed he now had or soon would have the whole of Gaul on his side, a coalition juggernaut of unstoppable power. He finished on a purely practical note, obliging his adherents to work on fortifying their camp, an unheard-of labour but from his perspective, a useful and instructive exercise.[26] Idleness always breeds discontent. Busy men grouse less.

Vercingetorix was industrious as well as eloquent. He re-equipped the battered survivors of Avaricum and demanded fresh levies from the tribes to make good his losses. He sent smooth-tongued emissaries to those who hadn't committed to win them over. He had promised Gaul total war and he intended to deliver. Anyone who thought they could safely waver would be disappointed. Caesar, equally, wasn't idle. He had resupplied from stocks in the captured city and allowed his men some respite to recover. Spring was now blooming and it was time to hunt down this elusive fox.

His allies, insofar as they could be trusted, the Aedui, now threw a civic spanner into the works. This was entirely domestic. Two candidates for the magistracy had both claimed a valid election. In law, there could only be one and the dispute was edging the nation towards civil war. Caesar, though he must have raged inwardly, could not let this state of affairs continue. Worse, the magistrate was not allowed to venture out of territory during his incumbency. He'd have to go there. He did, deciding in front of an assembly that Convictolitavis rather than his rival Cotus was the genuine case. He reminded the Aedui of where their loyalties lay and ordered a levy of ten thousand infantry and all available cavalry. He intended to use these Gallic auxiliaries to provide logistical support to free up his legionary detachments.

Satisfied with this he gave Labienus an independent command of four legions and a commission to move north against the Senones and Parisii. Caesar himself with the remaining six legions would march via the line of the river Allier against the Arvernian stronghold of Gergovia.

The Auvergne is a largely hilly and, in the south, mountainous region. It is bisected north to south by the Allier, which flows through some spectacular gorges. This is a primeval land of extinct volcanoes, nearly eighty of them, weathered down to jutting lunar stumps or *puys*, the highest of which is the Puy de Dome. This rich, mysterious landscape has an unearthly feel even today. The Arverni had grown wealthy on metalwork and stayed safe in their hilltop *oppida*, looming above fertile alpine pastures and dense covering of virgin oaks.

Both armies marched south, each on its own side of the swift-flowing river, swollen by the spring thaw. Vercingetorix made sure to break down all the bridges, camping always within sight but safely out of reach. The Gaul was not going to be caught out by superior Roman engineering. He posted sentries to make sure he would be warned of any pre-emptive moves. Caesar could not hope to get across, the river would not be fordable until the end of summer. So, he bivouacked near one of the broken-down crossings and kept two legions back while the others marched on next day. He thinned out the cohorts, spacing them to suggest his force hadn't diminished. This diversion worked. His engineers repaired the bridge and he got both legions over. He recalled the rest and they followed across. He had been humbugged but Vercingetorix would not be forced into fighting. He hurried his men on by forced marches till they reached Gergovia.

Avaricum had been strong but the Arvernian city was mighty, a second Troy. It was built on a broad flat-topped plateau that rises like the Lost World from the lower ground. Today, the village of La Roche-Blanche struggles up the steep ascent, pretty much over the ground the armies would contest. Until the time of Napoleon III, the village of Gergovie was named, rather unflatteringly Merdogne. The association with *merde* hardly glorified the memory of the fight: a new name was called for.

It took Caesar five days to catch up and by then Vercingetorix had seized all the high ground on and around the plateau. Every eminence was garrisoned and he had mobile forces of cavalry and skirmishers ready to spar with the legions. Caesar decided, wisely, against an all-out attack but a long drawn-out siege was equally problematic. As ever, he was having supply difficulties and his lines of communication were significantly extenuated.

For the Gallic army, this was both a campaign and a vast training exercise, learning how to fight like Romans. Vercingetorix had established a general staff system; all the tribal leaders reported to a daily conference and briefing. He kept them all on side, made sure everyone was singing from the same hymn sheet, while allowing his mounted gentry to show off their valour in daily skirmishing. This would get them the kind of adulation they craved, would keep their skills honed, but would not interfere with the strategic plan. Parading his infantry around their various outposts was another means of keeping up morale. He understood his men. They had plenty of courage but little patience. They had a grasp of tactics but very little knowledge of strategy. This was a new type of warfare for them; away from their tribal heartlands: a national army fighting for a common cause. The achievement was impressive.

What was Vercingetorix' overall strategy? There's no certain answer to that but we can infer that he was pursuing his policy of attrition, grinding the Romans down, so weakening their logistics and inflicting steady casualties through ambush, skirmishing and grinding siegework that Caesar would, at some point, no longer be able to keep the field. Vercingetorix knew all about political enemies and we can assume that he would have known that Caesar had plenty of those in Rome. If he stumbled just once and badly enough, they would be on him like a pack of hounds.

Caesar was watching and he had spotted the potential of the Roche Blanche south of the plateau. This could be pivotal. A successful assault there could threaten the enemy's water supply. Vercingetorix, reassured by the natural strength of the obstacle, had still installed a garrison, 'albeit not a particularly strong one'. Caesar seized the hill by a brilliant coup de main, a night attack. Always a risky strategy, yet in this instance, one which paid dividends. He put two legions there and dug a communicating trench or gallery from their smaller camp to the main base so troops and material could move unhindered between the two.

This was box office. Caesar was on the offensive. He might have been wrong-footed at the outset but, despite the odds, human and climatic, he had recovered fully, taken the fight to the enemy and now penned him inside his own fortress. He might have thought, having settled the magistracy on Convictolitavis, that the Aedui would be fully on side. But Vercingetorix was mounting a *geltkrieg* of his own and Caesar's treatment of the Aedui since the campaign began had played into his hands. The Aeduan magistrate put greed above gratitude. He was ready to cascade Vercingetorix' cash through the upper echelons, including the energetic young Litaviccus and his siblings. The defection of the Aedui would be a mighty blow, not only would it cut off the Roman supply chain: it would send a clear signal to any who remained undecided.

Litaviccus was put in charge of the infantry division levied as Rome's auxiliaries. His brothers went on ahead as his staff. Just under thirty miles from Gergovia and the siege lines, he delivered a carefully rehearsed speech claiming two leading gentry (Eporedorix and Viridomarus) had been treacherously executed on trumped-up charges. He magicked up a few 'survivors' to corroborate the tale. Those Roman sutlers unlucky enough to be with the column were tortured and killed.[27]

In fact Eporedorix was very much alive and well and had informed Caesar of Litaviccus' treachery. Caesar immediately grasped the serious-ness of the threat both to his rear and his supplies. He took out four of his legions and force-marched them to the Aeduan camp. He sent their own cavalry on ahead to expose their commander's perfidy. Most laid down their arms without demur obliging Litaviccus and his affinity to bolt for their lives. They headed for Gergovia where Caesar's slender force was under attack. Turning his very weary men around, with a bare minimum of rest, he marched them straight back again. Despite the odds, Gaius Fabius (the senior officer in charge) had, with the aid of artillery firepower, seen off all assaults on the lines.

Litaviccus had failed in his gambit but his spin reached the Aedui before Caesar's rebuttal and they gave themselves no time to confirm his story; 'some acted out of greed, others from motives of rancour or hasty imprudence (which are particularly characteristic of that people)'.[28]

We can sense Caesar's frustration coming off the page but, as with all his writing, this is still part tactics. He constantly proclaims the Gauls to be fickle and deceitful, even his allies. This may be so but these constant reminders shift the blame for any treachery onto their shoulders and exonerate Caesar. It is their weakness, not a failure of his diplomacy that is to blame. Even if that diplomacy is really just a thinly coated form of intimidation. That some people might resent this is understandable.

Nonetheless, the Aedui thought it safe to turn on those Romans seeded among them. Veterans, settled amongst the tribe, were summarily expelled and they, with a tribune who had been unlucky enough to be passing through, were attacked as they tried to withdraw. A running fight, costly to both sides, flared up. Once the tribesmen realised that their comrades, horse and foot, were with Caesar, they immediately calmed down. Litaviccus and his affinity were blamed. Many decided they'd gone too far already and that retribution was certain so they began to enter into negotiations with other states to defect. Caesar was well aware of his allies' duplicity and feared the conflagration must now spread. Accordingly, he prepared to draw off his forces from Gergovia and concentrate his field army.[29]

Not quite yet though – he'd spotted a weakness in the enemy disposition. From the smaller Roman redoubt on the captured knoll he saw that the Gauls appeared to have abandoned another previously garrisoned hill. He learned from scouts and deserters that the ridge, though narrow and forested, stayed level till it faded into the main plateau and the walls of the *oppidum*. Fearing further Roman gains, Vercingetorix had drawn his defensive cordon back to consolidate along the line of the main ridge. This rather imprecise description has baffled scholars since the hill Caesar refers to probably lay north-west of the eminence the Romans had just taken and garrisoned. Quite what the Gauls had abandoned and were now defending is by no means clear.[30]

Accordingly, Caesar sent out cavalry skirmishers and some spare muleteers carefully disguised as cavalry to ride around the hill and generally look busy. He also sent one legion up the hill and halted them where they were screened by woods. Vercingetorix and his staff would have had a grandstand view of all of this from the high point of the town. The activity was intended to draw out the defenders and persuade them to mask this flank in anticipation of a major assault.

Meanwhile, Caesar had stealthily moved legionaries from the main base to the forward post. He instructed his senior officers to attack the enemy's now largely abandoned camp in a rush, coming up from the south; no fanfares, colours shrouded. He gave strict orders that this was a limited offensive action not a general escalade. The ground was not favourable. In light of what occurred we are bound to suspect he may have edited his actual orders for the literary version. The Aedui were also detailed to mount a further attack from the east.[31]

Caesar tells us that his men would have to advance for about a (Roman) mile to reach the wall, but as the path zigzagged to ease the gradient the overall distance of travel naturally increased. Vercingetorix had thrown up a barrier, 'a six foot wall of large stones which ran lengthways following the contour line, to slow down the attack'. Below, the ground was bare but once over the wall, the Gauls' shelters and kit crowded the upper slope towards the town. Matters began well. The legionaries swarmed up the hill, breached the wall and took three of the defenders' encampments. Part of the haul was King Teutomatus of the Nitiobriges who was trying to get some kip in his tent when he was rudely awakened. He did manage to get clear, 'half naked on a wounded horse'. Both sides probably laughed.

Caesar now sounded the recall or certainly would have us believe he did. He felt he had 'achieved what he intended'. Which was what? Did he intend the men simply to fall back having beaten up enemy quarters, not much point in that? Or, did he simply expect them to regroup. Caesar himself was present, leading his old favourite the 10th. They halted, as did at least some of the others, even though separated by a defile or gully. The senior officers attempted to restrain their men but the soldiers' blood was high. It did seem as though they could sweep over the defences and take the town. Which, after all, would have brought the campaign to an end. Even if Vercingetorix survived the fall of his capital city, his prestige would not.

It is hard to discern precisely what Caesar had intended if not to take the place by a coup de main. Simply raiding the enemy camp was fine sport but tactically valueless and he would not go to such lengths, arranging such a complex diversion, unless he had a clear objective. It is difficult to follow this action precisely on the ground as his description is somewhat vague. But, having fooled the Gauls and got his forces literally beneath their walls, why not go on and finish the job? Caesar had form on risk-taking and the potential gain here was enormous. Did he perhaps, and for once, suffer a failure of nerve?

In any event, it was a total mess. There was panic in the town, women screaming, 'baring their breasts and leaning forward with outstretched arms they pleaded with the Romans not to kill them'.[32] Memories of the fate of civilians at Avaricum would still have been fresh. One determined centurion, in the mould of Vorenus and Pullo, got himself hoisted up and won a foothold on the parapet. But the attack was stillborn; there was no cohesion. Most had obeyed the trumpets and had already stood down. News of the raid had by now reached the bulk of the Gauls facing the wrong way, guarding against the feint. Vercingetorix showed admirable calm. He swung his men around, cavalry and infantry: sent the horsemen spurring on and marched his men back to defend their walls. The tide immediately began to turn, the Romans were tired and few in number: the Gauls were fresh, numerous and fighting for their homes. The women covered up.

Caesar could plainly see what was going wrong but couldn't do much about it. He did draw the reserve cohorts out from the forward base and draw them up at the base of the slope covering what would be the Gauls' right flank. He moved the 10th up to provide additional support. Lucius Fabius, the impetuous centurion, and his men were fighting for their lives. They lost. Others were dismayed to see what they perceived as enemy reinforcements on their open flank. These were in fact the Aedui, who were following Caesar's orders. Though their kit was naturally Gallic, they had left their right shoulders uncovered – the agreed signal. It was easy to smell treachery in the wind.

The scene was fast becoming a debacle. One wounded officer, Marcus Petronius, realising the fight was lost, bought time with his remaining strength for his men to get clear before he went down. Forty-six centurions died, along with seven hundred ORs. These are the casualties Caesar admits to but we must wonder if they were, in fact, much worse. The survivors got back to the 10th's blocking position and were spared a bloody chase as the defenders boiled out after them. Vercingetorix also avoided making the same mistake and kept his men in check. It was still a shambles and though Caesar tried to pass the buck onto his subordinates, it has to stop with him as commander in chief. Whatever he actually intended, he had got it wrong and suffered a personal defeat. Vercingetorix had beaten Caesar. And while Caesar might win a hundred battles, he could not afford a single defeat. Compared to the ferocity of his enemies in Rome, the Gauls were almost benign.

Next day Caesar paraded his men and harangued them over their recklessness the day before. Ramming home the point, he blamed the fiasco on their negligence rather than his. How convincing this performance sounded, he wisely doesn't say. He kept up appearances by holding his ground for another couple of days and drawing out his forces in battle order each morning. Vercingetorix wisely ignored this theatre and stayed safe behind his walls. Day three and Caesar was on the march, raising the siege and heading eastwards towards the Aedui country. He made good another slighted bridge and got his army safely across the Allier. Vercingetorix made no attempt to intervene. He had no need to. Matters seemed to be moving in his direction and, after all, as he had made it plain from the outset, this war was not about fighting pitched battles.

Failure at Gergovia unleashed the contagion of disaffection. First to swap sides were the Aedui. Caesar had acceded to their cavalry's request to return home. There was little point in having a mounted arm he could not trust and by hanging onto them he would just add more fuel to the fire.

At Noviodunum (not that settled by the Bituriges but what is today Nevers in Franche-Comte, an Aeduan township), the tribe had turned on Roman personnel. This was a serious blow, not just on account of the deaths of his soldiers: Caesar had lost most of his gear and a significant cache of grain. Those hostages he had taken from numerous tribes were also 'liberated', though their Aeduan hosts used them in turn as bargaining chips to sway more of the waverers. Having learnt from disasters such as Avaricum, they made no effort to hang onto the town but emptied the place and torched the shell.

Those two Aeduan gentry Eporedorix and Viridomarus had been the authors of the massacre at Noviodunum. Now they had decided to make common cause with Litaviccus and Convictolitavis. Caesar continuously comes back to his theme – Gallic deceit. No doubt this was real enough but it is also what his audience wanted to hear. For Rome these people were *untermenschen* – barbarians, childish, vicious and vindictive.

Eporedorix and Viridomarus stole what corn they could spirit away by boat down the Loire and burnt the rest. The great river was in spate and, having destroyed the bridges, they sent out flying columns of cavalry to keep watch and raise the alarm if Caesar looked likely to be able to cross over at any point. This was serious. But, as ever, Caesar was equal to the challenge. He got his men over the wet gap, finding a viable ford and using his cavalry as a breakwater to assist the struggling infantry, stumbling chest deep. Despite being vulnerable to concerted attack, the Romans reached the far bank without serious opposition. Caesar had won another round and the fields beyond were full of ripening corn.

He planned to move up through the Senones' lands to link with Labienus, whose detached legions had, under his highly competent leadership, completely defeated the northern tribes near Lutetia (Paris). Vercingetorix wouldn't be getting much help from the Belgae. With his whole army concentrated, Caesar might have mustered 40,000 men, predominantly legionaries. He was desperately short of cavalry and couldn't expect any more coming in from the Gallic tribes. He sent across the Rhine to hire in some additional German mercenaries, efficient light cavalry with fast-moving support infantry. As ever, the Germans were happy to oblige. They had no interest in assisting the Gauls in nation building. That was as bad a result for them as for Rome. Besides, Caesar would be paying in coin and that was always a powerful attraction.

He might have been impressed by his mercenaries' fighting spirit, rather less so by their ponies, which were in a deplorable state. A mounted man always commanded better wages than one on foot and presumably, everybody had grabbed whatever nags were going to boost their market value. 'When they arrived the horses they were using were hardly suitable, so Caesar took the horses of his military tribunes and the rest of the Roman knights and veterans [possibly those whose time in uniform had expired or simply longer serving men who'd acquired their own horses] and distributed them among the Germans.'[33] Though not mentioned, this is unlikely to have gone down too well; however needs must.

Having changed sides so dramatically, the Aedui begged Vercingetorix come to them and hold a general council. This would meet at lofty, sprawling Bibracte and the Aedui were aiming to have one of their own appointed as supremo. Their status demanded no less. Vercingetorix was clearly anticipating this bid but his prestige was still solid and he saw off the attempt. The assembly, which included representatives of most of the major players, unanimously endorsed his leadership. What choice did they have, what choice did they need? There were no credible contenders and he had already done more than any previous leader. This irritated the precious Aedui, particularly the ambitious duo, Eporedorix and Viridomarus, who began to repent of their haste. But they could hardly change sides yet again – certainly not so soon.[34]

Only three of the leading tribes were absent from Bibracte: the Lingones, Remi and Treveri. The first two were amongst the few who refused to join the rest and the Treveri cannily backed off, claiming they lived too far away and were already at grips with German invaders. What Vercingetorix wanted was more cavalry. He was satisfied with his swollen mass of infantry. He did not intend they ever be committed. Despite the great upsurge in support he was getting, he stuck to his strategic guns: there would be no pitched battles, the campaign would continue as one of attrition. He still intended, regardless of resources, to fight an asymmetric war. He would cement his allies' continuing enthusiasm by requiring hostages from them, plus their assurances that they would destroy their own stocks of corn. This level of sacrifice was essential if the scorched-earth policy was going to work.

His next target would be the province itself, Caesar's base, too long a part of Rome. If this region fell, Caesar was effectively marooned. So Vercingetorix levied 10,000 infantry from the Aedui and their clients the Segusiavi (whose lands bordered the province). He gave Eporedorix' brother a brigade of cavalry and sent them off to harry the Allobroges. Arvernian units were sent against the Helvii. Detachments of Ruteni and Cadurci would have a crack at the Volcae Arecomici. A cousin of Julius Caesar, Lucius Caesar, was the legate in charge of defending the province. He had 22 cohorts under his immediate command. Those indigenous tribes suffering from attack by their rebellious neighbours also fought back. The situation was ticklish but holding.[35]

Vercingetorix now possessed a very large cavalry force plus his own infantry and those he had levied from the tribes. Caesar provides no estimate of his total force but it must have easily been at least equal in overall numbers to Caesar's with a marked superiority in cavalry. He began to shadow the Romans. Caesar was marching towards the Sequani across the margins of the Lingones' territory. He was aiming for the province intending to forestall any further concerted attack. After three days' march, Vercingetorix had brought his forces to within about 9 miles of Caesar's camp.

He called a general staff conference. The Gauls faced a momentous decision. He explained that Caesar was making for the province and safety. He appeared to be conceding the campaign. This was all well and good but didn't of itself mean an end to the war. He knew Caesar would be back, with more legions. This wasn't freedom, it was just a respite. To attack now was essential. Using his superior cavalry he would swoop down on the Roman column. The legionaries would either have to fight to save their baggage and supplies (which would drastically slow them down, thus exacerbating their acute logistical difficulties) or they would have to abandon all their gear and get out as fast as possible.

He was confident the Roman cavalry would be too timid, too over-awed, to offer effective resistance. To boost his horsemen's morale and further cow the enemy, he'd parade all his infantry in front of their camp. Let these Romans see just how great was the combined power of Gaul, the pride of Gallic manhood, fighting for freedom and nationhood. Freedom they had had but nationhood or the idea of it was something Vercingetorix had conjured. It all sounded pretty good: 'The cavalry cried that they must be bound by a solemn oath; no man was to be received beneath a roof, or have access to his children, his parents or his wife, unless he had twice ridden through the enemy column.'[36]

With the benefit of hindsight, this must come under the heading of 'it seemed like a good idea at the time'. Vercingetorix was right – Caesar would not be just going away. He had nowhere to run to. If he left Gaul, defeated, six years of campaigning in ruins, his enemies would tear him to shreds. Retreating to the province was bad enough. To strike a decisive blow made good sense and Vercingetorix was, on paper at least, sticking to his concept of attrition. The blow to be delivered by his cavalry was aimed at hitting Roman logistics rather than bringing on a general engagement.

There was sense in this yet he was underestimating Caesar. All the years he had fought in Gaul, generally with the odds stacked heavily against him, he had never been bested. If Vercingetorix thought the man who had nearly conquered Gaul was going to slink off home to face the wolves, he couldn't have been more wrong. What he was in fact doing was giving Caesar a chance to show he was still a master tactician and to demonstrate to the tribes that the legend of his invincibility was no myth.

The battle fought the next day effectively decided the Gallic War. It led directly to the siege of Alesia and Vercingetorix' final defeat; Gaul would never find another champion. The question is where did the fight take place? Caesar is rather light on detail and doesn't give us a precise, identifiable location. Peter Inker has spent a great deal of time and research and has concluded that the fight occurred at Mont Reux near present-day Blerry-les-Belles-Fontaines. On that morning, Caesar had crossed into the lands of the Mandubii and as his extended column splashed over the small River Bornant he found his line of march blocked by a force of enemy cavalry. They had taken station west of the main camp, which is pitched on the east bank of the rather wider river L'Armançon behind them. A far larger mounted brigade was in reserve to their immediate rear on the slopes of Mont Reux.[37]

Caesar could not use his infantry effectively; they were strung out in column, so he sent his own cavalry forward with those feared Germans on the right of the line. Both forces were deployed in three divisions. A fierce cavalry melée spread over the valley floor. With tremendous élan, the Gauls spurred into the ranks of their opponents, but could make no headway. Like Ney at Waterloo, they regrouped, re-formed and charged again. The Roman cavalry had bought time for the infantry to shake out from column into line, baggage safe in the centre. If his horsemen were forced back by enemy pressure, the infantry could advance in support. Caesar probably had assumed the cavalry attack would be followed up by an all-out infantry assault. But no such initiative developed.

Vercingetorix had probably intended some form of hit-and-run spoiling attacks against the vulnerable column whilst it was lumbering along and otherwise unprepared. He could not hope that his cavalry, unsupported as they must have been, could take on the whole of Caesar's army. His infantry was stationed several miles away across the next river obstacle. This fight was pointless. Caesar realised his opponent had miscalculated and beefed up his cavalry by sending up his lightly armed skirmishers. His German hirelings were earning their wages. With their own infantry mixed in, they began to push the left wing of Gauls back up the slope. The morale of the Gallic force oscillated between furious valour and shameful panic. As the Germans battered inexorably forward, gaining the ridge, the Gauls lost heart and begin to pelt back towards their camp and the shelter of infantry spears.[38]

Fear on the left spread to the right. Despite a strong position on the crest, the rest of Vercingetorix' cavalry began to withdraw, ceding the high ground. This manoeuvre is difficult at the best of times, with morale crumbling it quickly degenerated into confusion, terror and then rout. The first the infantry saw of their proud horsemen, who had set off earlier with such confident boasting, was a disorganised rabble pelting towards them. Vercingetorix had fatally left too great a distance between infantry and cavalry and command and control structures were inadequate. During this campaign to date, the Gauls had learned much but not enough. Vercingetorix had blundered and his infantry, rather than moving up now moved back, trying to put the river between themselves and an inevitable Roman onslaught.

This onslaught did not materialise. Caesar did not commit his infantry. He allowed his cavalry the joy of their victory but decided against attempting to fight his way across the L'Armançon. His army had done enough. Quite enough: three of Vercingetorix' senior officers have been captured: Cotus, overall commander of the cavalry and Convictolitavis' former rival, Cavarillus his infantry counterpart and the turncoat Eporedorix, a galling and very uncertain outcome for these Aeduan leaders.

Vercingetorix withdrew all of his survivors, streaming towards the refuge of the Mandubii capital of Alesia. Caesar gave chase and accounted, he claimed, for three thousand from the enemy rearguard.[39] For the first time Vercingetorix had been badly defeated. For the first time Caesar had demonstrated absolute tactical superiority. Despite his leadership and training, Vercingetorix' army had failed to match their adversary's cohesion and discipline. He had failed as a general. His attack was badly planned and worse executed. Yet, compared to his next blunder, this was almost trivial.

CHAPTER 7

TIGHTENING THE VICE

It could be said of Caesar as of Rommel, 'between him and his troops was that mutual understanding which cannot be explained and analysed, but which is the gift of the gods'.

Michael Grant, *Julius Caesar*.

At the time in question, however, most of the Gauls who escaped including Vercingetorix, took refuge in the city of Alesia. Caesar laid siege to the city, but its walls were so high and the number of defenders so great that he was generally expected to fail in his attempt to take it. Then, in the course of the siege, Caesar was threatened by indescribably terrifying danger from outside, when the best warriors from tribes all over Gaul joined forces and marched in force to Alesia. This army consisted of 300,000 men and there were at least 170,000 fighting men inside the city, so that Caesar was trapped between two enormous forces and came under siege himself. He was forced to build two walls,[1] one facing the city and the other because of the new arrivals, since he felt that his situation would become absolutely hopeless if the two forces joined up.[2]

Plutarch was writing in the first decades of the 2nd century AD. Over that intervening period, the scale of Caesar's achievement had swollen. He himself recorded that he faced 80,000 warriors within and 240,000 without. Now, while we may have a view on that, Plutarch has definitely entered the world of pure fantasy. According to him, Caesar was facing the best part of half a million. In the nearly two centuries that had passed since the Gallic War, the fight at Alesia had taken on Olympian proportions, the measure of Rome's superiority, an Agincourt, Blenheim or Waterloo. Caesar is no longer just a soldier of Rome, he epitomises Rome. Alesia has become legend.

> There were a large number of reasons, of course, why the conflict at Alesia became famous: it was the occasion for deeds of daring and skill the like of which have never been seen in any other battle. But the most impressive thing was the way that Caesar managed to engage and defeat the huge army outside the city without those inside the city having the least idea what was going on – in fact, without even the Romans on guard duty on the wall facing the city knowing what was going on. The first they knew of the victory was when they heard from Alesia the men's cries of horror and the women's wails of grief at the sight, wherever they looked, of Romans carrying into their camp large quantities of shields chased with silver and gold, breastplates stained red with blood, and also cups and tents of Gallic design.[3]

Sometimes major battles, leading to a resounding victory for one side, still do not end wars. Neither Agincourt in 1415 nor Towton forty-six years later produced a concrete win. Flodden in 1513 resulted in a terrific thrashing for the Scots, the death of their king and a massive cull of magnates and gentry but still didn't end war between England and Scotland. Alesia, on the other hand, was decisive. Caesar certainly had another and final year of campaigning in Gaul ahead of him but the war was effectively over.

He would go on to win the civil war and become master of Rome and of the world but Alesia was Caesar's greatest tactical achievement. Prior to this climatic episode the campaign of 52 BC had been a very close-run thing indeed. If he had simply heaved a mighty sigh of relief and plodded on towards the sanctuary of the province, the war could have continued indefinitely. It was quite possible that his equally numerous enemies back home would have engineered his fall. Without victory in Gaul there would have been no Civil War.

Alesia was a clash of titans; two charismatic leaders of equal genius competing for domination of Gaul and the prize of determining the course of history – world history. Hollywood at its boldest and most dramatic could not have conjured up a more compelling plot, nor could the stakes for either have been higher. Both were aware of how fragile and vexatious their political support could be. Both needed a win.

It is unlikely the Mandubii, a confederation of tribes inhabiting the Bourgogne and Jura, clients of the Aedui, ever imagined their capital city might become such a battleground. Caesar tells us little of them and they had not really featured as players before. They were probably not players at all. Caesar tells us that Vercingetorix withdrew his battered and shaken force there after the battle. This was a port in a storm, whether he was invited or, more likely, simply requisitioned the place is unclear.[4]

The *oppidum* itself was not particularly large, occupying only the western flank of the massif. We have no clear idea of its normal, peacetime population, probably no more than a few thousand. Even if we're sceptical about Caesar's suspiciously large numbers, the Gallic army represented a many-fold increase in population, a takeover. Once Vercingetorix had established his headquarters in the town, the Mandubii were no longer masters of either their city or their destinies. Any who had misgivings would have been entirely justified. Any who feared the worst would see those fears bear bitter harvest.

Quite what Vercingetorix intended is unclear. Was he hoping for another Gergovia-style stand-off or did he not expect to be followed at all? Perhaps he anticipated Caesar would, having won the fight, simply continue his march to the province. His real mistake was to allow Caesar to regain the initiative and offer him a window to crush the insurgency once and for all. This wasn't an opportunity Caesar was about to decline. Here, now, after a frustrating, damaging and inconclusive campaign was the chance to make an end, to seize victory from stalemate. He could defeat his enemies in Gaul and silence those back home.

At the time it represented an enormous gamble for Caesar. He was committing his tired men to a further bout of campaigning, one that would tax their endurance to the limit. They would have to face a large enemy force, well entrenched behind Cyclopean walls with the very real possibility of a substantial relief army mustering to intervene. This one moment gives us the measure of Caesar's worth. Perhaps even more than the Rubicon, this is the test of his leadership. Failure means disaster. Nonetheless, he grasps the strategic nettle and follows Vercingetorix' demoralised army towards Alesia. As Caesar tells us:

The actual stronghold of Alesia was in an extremely lofty position on top of a hill, apparently impregnable except by means of a siege. On two sides the foot of this hill was washed by rivers, and for about three miles there stretched a plain in front of the town. Close by in every other direction more hills of equal height girded the town.[5]

The general and his staff would have surveyed the *oppidum* from the crests of surrounding hills Mont Rea and Mont Bussy (see Map 3). He decided at once the place could not be stormed; it would have to be blockaded. Vercingetorix' army comprised 80,000 infantry and 12,000 cavalry. Such a huge force could not be billeted within the town proper, which occupied the western rim, so most were bivouacked outside the walls, their tents and bothies covering the whole eastern side behind an improvised ditch and 6-foot-high rampart.[6]

At this stage Vercingetorix may not have been unduly alarmed. His field army remained intact and, for the moment, securely posted. Caesar had tried to winkle him out of Gergovia and had failed. Peter Inker estimates that the Roman army was made up of between ten and a dozen legions which, given the rigours of the campaign so far, cannot have amounted to more than 27,000 effectives, with perhaps nearly as many allied mercenaries.[7] This seems entirely reasonable. Nic Fields takes a view that Caesar's total force was under 50,000.[8]

Did Caesar face an enemy force nearly twice the size? He said he did and we cannot really argue; however, whilst his figure for Vercingetorix' cavalry is probably pretty accurate; he overstates the number of infantry. Simply feeding 80,000 men and an unspecified number of camp followers would be a major logistical feat and no previous Gallic armies had been in the field for so long or traversed such distances. Still, as the Gauls covered the whole of the plateau, their numbers were still considerable. Their general and his officers had comfortable billets amongst their hosts and, it can be assumed, a fair measure of goodwill. This would not endure. Starvation tends to sour relations.

Vercingetorix might have consoled himself into thinking matters were still going his way. After all, his losses in the recent fight would not have been that high and had fallen primarily among the elite of the cavalry.

He might have imagined he had time to summon fresh levies and to rest his tired and probably demoralised forces. Nevertheless, that worm of doubt must have gnawed. He had seen mighty Avaricum fall, Gergovia had been seriously threatened and he knew the Romans were masters of siege operations with several centuries of experience to draw upon. He could not have doubted the dynamic and inventive genius of his opponent.

Nor should we assume Vercingetorix was entirely supine. He would have at least attempted to plan an active defence. Writing centuries after, Vegetius describes how best to prepare for a siege. Livestock and supplies must be collected and got in. What can't be fed should be slaughtered and cured. Fodder for the horses needs to be collected. Whatever crops can't be harvested should be burnt to deny them to the enemy. The city should be filled and the countryside around wasted to increase the enemy's supply problem. All green spaces should be given over to vegetables. Food must be rationed by competent quartermasters while those who could not fight, the non-combatants, women, children, the old and sick – *bouches inutiles* – should be herded out. Necessity must triumph over humanity.[9]

All materiel needed for a successful defence has to be stockpiled, pitch and bitumen for incendiaries, iron, timber, sinew for bows and catapults; sling-stones and heavier boulders either for artillery or simply for heaving off the ramparts. Timber shutters or mantlets should be erected to offer protection from the besiegers' arrows. Wells, sufficient to provide an adequate supply of fresh water, preferably sunk deep enough so the flow cannot be dammed, are obviously essential.

Time was of the essence for both sides. Caesar had to work fast to complete his blockade and seal off re-supply routes into the city while Vercingetorix had to pack as much within the walls as he could. Both would have to work hard to feed their men. The longer a siege endured the harder it was for both sides. But, for the defenders, the noose must gradually tighten. We have to wonder when the Mandubii began to start repenting of their allegiance and resenting their increasingly desperate circumstances.

Caesar wasn't one to waste time. His legionaries were as at home with their tools as they were with their swords. Nothing he would tell them to do was in itself novel, except for the sheer scale of the undertaking. Their morale had probably risen after they had seen off the earlier attack, and now it was clearly they who had the upper hand. These Gauls had seen much of Rome's energy and competence, now they would witness more, far more. There would be no shock but there would be awe.

Vercingetorix had learned a great deal yet not quite enough. He had cannily avoided giving Caesar the set-piece, decisive battle he craved. His success in seeing off the Roman besiegers at Gergovia had blinded him to their true capabilities. It was the defection of the Aedui and the spreading flames that had driven Caesar off. Now he had no such distractions. Vercingetorix had put his head in the noose and Caesar was aiming to draw it tight.

Siegecraft was not invented by Caesar. His ingenuity represents a culmination of centuries of practice reaching back as far as the time of Troy (say 1250 BC). Scipio Aemilianus had flung a 9-kilometre ring of stone around Numantia in 134–133 BC.[10] Alesia raised the bar significantly. The limestone plateau, Mont Auxois, on which the city sat, is a spur spreading from much higher ground behind. The two rivers, Oze and Ozerain, both flowing from the Brienne, had scoured the land encircling the ridge and left it free standing, raised apart from the surrounding hills, Mont Rea, Montaigne de Bussy, Mont Pennevelle and Mont Flavigny, none of which was higher than around 1,200 feet (365 metres).

To the west, watered by a rough triangle of the two smaller rivers as they meandered into the Brienne, lay the flat Plain of Laumes, relatively lush meadow, ideal for cavalry 'and for about three miles there stretched a plain in front of the town'.[11] If Vercingetorix attempted to use his horsemen to break the ring, it would have to be here. West again and south, another rounded knoll – the Collines de Mussy-la-Fosse – rose to a similar height as the others. If a relief force did arrive, and Caesar had to assume it would, then this was the direction from which it must approach.

He set to work. With his engineers he scouted the circling hills, each a perfect site for a fortified camp, shallow rounded tops with generally good visibility, smaller versions of Mont Auxois itself. The first job was to secure the perimeter with a series of these bases, each around seven hectares, sufficient for a sizeable garrison of say 3,000–4,000 soldiers.[12] These, initially temporary marching camps [*castra*], eight in all, begin to form the ring, then they would be joined by the inner wall:

> The length of the siege works which the Romans had started reached ten [Roman] miles. Camps had been pitched at suitable locations and twenty-three forts built along the line. These forts were garrisoned in the daytime, to guard against unexpected sorties; at night sentries and reinforced patrols kept watch there.[13]

This was a herculean task. Even with the trained manpower available, to throw this massive collar around Alesia and then surround that with an outer line was an astonishing undertaking. Not just building the walls themselves but the logistical effort that underpinned the work. The whole job speaks volumes about the efficiency of the Roman army and the presiding genius of Caesar's guiding hand. Firstly, the men and horses must be fed and watered. Next, materials in vast quantities must be located, procured and finally transported.

A significant train of carts and wagons would be needed; drivers to drive, mules and horses to pull them. Forage and supply parties must be coordinated, guarded against attack and their haul distributed. The legionaries would not be building temporary barracks instead they would still be sleeping in their hide tents, all their sweat would be going into the ramparts. Vegetius laments that, in his day, the science of temporary fortifications has been for so long neglected:

> Nothing is found so safe or so indispensible in war, since if a camp has been properly constructed, soldiers spend days and nights so secure behind the rampart ... that they seem to carry a walled city about with them everywhere.[14]

This whole network of enclosures was intended both to hug the best contours and hem in the defenders. The forts or redoubts (*castella*) would act as buttresses and anchors to ensure all-round defence. They used the contours to provide additional, natural bulwarks.[15] To the north and south, following the flow of the wet gap barriers, his lines used the rivers as flooded ditches, coming as close to the beleaguered city as prudence and ground allowed.

Westwards, where the flat, even plain stretched towards the confluences, the walls stood further back, leaving a clear battleground between. Vegetius would have thoroughly approved:

> Camps ... should be built always in a safe place, where there are sufficient supplies of firewood, fodder and water and if a long stay is in prospect choose a salubrious site. Care must be taken lest there be a nearby mountain or high ground which could be dangerous if captured by the enemy. Thought must be given that the site is not liable to flooding from torrents... [16]

So before the encirclement proper was begun, before the first sod of any ditch was excavated, the men were securely placed, camps and forts within hailing distance of their neighbours and those further away could be contacted by signals. Labienus, as befitted his status as second-in-command, pitched his camp atop Mount Bussy, large enough to accommodate the Seventh Legion he commanded personally together with ancillary cavalry, artillery and other supporting arms. His position just overlooked the town itself (by a mere 15 metres) a perfect vantage for observation.

Vegetius is very particular on the layout of his camps, how these are to be constructed, even the aesthetics:

> Appearance should not prejudice utility, although those whose length is one-third longer than the width are deemed more attractive. Surveyors are cautioned that they must carefully work out the square footage so that the area enclosed corresponds to the size of the army. Cramped quarters constrict the defenders, whilst unsuitably wide spaces spread them thinly.[17]

Did Vercingetorix and his officers, from the lofty height of city walls look down and around at the ant-like figures scurrying so purposefully below and feel the first real frissons of alarm? This was Rome and this was what Rome did. She had in her already long history suffered setbacks, defeats even catastrophes such as Cannae but she had never been beaten. Vegetius goes on:

> A stationary camp is fortified with greater care and effort ... For each century receives a footage apportioned by the drillmasters and officers. The men distribute their shields and packs in a circle around their own standards and,

armed only with a sword, open a fosse [ditch] 9 ft. wide, or 11 ft. or 13 ft. or, if a major hostile force is feared, 17 ft. – it is usual to keep to odd numbers. The rampart is then raised between lines of revetments or barriers of logs and branches interposed to stop earth easily falling away. Above it a system of battlements and turrets is constructed like a wall. The centurions measure the work with ten-foot rods, checking that no one's laziness has resulted in digging too little or making mistakes.[18]

The tribunes supervise the work and ensure those who labour are well protected by those who do not, the cavalry and detached infantry, 'an armed cordon'.

Once the perimeter is constructed, the standards are set up followed by the senior officers' and tribunes' lodgings. As befits their rank, these will have soldiers detailed as batmen and camp servants. Tribunes don't go looking for their own firewood. Then the tents for infantry, cavalry and auxiliaries go up in strict order of place and precedence. Each century or squadron details four men for sentry duty during the hours of darkness. Nobody likes sentry duty and the long watches of the night are divided into three-hourly shifts, time being marked by a water clock. Trumpeters and horn-blowers call up and dismiss the sentinels. Chosen men, in Caesar's day called *circumitores*, keep watch on the watchers. Infantry keep watch from the walls while cavalry roam beyond. In daylight two shifts, morning and afternoon, carry on the patrolling.[19]

This is the system, it fits the soldiers like old gloves. They grew up with it and the veterans will hardly need telling. Vercingetorix will have looked out on this activity and must, by now, have been cursing his own folly. His men would have had little to do but stand to when ordered and husband their dwindling supplies. The townspeople must have been consumed with dread. Vegetius provides further instruction on the vital matter of supply:

> Among the things particularly incumbent upon a general, whether he is quartered in a camp or a city, is to see that animals' pasturage, the transportation of grain and other provisions, and the ministration of water, firewood and fodder are rendered secure from hostile attack.

The manual recommends garrisoning key points on the supply trail, existing features or if necessary, temporary camps or *castella*.[20] To feed a besieging force of, say, forty thousand men is a vast undertaking in itself; to accumulate the amount of timber needed is another Sisyphean task. All that wood has to be found, cut, dressed and transported. We can assume the country was fairly well wooded but by the time the siege works were finished, most of the area around would have been completely stripped of standing timber.

By the time both inner and outer walls were completed, their combined length was 25 Roman miles (37 kilometres), all reinforced and linked by a network of ditches, some 50 miles (74 kilometres) in length together with wooden observation platforms (possibly as many as 1,500[21]), the 23 forward redoubts and eight major camps behind. Past and current archaeological work has suggested Caesar's works were not quite as extensive or indeed even as complete as he suggests – he was not one to downplay his own achievement. Yet what was built was, by any standards, impressive.

The full encirclement of the town wasn't completed until after the cavalry fight on the plain when Vercingetorix' attempt to either interrupt or prevent the encirclement failed. At that point it became more evident than ever that the siege would be a long one and that Vercingetorix would be hoping for relief. Caesar had worked out his enemy's intentions, probably from the start though his deductions were confirmed by intelligence gleaned from deserters.[22] On the Plain of Laumes then he dug a 20-foot-wide, sheer-sided ditch with the main field fortifications set 400 paces (592 metres) back. This would serve to disorder any rush from the besieged and give the legionaries time to prepare to meet any assault on their lines.

In front of the ramparts a further two 'V' shaped ditches (collectively a barrier against assault or *titula*[23]), were dug to the same depth, 15 feet (4.57 metres) across, and he used both rivers to fill the inner fosse as a moat. The earthwork rose to 12 feet (3.55 metres) and was surmounted by a fighting platform and timber battlements. The join between rampart and parapet was protected by projecting stakes.[24] These obstacles were in fact fashioned from forked branches and sharpened. As Dr Fields points out, these 'stags' or *cervi* were a classical version of barbed wire![25]

TIGHTENING THE VICE • 133

Caesar confirms that timber observation towers were added 'at intervals of eighty feet'.

Dr Fields has considered an experiment in rampart building carried out by a team of today's Royal Engineers working on a reconstructed Roman fort at the Lunt in Warwickshire. The conclusion from this exercise was that to build a 300-metre stretch of Caesar's wall (just the rampart and not including superstructures), would have taken three hundred legionaries a full ten days.[26] That's an easy statistic but as Dr Fields further points out, one that represents a huge amount of sweat. The total circumference was 25 miles (40 kilometres), forming a truly remarkable feat that speaks volumes about the soldiers' fitness and their skill at this kind of work. This is where the difference between the two armies really shows – Rome's workaday warriors knew their stuff.

Caesar wasn't finished. The long lines of *circumvallation* and *contravallation* were vulnerable to attack from within and without so additional defences were added. Today, we'd just call these anti-personnel devices, Rome's version of the minefield. A belt of camouflaged pits laid out in chequer-board formation, hiding sharp, smooth poles, with typical gallows humour, the soldiers referred to these as *lilia*, 'lilies':

> Smooth stakes, as thick as a man's thigh and sharpened and tempered at the end were sunk into the pits; they projected no more than three inches [75 mm] from the ground. For strength and stability, earth was trodden in around them to a depth of one foot [300 mm] and the rest of the pit was covered with twigs and brushwood to camouflage the trap. Eight rows of such pits were dug at three foot [900 mm] intervals.[27]

US 'grunts' in Vietnam would encounter a 20th-century version of these traps cleverly concealed in conical pits intending to maim rather than kill. Tommies in the Second World War would become familiar with *panji* traps used by both sides in jungle fighting.

Thrown out in front of these pits were planted stakes with very nasty iron spikes or 'spurs' (*stimuli*). Stepping on either of these would have resulted in an agonising and disabling wound. This wasn't all. Between these outer fields of obstacles and the double-ditch another line of wicked obstructions were planted, aptly known as 'gravestones' (*Cippi*).

These comprised five rows of branches, lopped down and sharpened, dug down into trenches five feet (1.48 metres) deep and wound about together to form a vicious hedge.

There was more. *Tribuli*, basic but hideously effective calthrop-like spiked three-pronged devices were scattered at the front, potentially disabling man or horse. However they were placed, one sharp spike would be uppermost, very nasty. As well as the obvious damage to individual attackers these devices could inflict, they also served to slow down the impetus of any concerted assault, exposing the struggling attackers to the full weight of the defenders' shooting.[28]

This was that consummate professionalism the Gauls so obviously lacked. Caesar's orders were not debated, they were obeyed. The labour was back-breaking. The men would grouse endlessly but they could clearly see why they had to do what they were doing. Every metre that was added to the *circumvallation* increased the isolation of the besieged. The increasing pangs of hunger would begin to gnaw that bit more urgently. An added dividend from the lines of anti-personnel devices was that Caesar could afford to thin out those holding the line to beef up the foraging parties which, as the siege ground on, would have to range further and further behind the lines into potentially enemy country.

As every day passed the Gauls were reminded that Caesar now held the initiative. The Gallic temperament was not best suited to this type of positional warfare. There was little or no glory to be had, no beckoning feats of individual daring and prowess, just sweat and toil. Boredom and an increasing note of desperation would begin to erode the defenders' fragile morale. We know very little of what was happening inside the beleaguered town. The Mandubii must have been truly ruing the day they had allowed this vast plague of locusts to settle down behind their walls, the shanty town of tents and bothies filling the plateau. There is no suggestion of sickness amongst the defenders at this stage, though the smells must have been getting pretty ripe.

Vercingetorix was right to think Alesia very strong but he had missed the importance of the surrounding ring of hills, and how these commanded the entire site. The forts went up first. Each, as Dr Inker points out, differed in detail if not in substance as each was built by a separate legion that had its own idiosyncratic and no doubt jealously guarded preferences.[29] Labienus had pitched his standard on the top of Mont Bussy. Camps 15–18 (see Map 3) give a clear view over the valley of the little river Oze where it skirts the massif. Labienus could clearly view the plain and easily see across to Caesar's base across the valley (Camp B). All-round vision and mutual support are key features of such operations – a lesson Vercingetorix' descendants would forget as recently as 1954 at Dien Bien Phu in Indochina, with evil consequences.

These primary regimental bases were augmented by smaller, flanking camps. Some such as Fort 15 (see Map 3) were, by comparison, diminutive, in this case only half a hectare. As the archaeological finds confirm, this was most probably a shooting platform for archers. Fort 18 on the western rim of the same high ground and again small at only 0.7 hectares, probably housed other specialist troops.[30]

Caesar had pitched his tents on Mont Flavigny. He could also overtop Alesia and look down the Ozerain valley. The high vantage obviously facilitates signalling so the general could direct the entire battle from his command point. Slightly larger than Labienus' position at 7.3 hectares, the camp could easily hold a whole legion. Satellite camps also flanked Caesar's headquarters, probably intended to house commanded formations or *vexillations*. The camps, like the main *circumvallation*, were protected by ditches and obstacles, gateways carefully sited and protected. The forts were themselves a network of carefully chosen mutually supporting positions, 'fire-bases' in modern terminology.

The flat plain was to be covered by a pair of big camps. Camp K to the south, stood at the foot of Caesar's hill and housed, appropriately for the ground, cavalry. It covered the Ozerain valley and that of the wider Brienne. To the immediate north Camp H performed the same function for the Oze River. Between these two bastions a line of smaller bases gave clear notice of Caesar's intention to bottle up the defenders and deny them the plain.[31]

Further east, the plateau was isolated by additional redoubts. One (Fort 13) sat on the forward lip of Mont Penneville, sealing off both valleys. Camp G bottles up the re-entrance along the course of the little River Rabutin.[32] This is a vital junction, the link between Mont Bussy and Mont Rea. This high ground is covered by two smaller camps, one on the top and one at the base. It couldn't be predicted at this stage but this sector would become the crucible.[33] Meantime, Vercingetorix was penned in, the ring of bastions effectively severing his communications with the rest of Gaul.

All this labour did not go uninterrupted:

> After work on the siege had begun, a cavalry battle took place in the three mile stretch of plain which we mentioned above as lying between the hills. Both sides fought fiercely. When our men got into difficulties Caesar sent the Germans to their assistance and stationed the legions in front of the camps to prevent any sudden invasion by the enemy infantry.[34]

What was Vercingetorix hoping to achieve by sending out his cavalry? Did he hope they could drive the Romans away without infantry support or was this just a morale booster, a chance to ease the sullen frustrations of the siege, a chance to be proactive rather than passive?

If we allow Vercingetorix his 12,000 cavalry, for he surely had not been able to make good the losses his mounted arm sustained at Mont Reux, what exactly could they achieve by attacking across the Plain of Laumes? Unsupported, they weren't going to drive the Romans away, the digging might be interrupted but it wouldn't be stopped. Even if they brushed aside Caesar's own cavalry screen, they would stand no chance of getting past the legions. This then was a raid, a classic attack on enemy quarters to improve your side's morale and dint his. Perhaps, if the cavalry could successfully harass the besiegers, they'd abandon the attempt. It rather smacks of desperation.

Once combat was joined, Caesar leaves us pretty short on detail. Initially, it seems his allied cavalry took on the Gauls without the Germans being committed. Having the legionaries stand to was a precaution against a secondary assault by infantry, so he was assuming Vercingetorix might attempt a full-scale break-in. The soldiers didn't intervene though, other than, by their presence, adding moral support to their comrades on horseback.

'When our men got into difficulties' – at some point the Gallic horse, possibly by sheer weight of numbers, began to push Caesar's allied cavalry back. Then he threw in his Germans; fresh, brimming with ferocious élan and confidence, they tipped the scales. It is clear they possessed discipline and cohesion in far greater measure than their adversaries and, so far, the Gauls had never succeeded in getting the better of them. By the time they were committed, the cavalry battle would probably have broken down into a series of untidy, swirling melées, knots of horsemen contending with lance and sword; difficult for the Gauls to rally and re-form to meet this new, if surely not unexpected, threat.

It's hard to see what else Vercingetorix could have expected. He had had painful experience of just what the Germans could do and Caesar doesn't suggest any new or varied tactics. The result was never really in doubt. 'The enemy were routed. There were so many of them they got in one another's way as they fled; they were crushed together in a heap at the gates, which they had left too narrow'. Fired with bloodlust, the implacable Germans pursued their panicked foes to the very walls. Some of the Gauls, Caesar tells us, jumped off their horses, tried to wade the ditch and climb the wall. Caesar ordered the stationary legionaries, those nearest the town, to make a demonstration, which convinced the defenders they were about to suffer a full-scale infantry assault. Vercingetorix closed the gates, shutting out many of the scrum trying to shoulder their way back in. The Germans took full advantage, killing men and taking horses. All in all they were really earning their wages.[35]

Having thinned and chastised their beaten opponents, the Germans withdrew in good order as Vercingetorix' men boiled impotently on their walls. Caesar avoided the error of Gergovia and did not attempt to follow up with an all-out attempt at an escalade. This fight was all about method. Caesar had won another round, moreover he had tightened the vice and it was really beginning to bite. But he was aware this fight was far from over. In fact it was just about to really begin.

'Vercingetorix now decided to send all his cavalry away by night before the Romans completed their siege works. As they left, he told each of them to go to his own people and muster for battle all the men of an age to bear arms'.[36] He was upping the stakes. Caesar wasn't going to give up so he would have to be driven off. The besieged couldn't hope to achieve this, the cavalry's failure had clearly illustrated that. What was needed was a relief army, one so massive, so overwhelming a juggernaut that it would smash clear through Caesar's lines and finish the war once and for all. It was make or break … 'any hint of negligence in them would bring about the deaths of 80,000 picked men, as well as his own'.[37]

CHAPTER 8

THE RELIEF AND FINAL BATTLE

The Duke of Wellington remarked that the 'want of power to reward' was a fatal handicap for a general, and Caesar was always aware that his soldiers, like those of other commanders, might at some stage or other become uncontrollably impatient for remuneration; and this applied most of all to the legions he had raised specially and temporarily for the purpose of the war – 'if you lack soldiers, you will have no money', he said; 'but if you lack money there will be no soldiers'.

Michael Grant, *Julius Caesar*.

Caesar led the Gauls in triumph,
Led them uphill, led them down,
To the Senate House he took them,
Once the glory of our town.
'Pull those breeches off', he shouted,
'Change into a purple gown!'[1]

It was now stalemate. Vercingetorix was effectively bottled up. His cavalry had again failed the test, had been routed and humiliated. He had sent them away with a desperate summons to Gaul – come to our rescue or see us destroyed. This wasn't an ideal form of generalship. Vercingetorix had begun his campaign as one of rapid manoeuvre. Time and again he had rightly stressed the perils of becoming bogged down in positional warfare against a superior opponent. Now, he was trapped, the noose of *circumvallation* tightening day by day as Caesar's legionaries dug and built. The message was soon abundantly clear even to the dimmest warrior. While the cavalry had got clear away, the infantry could not.

Once the plan was adopted, Vercingetorix had barely enough corn for thirty days, though by practising economy it could be made to last a little longer ... He demanded that all corn be sent to him, and decreed the death penalty for those who disobeyed.[2]

Now the Mandubii, his hosts, began to appreciate the full extent of their own crisis. All livestock was ruthlessly requisitioned and parcelled out to the fighting men. Their city would be a shambles, picked clean by this plague of locusts, their streets fouled and squalid, any control over their own destinies lost, just pawns in a savage duel of titans.

Vercingetorix pulled his outposts back under the shelter of Alesia's walls and bunkered down for a close siege. Quite where these vedettes had been stationed is unknown, possibly on the Plain of Laumes, though they would have been vulnerable there to Caesar's cavalry. Among the defenders, morale must have plummeted. They were effectively impotent. According to Caesar they still, even minus cavalry, outnumbered the besiegers by two to one yet they did not attack. Stuck, brooding and increasingly hungry in their rough bothies covering the plateau, they could only watch as their enemies laboured purposefully and extended their works, a dazzling double line of dense obstacles and uniform ramparts rising around them. Caesar lets us know he was well informed of conditions inside the ring by 'deserters and prisoners'.[3]

While he might be ahead of the game, Caesar had no grounds for complacency. He was aware that Alesia would still be a very tough nut to crack, too strong for an all-out assault. He would have to wait until hunger compelled the enemy to surrender. Before then, he could be sure that he would have to beat a relief force, bound to be substantial, possibly massive, perhaps the largest single army he had ever had to face. Vercingetorix would attempt to break out as the relief tried to break in. Caesar would have to fight, heavily outnumbered, on two fronts simultaneously.

'While this was going on in Alesia, the Gauls called a meeting of their leaders. They decided not to follow Vercingetorix' proposal that all men able to bear arms should be called up, but rather a certain number from each state'.[4] The logic of this was that such a grand *levée en masse* would create an unwieldy and all-consuming monster that could be neither fed nor directed. Clearly this was sensible so the council opted for a quota system. Each tribe or tribal confederation would be required to produce so many warriors according to their resources.

Caesar gives us a detailed list of these quotas (see Appendix 1). The Aedui and their clients, as befitted their status were obliged to find 35,000 recruits, as were the Arverni. Major nations such as the Carnutes and Bituriges had to find 12,000 each. Relatively minor peoples such as the Raurici and Boii only had to raise 2,000 each.[5] Only the quarrelsome Bellovaci who were supposed to supply 10,000 spears demurred, cannily asserting they would fight Rome in their own way and not under anyone else's banner. Caesar makes no comment but this rather sounds like fence-sitting!

One who was able to influence them was Caesar's erstwhile ally and client, wily Commius of the Atrebates.[6] Despite his previous enthusiastic collaboration, his influence was still strong enough to persuade the Bellovaci to send a token force of 2,000 for the sake of unity. Commius scooped up a senior position, as did the Aeduans, Viridomarus and Eporedorix, together with Vercingetorix' Arvernian cousin Vercassivellaunus. Those supplying the most spears obviously commanded the top jobs. Once this vast host was mustered Caesar informs us, there were no fewer than 240,000 infantry and 8,000 cavalry.[7] 'They all set out for Alesia eager and full of confidence'.[8]

This is a truly colossal number. While the figure for cavalry is credible, the number of foot seems rather less so. Yet we have only Caesar's account and tally to work from. He is specific on the numbers being levied but it is unclear if this full paper muster actually translated into boots on the ground. He does not say. Perhaps he did not know, but there would be other tribes none too keen to serve under the banners of the Aedui or Arverni, who were equally likely, if successful, to oppress them as Rome had been.

Caesar had won so often in the past by exploiting just such regional and tribal discords. To what extent the concept of nationhood or national emergency appealed to smaller tribes, we can't say. It would be safe to assert, we think, that not all came willingly. In reality, the senior officers would be aware they could rely on their own men but less so upon others. Old resentments die hard.

Caesar is tantalisingly brief in describing this great relief army. He gives us tribes and numbers but nothing else. How were the tribes mustered? How were logistics provided? What was the line of march? Many had to cover considerable distances and surely there must have been a number of muster points where local contingents formed individual corps and then marched via the river valleys towards a point of concentration.

How many ancillaries and camp followers were needed or allowed? Alesia lies south central and to the east, practically in the Jura. Probably mighty Bibracte was the muster point, certainly for the Aedui and their clients and also perhaps for the Arverni from further west. Equally so the central nations such as the Carnutes and Bituriges. Those from the northern and western marches had far further to travel. Their journeys would take several weeks, assuming they had mustered nearer home in full corps strength.

It is not recorded who organised this vast effort, how supplies were gathered and distributed. Most would, we can assume, have been responsible for provisioning their own contingents. Men would have brought their basic war gear. We don't know whether there was any central quartermaster organisation to distribute arms and armour to those who were less well equipped. The whole examination is a fascinating one and it is frustrating that Caesar doesn't explain more, but of course his commentary isn't about the Gauls, it's all about him.

Nonetheless, the accumulation of the relief amounts to a unique and monumental effort and speaks volumes about Vercingetorix' prestige. No leader before could call into being such a colossal effort. The idea of a national *levée en masse* doesn't really recur till the dark days after the Revolution of 1789 when the energetic and brilliant Lazare Carnot mobilised the entire nation to resist invasion and lays the foundations for Napoleon's greatness.

'They all set out for Alesia eager and full of confidence …'[9] And well they might, whatever the actual size of the field army, it was clearly very large and it must have seemed, as Caesar suggests, that no force on earth could withstand such a juggernaut. These huge numbers combined with the substantial contingent bottled up in the city would crack the Roman siege. Even mighty Caesar couldn't withstand such an overwhelming and concerted attack.

Inside the beleaguered town, hopes had begun to fade. They had no news of this great levy and their 30 days' supply of corn was gone. Vercingetorix called or allowed a council that certainly debated surrender. Those with fight left in them advocated a sally while they still had strength. One of the Arvernian gentry, a grizzled much-respected veteran called Critognatus, put forward his own solution. He lambasted those faint-hearts who were craven enough to think of throwing in the towel. He was just as scathing towards those who wanted to sally out to do or die. Theirs was just another face of cowardice.

He pointed out that their survival wasn't just a matter of preserving their own necks. They were the vital spear-point of Gaul. If they failed, the cause of freedom died. They had a duty to their nation to bear whatever hardships fate threw at them. They simply had to hang on, to grit their teeth, sit tight and wait for the relief. If they did not, all of the Gallic tribes would pass beneath the yoke. The mere fact the Romans were labouring so hard on their elaborate defences was surely proof enough of how much they feared this mighty storm that was rising behind them.

As for hunger, the obvious solution was to use the flesh of those too old or weak to fight as sustenance for those who could. The future of Gaul justified a spot of cannibalism.[10] That probably shut everyone else up. It was the most draconian remedy yet one that made most sense. The imperative of national liberty justified any means whatsoever. If eating their hosts avoided the rest becoming slaves of Rome then so be it.

Grittily realistic as this apocryphal solution may have been, it was still a dish too far for the rest. Vercingetorix was ruthless but perhaps not that ruthless. A compromise was decided upon. All those who couldn't fight – the *bouches inutiles* – would simply be expelled, driven out, herded into the no-man's-land between besieged and besiegers. And so the

Mandubii suffered the final working out of their devil's bargain. Their fellow Gauls, to whom they'd given shelter, now drove them out into the wasteland, the empty tundra between the armies. Vercingetorix might have kidded himself that Caesar would let them pass and allow them not to become beggars in their own land.

The desperate fugitives, children dragging at their tattered robes, begged to be allowed through, willing to accept submission and slavery. For the individual legionaries, this was an opportunity, not to show humanity but to pick up some walking booty. Caesar promised them they would be rewarded with slaves from those still inside but these poor, desperate, wailing refugees stayed where they were. Having dealt with the issue, Caesar forgot about them.[11] They would be forced to huddle, without food, sanitation or shelter between the lines, increasingly listless spectres as events moved on without them. The forgotten – abandoned by their own side – watching beneath the walls of their homes as they and their children slowly starved; it was a horrible fate. The universal reality of war throughout the ages; the innocent are always the main victims.

Caesar would have coldly calculated that the dismal presence of these emaciated, despairing wraiths would further demoralise the Gauls. After all these were their own people and so awful an expedient would have weighed heavily on many. These were the people they were supposed to be fighting for not sacrificing.

We get no information as to the time scales involved. We know only that Vercingetorix had 30 days' supplies within Alesia when he sent away his cavalry and that the relief force did not arrive in that time. Expelling the hapless civilians would have helped eke out the remaining provisions but we don't know how long elapsed between this enforced exodus and the arrival of the army. If the riders sent out initially had only say four weeks to reach their own people, for those peoples to convene, agree a strategy and appoint officers, then to begin assembling so massive a force, to concentrate and move that army to the point of contact, well that's a pretty tall order.

We can assume that the big players, the Arverni and Aedui, by no means natural allies, were jointly in the driving seat. They were both centrally placed and Bibracte was the natural seat of operations. Still, to get messengers out to all of the tribes including those of the far west and north, for those peoples to muster, to arrange their own supply lines (as it must be assumed no central commissariat existed), had to be time consuming. For lines of approach and points of concentration to be identified took time. The contingents could only move as fast as a man can walk. It was summer, high summer by now, so the roads would be dry and easily passable yet it must have taken several weeks for the Nervii say, once they mustered, to reach Alesia. It is almost inconceivable that the whole process could have been accomplished in anything under a couple of months and even that would be impressive.

Yet they made it and the combined army must have presented in the much-overworked phrase a truly 'awesome' sight. Not even Rome had seen so many spears on the march at once, a host of biblical proportions. We know the English army of Edward II in 1314, heading for Stirling and disaster, perhaps 20,000 strong, needed 20 miles of road; in 1914 the average foot battalion of a thousand required a mile or so. On that basis, the relief army would have extended for over 200 miles. It would take days just for all the contingents to arrive.

'Meanwhile Commius and the other leaders entrusted with the supreme command reached Alesia with all their forces. They occupied a hill outside, less than a mile from our fortifications, and took up position there... '[12] Next day, as Caesar tells us, the Gauls deployed all of their cavalry on the Plain of Laumes facing the outer rampart of the *circumvallation* and filled the whole of the plain. The infantry, this astonishing mass, this massive steel-tipped phalanx, like an avalanche waiting to explode, filled the rising ground behind.[13] For the hungry defenders this must have been a tremendous boost. Their suffering and tenacity were at last rewarded. The sheer size of the relief army would have fuelled a heady elixir of optimism, charged by a surge of pent-up aggression 'everyone was stirred to a state of rejoicing'. It was finally time to strike back!

Clearly Vercingetorix had been planning for just this. We can surmise he'd been keeping the men's morale up by rehearsing and training for the break-in. He paraded his men on the plain facing the inner face of Caesar's lines. They'd made ready with 'wicker hurdles' that they used to fill in the outer ditch, necessary preparation for any major sally.[14] Caesar riposted by fully manning both lines of defence, so his infantry were ready while he then unleashed the cavalry. From their various vantages both sides had a grandstand view of this dense arena. Infantry remained as spectators as the horsemen collided.

Commius had been learning from the Romans too and was copying the German tactic of mixing light infantry and some foot archers in with his mounted men. 'A number of our soldiers were unexpectedly wounded by these men, and began to leave the fighting'. Caesar gives us this detail as a kind of throwaway remark. As ever, he adroitly sidesteps the fact he plainly hadn't seen it coming. After all Commius, until this point, had been a trusted ally and a clever one. Seeing their fellows beginning to win the upper hand, the Gauls cheered them on, their shouting echoing around the plain and ring of hills, a tornado of sound. 'It was impossible for any deed, be it courageous or cowardly, to be concealed'.

The fight sprawled on all afternoon, almost till dusk. We are not sure precisely what time of year this was but probably high to late summer with darkness falling at around 2000 hours. As Caesar tells us the engagement began at noon, that's seven or eight hours of combat. This obviously wasn't continuous, horses would have been blown and men exhausted. While he doesn't say so, we can assume that the fighting was patchy and sporadic, individual bodies and knots of horsemen swirling together in a melée. Casualties on both sides, till this moment, were probably fairly light even if the Gallic archers had managed to empty a few saddles. At the crucial moment, Caesar won the upper hand. As before, it was the gift of his incomparable Germans.

On this very point, Vegetius has some sound advice:

> The general should know against which groups of the enemy he should set which of the cavalry. For some obscure, or indeed, one might say, divine reason, some men fight better against others, and those who have conquered the stronger are often themselves defeated by the weaker. But if the cavalry are outnumbered, the ancient custom should be adopted of mixing in with them very swift infantry

with light shields, specially trained for the purpose ... if this is done, no matter in what force the enemy cavalry turn out, they cannot match the mixed formation. All ancient generals found this to be the only answer. They trained young men who were outstanding runners, placing them one between two horsemen, on foot and armed with light shields, swords and javelins.[15]

He goes on to offer another pointer to success; holding back key reserves, the elite of the mounted arm and throw them in at the tipping point both in the centre and on the flanks. Otherwise unattached officers should be sent in with them. The reserve can be used to prevent enemy breakthrough, to punch though his lines or reinforce success as circumstances demand. While he was writing centuries after Caesar it is clearly great generals such as him who have influenced his tactical doctrines.[16]

Caesar informs us the collapse and rout was both swift and complete. As Vegetius advises, the Germans massed their reserves for a decisive punch and then charged. The tired Gauls were presumably not expecting this, though they'd suffered the same treatment before. Their cavalry shuddered and recoiled, leaving their pesky archers completely in the lurch. The bowmen were simply ridden down or dealt with by the accompanying light infantry, 'surrounded and killed'. The Germans didn't give pause, harrying the retreating Gallic cavalry 'right up to their camp'. Grandstanding has its downside. There would be no more cheering from the Gauls on that day. Caesar had won another round and his siege lines had not even been shaken. Vercingetorix' proposed sally from the town remained a stillborn exploit.

The respite was only temporary. Both Commius and Vercingetorix, while they knew they couldn't communicate directly, were aware they had to strike fast and decisively to break the deadlock. There can't have been much food left in the town by this time and the enormous host on the hills outside would quickly consume everything they had brought. Caesar doesn't tell us about his own supply situation. While this clearly wasn't critical, he was himself penned in to a large extent. To what degree his foraging parties could operate beyond the shelter of the lines is uncertain.

Undeterred by the failure of their cavalry, the relief army began making preparations. If imitation is indeed a form of flattery then Caesar was being flattered. The Gauls were getting ready for a major infantry assault. No mad, careering rush full of dash and fire. If very little else, this would be done in the best Roman manner: 'the Gauls manufactured a large quantity of wicker hurdles [fascines], ladders and grappling hooks'.[17] This was to be a night assault, a very tricky operation at the best of times. Darkness breeds confusion even in the age of hi-tech communications. In the classical era, this was very much worse. Commanders struggled to communicate with sub-units even in daylight. To do so in the confusion of night was nigh on impossible.

That doesn't necessarily mean it was a bad idea. There was clear logic in using darkness to mask the attempt. At night, the Romans would be very uncertain about the overall direction of the attack. Was any section of the line facing the main effort or just a diversion? If local commanders rushed reinforcements to one spot, they would be uncovering another. Furthermore, that superior firepower which the legions relied on would be substantially diluted – obviously, it is much harder to hit a specific target when you're shooting blind.

If, as they seem to have managed, the first wave could get over the dead ground unseen and begin neutralising at least some of the serried obstacles, casualties from wall-mounted artillery would be significantly reduced. As the attacking formations began to infiltrate the minefields, they released a huge shout, the clarion sounding through light summer darkness to alert those immured in the town that were waiting for the signal. How many were deployed in this assault we don't know, possibly Caesar never actually knew. What we can be sure of is that these would be picked men, the bravest and the best who would have been under no illusions as to the riskiness of their mission.

In command of the threatened sectors of wall were Mark Anthony and Gaius Trebonius. Both had trained and drilled their men for just such a moment. Both were seasoned fighters, not given to panic. The Gauls covered their infantry with a hail of missiles, intended to keep the defenders' heads down while sappers dealt with the obstacles. Caesar's legionaries responded with vigour, using their artillery, slings (throwing 'large' stones[18]) and javelins. How long this initial duel lasted is not told but Caesar implies his soldiers rapidly gained 'fire ascendancy'… 'They frightened off the Gauls'. Even in the darkness, which hampered both sides, the Roman artillery was already ranged and they had the additional advantage of greater height for shooting.

Caesar concedes that the sheer weight of enemy projectiles caused 'many casualties' and the Roman officers began drafting in replacements, robbing men 'from towers further away'. As the Gallic infantry struggled forward, many would inevitably be disabled by the ingenuity and density of the obstacles. Each man who went down thrashing in agony would become a further impediment to his comrades who were sure to be under orders not to stop and assist their wounded. Inevitably, the fight came to close quarters as the Gauls, reaching the ramparts, swarmed upwards to the fighting platform, using ladders or simply lifting men up, covered by shields. Some would chuck grappling hooks looking to pull down sections of battlements.

It was now the classic soldiers' battle. Mark Anthony and Gaius Trebonius could feed in reinforcements as men were wounded or became exhausted but survival depended on the fighting skills of the legionaries. This fight was hard fought, no quarter asked or given and intensely bloody. The balmy night air racked by the clash of steel and screams of dead and dying. Men generally don't die quietly or necessarily quickly. Relatively few wounds would be instantly fatal. Anyone who went down would probably suffer a rain of hacking blows, the fighting platform soon slick with blood, gallons of it, spilt brains and entrails.

We don't have any firsthand accounts or memoirs from Caesar's men and certainly not from their opponents. Archaeological evidence from mass graves unearthed on the sites of medieval battles suggests most fatal injuries were caused by blows to the head. Mute remains from grave pits testify to this, the bodies of the English dead from Otterburn in Northumberland (1388), whose remains were found beneath the nave of Elsdon church in the 19th century, from Visby in Sweden (1361), and from Towton in north Yorkshire (1461). Slashing and stabbing wounds, though ghastly, were not always fatal and more victims probably recovered than might be expected. Complications such as peritonitis or blood poisoning, however, were invariably fatal. Many injured would be left lying on the field exposed to the rigours of climate and the tender mercies of scavengers. The Towton mass grave, excavated during the 1990s, has provided a grim insight into the sheer nastiness of 15th-century warfare. Some 43 skeletons were unearthed; most of these had suffered a series of horrific head injuries, puncture wounds and calamitous fractures with evidence of specific and deliberate dagger thrusts to the back of the skull, either a *coup de grâce* or cold-blooded execution. In either event the victim had no head protection at the fatal moment.

The fighting for the individual combatants would have been disorientating. Most veterans the authors have interviewed over the years, when they can recall details of what was happening, can only recollect that which went on immediately around them and not always accurately. The red mist doesn't make for precise reportage. Time is meaningless, noise and heat terrific. Men fighting in armour produce great clouds of steam and rivers of sweat; dehydration is as much of a hazard as their enemies' blades. Morale is fickle. Men who have fought like lions only a moment before can break and run like rabbits.

This was also the type of close-quarter combat at which the legionaries excelled, a distillation of all their drill, training, and experience. Their armour and weapons were specifically designed for just this and each man had long, slogging hours of practice behind him. It paid off. The battle lasted all night until the first rising glow of dawn showed that the defences, battered and slighted in many places, were nowhere breached. The attack had failed and, in the creeping light, the assault parties risked being taken in the flank by Roman units from the camps higher up, fresh and no doubt eager. The Gauls had had enough. It was another failure, a brave gambit, well conceived and competently executed but it hadn't worked.

What definitely hadn't worked was the plan or intention to coordinate the attack from beyond with a sally in force from within. 'While this was happening those inside the town fetched out the equipment Vercingetorix had made ready and prepared for a sortie, and filled in the first set of trenches'.[19] For whatever reason, their timing went completely astray and by the time they were ready to attack, the main assault had failed. They filed back into the city without having struck a blow. It was a massive failure. Had Caesar's lines suffered a double attack, from both sides at once, sheer weight of numbers and increased pressure just might have punched a hole in the *circumvallation*, which would have been pivotal. Vercingetorix' trapped army could have moved quickly through the breach, a corridor to salvation, kept open by the relief force and then got clear. There would have been losses but not catastrophic ones. The whole nature of the battle would have shifted. Caesar would have been penned impotent within his own, now half-redundant lines. Even if he had then taken the empty town, what would have been the victory, a stripped, abandoned settlement, empty of sustenance?

It is hard to identify from Caesar's sparse prose why the effort foundered so dismally. Vercingetorix would have been fully aware that this was the decisive moment. He could have won, he could have survived and, at the worst from his perspective, the campaign of 52 BC would have ended in a draw. Why we cannot say but he failed the test and that must have been a moment of unimaginable bitterness for him.

Dawn would have revealed a scene of unalloyed carnage, overlaid with the stench of blood and entrails, blended with piss and shit. The carefully engineered pits and hedges would have been topped with corpses. Whether the Gauls were able, as they withdrew, to collect all their many wounded we can't say. Probably so, the weary defenders made no effort to follow and harry and most of their available arsenal of missiles would have been used up. Caesar gives no note of casualties. His own would not have been light but the Gallic relief would have lost far more. For any wounded left behind, their fate was sealed. For the Roman wounded there would at least be medical attention.

Caesar's armies were, of course, in the field long before the age of the great Roman surgeon Galen (129–c. 200/216 AD). Nonetheless, the legion possessed sophisticated and efficient medical services. Normally, the organisation and administration of these was the responsibility of the camp prefect (*praefectus castrorum*) and this would extend to active service. The medical staff sergeant, orderlies and dressers were classed as *immunes* – exempt from heavier duties. They would have been busy that morning.

It was the father of medicine, Hippocrates, who had observed that 'He who desires to practice surgery must go to war'. It was the influence of Greece and Greek surgical techniques that informed much of Rome's military medicine. While first-class provision dates from Galen's time, basic care in dressing and treating wounds was available in Caesar's day. Rome had, after all, invested heavily in her soldiers.

'The Gauls had now suffered serious setbacks on two occasions, and began to discuss what to do...' What indeed? Their cavalry were beaten and the attempted break-in must have taken a heavy toll of their best men. Whatever the actual size of the relief force (even if we accept Caesar's numbers), by no means all of that quarter of a million men were elite warriors, probably only a relatively small percentage. These would be proven men of worth with full weapons and mail – using unarmoured men for such close combat would have been pointless.

Commius had by now realised that the *circumvallation* was very strong indeed and that head-on assaults, however well planned and set up, were simply not going to succeed. What he needed to find was the weak spot in Caesar's armour, the gap in the cordon. His scouts would have been active and it would be from them that he learnt, potentially, of just such a place.

His eye and those of his fellow commanders fixed on the lines north of the town where Mont Rea sweeps down to fade into the Plain of Gresigny. The gradient here was steep, too steep for Caesar to build effectively. The topography at least appeared to work in his favour and he had placed a camp at the base of the hill. So far so good but this fortlet was only linked to the rest of the lines on the eastern flank. The little River Oze runs to the south-west. North of the redoubt the outer wall did not exist, the slope makes it nigh on impossible. This then would be the place, the hinge on which the fate of Gaul would pivot. A strong diversion on the much fought-over Plain of Laumes could keep Caesar's attention fixed while the real attack went in here.

> There was a hill to the north which our men had been unable to include in the siege works because of its large circumference; they had been obliged to set up the camp on ground which, because of a gradual slope was slightly disadvantageous. In charge of it were the legates Gaius Antistius Reginus and Gaius Caninus Rebilus with two legions.[20]

Caesar goes on to tell us that the Gauls' attack went in at midday and involved some 60,000 picked men, chosen from those tribes with the highest reputation for courage and stamina. By this we can probably assume the attackers were mainly Arverni and Aedui. The Arvernian Vercassivellaunus would lead them; as Vercingetorix' kinsman, he could be counted on for maximum effort.

Again, this was well planned. If we can discern a guiding hand behind these moves, it has to be Commius; very few in Gaul could have had better insight into the ways and capabilities of Rome. 'During the first watch,' Vercassivellaunus led his corps, taking them, we can assume, to the north of Mont Rea. The march took all night and the storm-troops had to be ready before dawn could give them away. Moving so many fully armed men without being detected under the very noses of Roman sentries and possibly mounted vedettes, was a tough assignment and a very considerable feat. They had to remain invisible until it was time to attack. Speed and timing would be of the essence.

That dawn would have brought an uneasy calm. Both sides, down to the dimmest spear-carrier, would have been aware that the decisive moment had to be near. Caesar, the grand impresario, had called up this huge cast onto the stage he had built. It was time to see how they all performed. So far, he was ahead on points. He had beaten Vercingetorix and bottled him up, wrested back the initiative he had never really quite grasped all season. He had kept him penned up, defeated his cavalry, and sealed the place up tightly. So far, he had successfully seen off the best efforts of the relief to fracture the ring. He would be aware he still had no grounds whatsoever for complacency. The Gauls would have to make one supreme effort to punch through and that had to be linked to a major sortie by the defenders. Both forces outnumbered his. If they could join, Vercingetorix could still be the winner.

The tactics were quite straightforward. Down on the plain the cavalry and infantry would make a demonstration in front of the defences already battered from the night attack. While Roman attention was fixed there, the main infantry assault would go in against the vulnerable hinge. For all their constant vigilance, it seems the besiegers had failed to detect the flanking movement of Vercassivellaunus' picked corps. So the essential element of surprise remained theirs.

Commius and the rest of the war council had learnt from their mistakes. To focus on a single massive blow against the defences would never work. Caesar could concentrate his forces at the point of contact and utilise fully his soldiers' superior drill, training and kit. What might work would be to launch a series of attacks at different points, applying pressure all around the walls so Caesar's forces would be pinned and denied their essential flexibility.

Attacking on the plain, despite the earlier defeat, made sense. It was here the Gauls could best deploy their superior numbers. The defences would certainly have been weakened in the last attack and many of the anti-personnel devices neutralised. There wouldn't have been time to fully replenish them. Coordination with the defenders inside would be far easier in daylight so the attack could come from both sides at once. That was obviously going to be essential: 'Vercingetorix saw his men from the citadel of Alesia and marched out of the town, taking the wicker hurdles, poles, shelters,[21] siege hooks and the rest of the equipment he had had made ready for the sortie'.[22]

By noon, as the sun reached its zenith, fighting broke out on all fronts, 'on every side and every expedient was put to the test'. Montgomery might have called this a 'crumbling' operation, wearing down the enemy's defences by savage attrition till the dam burst somewhere along the line. Caesar had the benefit of interior lines and a well-practised command and control structure. 'Both sides realised this was the very moment for putting their utmost effort into the fight...' Caesar had the additional advantage that his command post on Mont Flavigny sat on higher ground and he could see the whole battle unfolding at once.

As the Gauls streamed towards the battered defences on the plain, evidence of the previous night's failed attack would have been everywhere. Loads of abandoned kit and piled bodies, frozen in the unnatural sack-like poses of violent death, of their fellow warriors attested to the fury of the fight. Their men died in droves but showed no lack of courage, anything but. These fresh waves began the laborious and dangerous business of filling in the ditches and dismantling obstacles. This time the Roman artillerists had a clear target, bolts thudding into flesh as the Gauls struggled forward. Many would be shot down but as each man fell, another would step forward. For the first time Caesar's lines of *circumvallation* were under simultaneous attack from both sides.

Even for experienced and hardened legionaries this would have been distinctly unnerving. In battle, generally, you only have to worry about the enemy directly in front of you. Here, you are aware there are masses of them behind you and that your survival depends, not just on your own skill and luck, but that of those covering your back. In front of you the snarling faces of an enemy stirred to the point of fanaticism. If the line fractures at any point you will surely be overrun:

> The shouting which arose behind them was effective in frightening our men as they fought, for they realized that the risk to themselves depended on the courage shown by others: after all it is usually the case that what is unseen is more effective in disturbing men's minds.[23]

Using their defensive gear, masking the obstacles, coming on regardless of casualties: the Gauls smashed against both faces of the ramparts across the corpse-strewn plain. The pressure was intense. Again, it was a soldiers' battle, the men streaming sweat, scarcely aware of what was happening outside their immediate peripheral vision. Those attacking would again be the elite, well harnessed in mail, skilled and determined. Here was the place a man might earn undying fame, the greatest battle Gaul had ever seen. The legionaries fought as they always did, using shields to parry the slashing strokes, jabbing with their short swords, the blades soon growing blunt as they jarred off bone and punched through tissue.

Men would lose all sense of time, the red mist like a curtain, hard to rotate individual fighters in such a narrow, confined space, parched, over-heated and increasingly tired. Both infantry commanders on the spot, Marcus Antonius and Gaius Trebonius, were able to whistle up reinforcements from less beleaguered sectors. Officers would have made sure water reached their soldiers. An armoured man, however fit, can only fight for a limited period. He will dehydrate very rapidly. Caesar doesn't discuss this minutiae but he would have had a system. Probably vats of fresh water were placed along the lines and/or there would have been orderlies taking flasks around.

Vercassivellaunus timed his strike to perfection. Unseen and unsuspected, his fresh troops, rested after their tiring night march, struck home like a tidal wave:

> the unfavourable downward slope of the site played a crucial part. Some of the enemy threw missiles, others formed a 'tortoise' and moved up close; exhausted troops were continually being replaced by fresh. They all threw earth on to the defences which gave the Gauls a means of ascent as well as covering over the devices which the Romans had hidden in the ground.[24]

This was the red-hot crucible of the battle. Those two legions defending the camp were partly isolated from the rest and the nature of the downward slope, as Caesar describes, facilitated the attack. Quite clearly Vercassivellaunus had also been studying Roman methods, and he'd trained his men in forming the 'tortoise' (*testudo*), that bristling phalanx of locked shields. It was the nearest thing ancient armies came to an armoured personnel carrier. They prepared bags of earth and stones to spread a blanket over the field of obstacles with sufficient left to form an assault ramp. This was a meticulously planned and brilliantly executed move. It certainly looked like it was going to work.

The Romans fought back doggedly, even with the *testudo*, their artillery would have taken a steady toll of the attackers. Vercassivellaunus understood the need to come to contact as rapidly as possible, to deliver his punch at maximum velocity. For the legionaries on the walls, it was a nightmare scenario. Their obstacles had been countered, their ramparts scaled and a seemingly inexhaustible flood of enemy was surging over and around them as inexorable as a raging spring tide.

Caesar was watching. He could see his two legions were facing odds at best of probably six to one and both legates were fully committed. Every man who could stand was on the walls. And those walls would have been crumbling; grappling hooks would be wrenching aside whole sections of the superstructure, a rain of spears falling on the exposed defenders. 'When he realised what was happening Caesar sent Labienus with six cohorts to help the men in trouble.'[25] His orders were precise. Titus

Labienus, his second-in-command, was to bolster the existing defence and if, and only if, it proved impossible to contain the potential break-in to fall back, regroup and immediately counter-attack.[26]

Labienus pulled together all available forces and marched them down from Mount Bussy, safe to deploy as they were covered by both lines of *circumvallation*. Leadership counted now more than ever, time for that touch of Caesar in the afternoon. He knew he could rely on Titus Labienus, a highly able commander – the fatal rift is certainly not yet apparent. Summoning up his personal bodyguard, the Roman general cantered down from his eminence onto the boiling plain below; the line was holding but the pressure remained intense. He treated his battle-weary soldiers to a terse oration. He, Julius Caesar, his old red cloak streaming, is their talisman, the magic of his charisma enabling each man to draw from deep within those final resources of resilience and stamina.

'Inside the Roman lines, the enemy abandoned hope of success on this level ground because of the size of the defences...'[27] Caesar's timely intervention had forestalled a deepening crisis on the plain. The fury of the attacks, certainly those from the besieged, began to ebb, receding like a sucking tide. Vercingetorix must have been dismayed to see this new spurt of vigour and his men retreating. If he was, he didn't show it; rather praising his warriors for their tremendous efforts and re-deploying the survivors to attack up the slopes of Mont Flavigny. This was a shrewd gambit. He would have seen how sections of the walls would have been thinned to reinforce the legionaries battling on the plain. Up the hill they charge; 'a hail of missiles from the defenders on the towers scattered them...'

But only for a heartbeat, the volleys may have slowed the onslaught but it didn't deflect it. The officers and veteran legionaries laid into the waves of attackers with javelins and then with their swords. As with the other camp, Vercingetorix' men had learnt new tricks and were well prepared to tackle the belts of obstacles. Hooks tore at the battlements as the Gauls surged forward, men falling but more coming through. And again it was hand to hand, lunge, cut, thrust, parry; blood and entrails spilling and sloshing.

Caesar reacted with customary lightning reflex, sending his household men and whoever he could spare from the plain to bolster the hill. '[He] sent first the young Brutus with some cohorts then his legate Gaius Fabius with more, finally, when the fighting grew more fierce, he came in person...'[28] He pushed this steady stream of reinforcements in from between the walls to bolster the outnumbered defenders. This finally, and only when Caesar himself joined in, tipped the scale. The crisis on the mountain peaked and then began to subside. There were now too many swords on the walls, too many fresh *pila* finding their targets. The attack ran out of breath. Those Gauls who made it onto the fighting platform were hurled back dead or wounded, the luckier ones just jumped and run for it.

This wasn't victory, only a respite. The defences were by now badly degraded at several key points. Caesar needed to keep the flow of available men moving to counter each new threat as it emerged. On the plain the relief army, undeterred by Vercingetorix' failure from inside the lines, were still bashing away at the crumbling rampart and showed no signs of retreating. Labienus meanwhile was in serious difficulty. The couple of cohorts he had been able to deploy hadn't been enough to halt the offensive. Vercassivellaunus' raging warriors had the scent of victory in their nostrils.

Up on Mont Flavigny, Caesar could plainly see that the position at the foot of Mont Rea opposite was fast unravelling: 'Then Caesar made for the place where he had sent Labienus. He withdrew four cohorts from the nearest fort and ordered one section of the cavalry to follow him, the rest to move round the outer defences and attack the enemy from the rear'.[29] This was the absolute crisis; the battle, the campaign, the entire six years of war hung in the balance. Vercassivellaunus was on the point of breaking through, an irresistible rush of warriors about to hack a huge gap in the defences. The besieged and their relief would be united. Gaul would have won and Rome would have lost.

'Caesar hurried to join in the fighting. The conspicuous colour of the cloak he habitually wore in battle proclaimed his arrival'.[30] This was perhaps the key. Caesar could lead his men in person during the decisive clash. Vercingetorix couldn't, he was 'banged up' behind the walls, just a spectator. Vercassivellaunus' corps, poised on the very point of breaking through would have clearly seen Caesar approaching. He had drummed up four infantry cohorts and as he spurred across the plain he ordered up his cavalry. Some as infantry support but the rest formed up for a mounted sortie to threaten their attackers' flank and rear. He intended to both bolster the defence and assume the offensive at the same time. His well-oiled command and control mechanisms and the inestimable benefit of interior lines made this brilliant counter-stroke possible.

But these manoeuvres would need time. The cavalry would have to ride around the circuit of the defences, anti-clockwise, over the high ground, before they'd be in place. Caesar had to hold back the storm till then. From his own command post Vercassivellaunus could plainly see what was happening so he threw in his final reserves, leading them in person. There was little more either general could do. Caesar's men joined with Labienus' exhausted legionaries and fought on. The grim, brutal attrition continued, 'our men threw their spears then fought with swords'. If the Gauls battered their way through before the Roman cavalry got around to attack them, they might still win the battle. Caesar's line was stretched as taut as a bowstring.

The legionaries hunched beneath shield rims, their blood encrusted swords ready. As Peter Inker observes, this type of close fighting favoured their stance rather than the looser Gallic formation that needed space for each warrior to deliver slashing blows, which was more tiring.[31] This type of slogging match was just what the Romans do best. Then '... suddenly the cavalry was glimpsed in the rear; more cohorts were advancing. The enemy turned tail and the cavalry charged them as they fled.'[32] In almost an instant, the battle swung from crisis to carnage, from contest to rout. The appearance of Caesar's cavalry hacking at their flank and seemingly about to cut off their line of retreat was too much for the tribesmen.

As ever, the rot would not have started at the front. The man fighting for his life in the first rank has no time to see what is happening – he is focused on the fellow three feet away who's trying his very best to disembowel him. Very disconcerting then to feel the press behind him start to unravel as panic grips vast swathes of those at the back, many of whom won't have struck a blow: 'massive slaughter followed'. Both sides would have lost in the melée but the real killing starts when one side, in this case the Gauls, begins to run. Those lions who had struggled for hours to hack a path to victory suddenly degenerated into a vast horde of lemmings. And lemmings they were, because a tired man on foot isn't going to outrun a horse.

As they streamed back up the funnel, Mont Rea on their left, up the narrow valley of the Rabutin stream, they were hacked down and trampled in their hundreds, probably thousands. It was pure murder. Weapons and kit were chucked away in the contagion of fear, those proud badges of rank and nobility, the tokens of a warrior elite, become just so many souvenirs.

Sedulius, chief of the Lemovices was one of the many gentry who died. Vercassivellaunus was captured. He and 74 looted standards were part of the vast haul of booty.[33] Vercingetorix and the defenders must have watched with sick horror as this vast, proud army, the pride and hopes of Gaul, descended into a panicked rabble, sword-fodder for Caesar's terrible Germans. The rest of the army simply bolted with them, a huge, streaming tsunami of terrified and broken humanity heading for the hills and for home, many without a backward glance.

On the broken ramparts, Caesar's men watched as the cavalry did their business, turning flight into massacre, watched as the Gauls fled back across the corpse-strewn plain, abandoning their camp, their baggage and gear. The men would have been stunned, slumping into that black hole of numbed exhaustion that follows action. They would probably have not been too tired to collect weapons and armour. Many years later Colonel O'Sullivan, Prince Charles Edward's dyspeptic chief of staff, remarked after the Jacobite win at Falkirk that, with so many Hanoverian dead or prisoners, gold watches could be bought cheaply. We can imagine that fine Gallic swords, helmets and harness were in very plentiful supply after Alesia and pieces would have changed hands for small change.

The pride of Gaul was humbled. Caesar gives no figures for either side's overall casualties. His own cannot have been light but the Gauls would have suffered many times more including a fair cull of gentry. The battle was over as effectively was the campaign. The war would continue through the next year but Rome had won. Caesar had won and Vercingetorix had lost. He would get no second chance. In many ways his campaign had been masterly but not quite masterly enough. There was now only one master in the ring and he hadn't finished, not yet.

CHAPTER 9

LEGACY

Unmistakable signs forewarned Caesar of his assassination. A few months previously the veterans who had been sent to colonise Capua under the Julian Law were breaking up some ancient tombs in search of stone for their new farmhouses – all the more eagerly when they came across a large hoard of ancient vases. One of these tombs proved to be that of Capys, the legendary founder of the city, and there they found a bronze tablet with a Greek inscription to this effect: 'Disturb the bones of Capys, and a man of Trojan stock will be murdered by his kindred, and later avenged at great cost to Italy'.[1]

The Ides of March fell upon the 15th of the month. It was Caesar's close friend Cornelius Balbus who told him the story from Capua. Just after the 55-year-old dictator learned that a herd of horses which he had dedicated to the river Rubicon, a tribute and acknowledgement to that fateful crossing, didn't like to graze in the valley, as though it was somehow accursed. In the course of sacrifices, the augur or seer Spurinna issued that famous warning 'beware the Ides of March'.

On his last night on earth Caesar prophetically dreamed he was soaring towards the Elysian Fields and shaking hands with Jupiter himself. You wonder if he viewed this as a meeting of equals.[2] And why not, this was Caesar, the man who had outstripped any of his contemporaries, the late developer who had taken Gaul and then, in the Civil War, the Republic itself. Crassus had gone to his shameful death at Carrhae, Pompey had been defeated then nastily butchered in Egypt. Julius Caesar was the first citizen of the known world.

Calpurnia, his wife, also dreamt. She saw one of the great honours voted him by a pliant senate, a gable, collapsed with Caesar crushed beneath.[3] Suetonius suggests that his health was failing and that he was well aware of the conspirators' intentions – a form of suicide by assassin theory, 'some of his friends suspected that, having no desire to live much longer because of his failing health, he had taken no precautions against the conspiracy'.[4] We cannot say if this is so. Certainly such distinguished biographers as Adrian Goldsworthy do not see Caesar's health as irreversibly declining. Surely, his epilepsy had worsened and he was a good age by the standards of the time. Yet there were no signs that his incredible energy levels had declined.[5]

In the event and on the day, Caesar did hesitate. He felt unwell and the Senate had been in session for an hour when he arrived. He left home at around ten in the morning. Some passer by pushed a note into his hand. This contained details of the plot but he didn't read it, merely added the missive to the bundle of papers he was already carrying. Presuming, we conclude, that it was another request from a client. There's an irony in that. As he passed Spurinna, who'd earlier warned of the Ides of March, he quipped that the day had come and all seemed well. Come yes, replied the seer, but not yet gone![6]

As he took his seat, the conspirators, their nerves already stretched to breaking point, crowded round, 'as if to pay their respects'. Tillius Cimber, who had agreed to lead the attack, pressed close as though to pose a question. Caesar waved him back, signifying he should wait. Cimber grabbed hold, trying to pinion the dictator. Caesar protested but one of the Casca brothers, seizing his cue, lunged from behind inflicting a glancing wound beneath the throat. Caesar fought back, grabbing his assailant's arm and jabbing his sharp stylus into the attacker's flesh. He tried to prise free but took a second thrust to the chest (the fatal wound).

Surrounded by a frenzy of slashing blades he pulled the upper hem of his toga over his face so his enemies might not see his death convulsions. He was stabbed and hacked by twenty-three furious blows. He didn't utter a sound unless it was the famous rebuke to Brutus as he struck, 'You too my son'.[7]

The master of the world died in a river of his own blood, brought down by his fellow senators in a squalid act of murder: Almost all authorities, at any rate, believe that he welcomed the manner of his death. He had once read in Xenophon's *Boyhood of Cyrus* the paragraph given by Cyrus on his deathbed, and said how much he loathed the prospect of a lingering end – he wanted a sudden one. And on the day before his murder he had dined at Marcus Lepidus' house, where the topic discussed happened to be 'the best sort of death' – and 'let it come swiftly and unexpectedly', cried Caesar.[8]

A dozen years earlier Caesar had presided over the inevitable aftermath of his greatest victory at Alesia, one of the most remarkable feats of arms in military history. He had, after an intense and close-fought struggle, overcome the greatest Gallic rebellion and threat to his conquest. He had turned the tables, defeated his gifted and charismatic opponent, bottled him up, penned, contained and starved him. He had seen off a mighty relief force and compelled the demoralised survivors in Alesia to surrender.

> The following day Vercingetorix called a council and argued that he had undertaken this war not in his own interests but for the liberty of all. Since they were forced to yield to fortune, he went on, he was putting himself in their hands, ready for either outcome, whether they wanted to make reparation to the Romans by putting him to death or to hand him over alive.[9]

They decided to throw him to the wolves, and sent envoys to Caesar who ordered them to disarm and send out the principal officers. Ever the consummate showman, Caesar had a dais built so the defeated could grovel in the dust to best advantage.

> And the leader of the whole war, Vercingetorix, after putting on his most beautiful armour, and decorating his horse rode out through the gate. He made a circuit around Caesar who remained seated. And then leaped down from his horse, stripped off his suit of armour, and sitting himself at Caesar's feet remained motionless, until he was delivered up to be kept in custody for the triumph.[10]

His captivity lasted for six dismal years till he made his final public appearance as star exhibit in one of Caesar's triumphal shows. That complete, he was quietly strangled in the Tullianum jail. The price of failure was high. And Vercingetorix was far too dangerous an opponent to hope for any of Caesar's noted clemency.

Though he spared the Aedui and Arverni from the worst consequences (he needed them as allies) he enslaved the rest. Each soldier, as promised, got a slave as booty. The value of the weapons cache would form a tidy bonus for Caesar. Having stamped on the ashes, he set out for the land of the Aedui to bring them back in line. The Arvernians were falling over themselves to pledge whatever needed pledging. He took large numbers of hostages but did return his prisoners of war (around 20,000), to both tribes.[11] Next, he sent the legions into winter quarters whilst he himself took up temporary residence at Bibracte, just in case anyone hadn't got the point. His victory won him twenty days of thanksgiving in Rome. His political enemies would also be silenced, at least for the moment.

To all intents and purposes, Caesar was done with Gaul. Despite the scale of his victory, the war wasn't quite over. With his forces distributed and generally keeping an eye on things it was time to put some stick about amongst those truculent tribes who remained troublesome. He launched a series of short, sharp shocks directed against, particularly, the Bituriges and Carnutes. For the spring campaign of 51 BC he focused on the Bellovaci, Eburones, Treveri and those stubborn Carnutes.

The most significant episode was the siege of Uxellodunum,[12] conducted by Caesar's legate Gaius Caninius.[13] This proved a very tough nut indeed and the defenders had clearly learned much from the Alesia debacle. Finally, the place capitulated. The survivors trusted to Caesar's habitual mercy and they received some. They weren't killed, but the hands of all those who had borne arms were cut off in retribution.[14] All of Gaul needed to understand the price of continued resistance. The Gauls got the message and the war was effectively over.

Caesar went on to fight and win the Civil War against Pompey, winning decisively at Pharsalus. He took Egypt and campaigned in Spain and North Africa. His victory was finally complete. He had matched Alexander though his legacy looked just as shaky after the Ides of March. More civil war followed as his heir Octavian and Mark Anthony fought and defeated his assassins, before uneasily dividing the spoils. Anthony, Caesar's flawed shadow, became adrift in Egypt.

Octavian – Augustus – stayed calm and swept the board. The Republic was dead and the Empire was born. This and, perhaps, the success of the *Pax Romana* in Gaul were Caesar's true gifts.

In one sense, Caesar's conquest was a larger-scale extension of the kind of domestic wars the Gauls excelled at. His annexation was not about the invasion of a hitherto united, peaceful or in any way centralised society. He just did what they were already doing but did it rather better. Gaul and the Gauls undoubtedly suffered a great deal but Caesar almost certainly, as discussed, exaggerated casualty figures and he was never short of willing Gallic allies. Part of his skill lay in the way he exploited existing tribal differences to his own advantage, parochialism winning out over any notion of cohesive and concerted action.

Vercingetorix was unlucky in that he came too late. Had the Gauls possessed a national leader of such a high calibre in 58/57 BC, Caesar might have found the job beyond his resources. What is perhaps remarkable about Vercingetorix was not that he ultimately failed but that he came so close to success and achieved so much in so short a time when the pattern of Roman conquest was already so strongly imprinted.

'Frightfulness' – the use of terror tactics as policy was already well established in the classical world. There was no real dividing line between military and civilian personnel. Caesar knew about terror, the mutilation of the survivors of the siege of Uxellodunum is a case in point and that was marketed as leniency! He could have killed them all. The Gauls themselves were just as susceptible to bloodletting.

Vercingetorix massacred Roman traders and administrators in Cenabum, just to show that this was total war, that there was no such thing as a civilian. While he demurred at the proposal at Alesia that the non-combatants be recycled as a ready supply of protein, he agreed to their expulsion. In the history of siege warfare the fate of such *bouches inutilés* has never been a happy one. Caesar, like Henry V, refused to let them pass so they were condemned to a lingering and horrible death between the lines. Nor were they re-admitted. Both sides were responsible for their fate.

Men, women and children died in sieges, in battles, in casual raids and forays. If they lived it might very well be as slaves. While the modern world views slavery as anathema, that was not the view in the classical world. Neither Roman nor Gaul would have expected anything different. Also, scorched earth strategies were carried out by both sides, leading to many deaths by starvation. For Rome, as the wars were fought in Gaul, it was the locals who suffered, especially those who depended on the agricultural economy. Destroying crops and lifting livestock would have an especially devastating effect, initially on the rural population and then on those in the great trading and production centres who depended on rural surpluses for both exchange and subsistence.

Could the conflict for either side be defined as *jus bellum iustum* – a 'just' war – by either side? And if so does this mitigate the colossal price paid for ultimate victory? Long after Caesar and Vercingetorix, Thomas Aquinas laid down three criteria or tests that must be satisfied before a war may be viewed as 'just':

> Firstly the just war can only be waged by a properly instituted authority such as the state; 'Proper Authority' striving, as it is assumed, for the common good which is a lasting peace which endures for man's universal well-being, thus promoting, through force of arms, God's true intention.

> Secondly, the war must be initiated for a good and just purpose rather than simply for gain or territorial expansion – 'Just Cause', for the sake of restoring some legitimate right that has been denied such as territory overrun, goods seized or punishment for evil perpetrated by an enemy state or rogue elements.

> Thirdly, and perhaps most testing; peace must be the central motive even in the midst of conflict, this is defined as 'Right Intention'. The state must fight for the just reasons it has expressly claimed for declaring war in the first instance and this ideal extends to ordinary combatants.

Caesar could certainly say he had just cause for his intervention at the outset. Both the Helvetii and Ariovistus posed a 'clear and present danger' to the interests of Rome and her allies. The Gauls would undoubtedly have agreed. From that next year though, 57 BC, Caesar was on an opportunistic mission of his own devising – like the mythical Kurtz in *Heart of Darkness* and its screen realisation *Apocalypse Now*. He was initiating a private war, beyond the effective recall of the Senate and justified, in pragmatic terms, by the flow of booty and slaves. This war wasn't 'just' – quite the opposite. The central character in Coppola's film wearily comments that complaining of atrocities in Vietnam is like handing out speeding tickets at a grand prix, irrelevant.

Rome, of course, escaped any ill effects. Slaves, loot and revenue flowed into Republican coffers. Caesar pump-primed a series of large-scale civic infrastructural works from the proceeds of the war, none of which stood him in bad stead. Merchants, traders and general carpetbaggers were drawn to follow Roman armies like moths to the flame. War is devastating but it opens up vast new horizons to hardy and unscrupulous entrepreneurs.

Could Vercingetorix, for his part, claim his war was just? Probably yes. He was fighting to free Gaul from a ruthless foreign oppressor and certainly claimed he was not acting out of personal ambition, though some manner of high kingship was clearly his goal. His methods were ruthless and resulted in excessive suffering among his own people. On the other hand, Caesar was a world-class opponent and this war was never going to be gentlemanly.

More than seventy years ago, British bombers attacked the German city of Dresden, a raid that sparked almost immediate controversy. Arthur 'Bomber' Harris was an advocate of what was termed 'strategic bombing'. From 1940 the Luftwaffe had attempted to break Britain during the Blitz. Happily, even though it did not seem so at the time, Goering's air force, a superb tactical arm, was not well designed for the strategic role, his twin-engined bombers didn't have the necessary range or payload for the job. By contrast the Allies did; most famously the four-engined Avro Lancaster. Harris was unequivocal and brutally honest as to its role. During the war, precision bombing of the exactness needed to pinpoint target enemy factories and installations wasn't possible. His approach, echoed by Carl Spaatz of US Eighth Air Force, was that the RAF would relentlessly target German civilian workers, kill them and their families, deprive Germany of her labour force and so decimate and overawe the people that their will to continue the war would falter. A vast amount of damage to German infrastructure was inflicted. Tens of thousands died but the bombing campaign didn't win the war. It did force Germany to hold back hundreds of thousands of troops for homeland defence and expend precious and dwindling resources that could otherwise have been deployed west against the Allies or east against the Russians. Harris, it must be said, did not particularly intend or wish to bomb Dresden, the raid was ordered because the city formed a communications hub, channelling men and materiel into the fight raging in the east. Although the same cannot be said of Magdeburg. That medieval city burned precisely because it was made of wood, a blow to Germany's past as well as her present.

It was the Luftwaffe, attacking Coventry, which had first used incendiaries to ignite fires and result in greater damage than could be achieved by high explosive alone. The resulting firestorm was referred to by Axis pilots as 'Coventration'. Dresden got truly coventrated – the ancient timber structures of the city centre were engulfed in a whirlwind of unstoppable fire, whipped to hurricane strength by its own intensity. At Coventry, nearly six hundred people died. Goebbels claimed that 250,000 perished at Dresden. While this number was pure propaganda, the actual figure was around a tenth of that – still rather more than an eye for an eye.

Essentially, the ongoing debate questions to what lengths liberal democracies, fighting for freedom and justice, can go to win. Nazi Germany was a formidable and terrible opponent, both the most evil and potent dictatorship in history (with the possible exception of Stalin's Russia). Can the strategic end justify the tactical means? The discovery of Belsen with all its unimagined tableaux of horror went a long way to silencing early qualms about Dresden. The clear assessment was that a people so dedicated to deliberate cruelty deserved no better. Germany intended to enslave Great Britain, can it be said any means of defeating such fearful tyranny is justified? Caesar might have used the same argument. The tone of his writing suggests it: the Gauls were backward savages, what was done to them was necessary for civilisation to prevail.

More recently, Operation *Enduring Freedom* was the conquest of Iraq undertaken by an allied coalition, primarily US/UK, to unseat the dictator Saddam Hussein. Militarily the conquest was swift and successful.

Saddam was eventually, and after a fashion, tried by a rigged court and then clumsily hanged. The whole process became bloodily unstuck when it became obvious that there had been no thought given as to how Iraq might be safely governed after the invasion. Plenty of rhetoric about 'democracy' but no clue as to how this might be established; the consequences of this bungled intermeddling continue to resonate very loudly.

In the 21st century, there have been calls for the inclusion of a third facet of just war theory – *jus post bellum* – the morality of post-war settlement and reconstruction. Rome, it has to be said, knew how these things were done. The second and essential element of conquest was assimilation – the Gauls had to realise that being a part of this vast multi-national corporation was in fact a good thing. Ultimately, they would be winners not losers. The Romanisation of the formerly independent Gaul endured for half a millennium and was disrupted by external not internal forces. The era would be viewed in retrospect as a golden age, one that future rulers would attempt to revert to, not escape from.

The Civil War prevented Caesar himself from undertaking this process. It was left to his highly competent successor Augustus. Caesar had to be content with simply extending the policies he had already tested – favouring the tribal elites, fostering goodwill through concessions and granting monopolies. Subsequent senatorial commissioners could build on this, focusing individual tribes' loyalties by using the existing *oppida* as bases for Romanised civic settlements, imposing Roman-style administration and law, future *civitates*. Yes, there were taxes to pay but these were not unduly onerous and peace, even prosperity, were lasting dividends. You could argue Caesar did not 'conquer' Gaul in the enduring sense. What he did do was to defeat the tribes and establish control, the platform or foundation to be built up by his successors.

Part of Rome's skill in fostering assimilation was to build on existing foundations rather than try to impose new ones. The tribal elites retained their status: warlords became civic dignitaries. Their fortunes swelled rather than shrank. The idea of local rule managed through existing oligarchies was part and parcel of Rome's policy. While dictator, Caesar also founded a series of veterans' colonies, mainly in the province. These served a dual function. His legionaries were rewarded for their good service and a hard core of experienced fighting men, now with a stake in the land, was established. There would be no Gallic Boudicca to vent her rage on the townships. Flare-ups did occur of course. A rebellion sparked in 21 AD, possibly as a consequence of a fiscal dispute over tax collection,[15] but there were no mass risings.

Even though the campaign of 51 BC saw Gaul effectively conquered, Agrippa needed to undertake further military action 12 years later. He consolidated by extending the road links. Building roads, at which Rome excelled, provided the arteries for commerce and the benefits of the peace. Augustus was careful to extend his own Imperial grip on the region, dividing the province into three administrative districts: Aquitania, Gallia Belgica and Gallia Lugdunensis (chief city of the third of these being Lugdunum (Lyons)). In 9 AD Varus led his legions to annihilation in Germany, thus ensuring that the Rhine would stay as the frontier. A chain of fortresses with their adjacent civilian sprawl (*vicus*) marked the line: Strasbourg, Bonn, Mainz and Regensburg all started life as Imperial outposts along the line (*limes*).

Alesia was not abandoned by the Mandubii, despite their terrible sufferings. It remained both a tribal centre and a thriving Gallo-Roman town. It was a prosperous place with a 5,000-seat theatre erected in the north-west quadrant (relatively modest, that at Autun held four times as many patrons). A temple dedicated to Jupiter and Taranis (the Celtic god of thunder), dates from the 2nd century AD. Artefacts recovered from the site dating to the following two centuries reveal evidence of the cult of Cybele (an Anatolian Mother Goddess).

The town could boast an impressive basilica housing the courts and council chamber or *curia*, which surrounded an open forum, lined with shops. North of the public space was a monument to the patron god of craftsmen Ucuetis and his consort Bergusia, evidence the settlement was a centre for bronze and metalwork, probably the basis for its prosperity. The whole place embodies the transition from Celtic capital to Romano-Celtic township – *Pax Romana* exemplified.

Once wars end they become history. Napoleon once trenchantly observed – 'history is but a fable agreed upon'. His nemesis, the Duke of Wellington, agreed in that writers could as easily describe the course of a ball as a battle. Happily, historians have demurred.

In 1995 Michael Dietler wrote a very interesting article on the way history, particularly archaeological history, can be used to foster, indeed construct, what he later called 'memory factories', places where what we perceive to be our identities can be lodged, can become the stuff of collective memory. He suggested that language, objects, places and persons have all been cited to 'have been differentially emphasised to invoke antiquity and authenticity at each of these levels in the process of constructing emotionally and symbolically charged traditions of Celtic identity'.[16]

What particularly catches one's attention is the timing of his articles (1994 and 1998).[17] Europe was dealing with the trauma of the Balkan wars, triggered by the resurgence of savage nationalism in the wake of the break up of Yugoslavia. Archaeology, history and myth were cited as a justifying narrative for brutal ethnic violence. The spectacle of determined attempts to destroy historical buildings, monuments and documents confirmed how important those narratives were perceived to be. Destroy the library and you destroy the nation. The Sarajevo librarians who risked (and gave) their lives to save the historic collection in Vijećnica were doing more than saving books, much as that matters.

Dietler argues that appeals to an ancient Celtic past (usually presented as unified) bolstered three aspects of French national identity: pan-European unity in the context of the European Community (EEC), retaining a specific identity whilst taking on a new characteristic (that of an EEC member), and allowing for regional resistance to nationalist hegemony. 'Invented traditions'[18] abound throughout the Alesia story as it has been presented over the last 200+ years. You could even say that the modern version of Vercingetorix is an invention.

First Alesia, then Gergovia and Bibracte have all been the subject of political attention in the 20th century. The three *oppida* considered by Dietler can all be seen as validating the national myth – making it seem real and rooted in concrete locations.[19]

Napoleon III had spotted the potential of the Celtic myth that had emerged during the French Revolution. Many have argued that the revolutionaries of 1789 characterised the class struggle as a battle between the descendants of the Celts (the good guys) and the Germanic Franks who had conquered them in the 5th century (the nobility). Which, of course, had the added benefit of ironing out strong regional sensibilities and differences – even languages in some instances... This was particularly valuable when tackling the profound nature of those differences in parts of France that already defined themselves as inheritors of the Celtic past e.g. Brittany.

The 'war of the two races'[20] was a theme of France's revolutionary past that also found expression in the consideration of her colonial legacy and the issues raised by a multicultural present. Napoleon I had grabbed the concept of a war of two races, using it as a justification for expansion. In conquering the rest of Europe, Napoleon could be seen to reunite the old Celtic heartlands. He founded the Académie Celtique – founded to document and promote Celtic language, folklore and archaeology, in part to gather the evidence needed to cement his theory.

The historians of the second republic, in pulling Vercingetorix from obscurity, provided an appealing emotional focus for an emerging sense of unified nationality and class coherence. Napoleon III literally rooted this sense in the landscape, authenticated by archaeology. It is no accident that the teaching of history became mandatory in French schools in 1867.

Napoleon III can reasonably be credited with the titling of Mont Auxois in Burgundy as the site of Alesia. Dietler describes it as the 'linking of a place, an event and a historical figure from an ancient text to a modern landscape'.[21] His attention captured by the discovery of a hoard at the site, the Emperor funded further investigations that rapidly found evidence of fortifications.

At the time Napoleon III became interested in Alesia he was writing a biography of Caesar and was stirred to see Vercingetorix as a pivotal figure in the history of France, the first to endow a sense of nationhood. The perceived success of Colonel Henri Baron Stoffel's excavations, carried out over four years, 1861–1865, was sufficient evidence for him. Up went the impressive statue, 6.6 metres tall, sitting on a 7-metre-high stone pediment. It is the perfect example of 19th-century slush. Vercingetorix' flowing cavalier hair and bold moustaches, rather imaginative pearl necklace, anachronistic Bronze Age harness and sword with Dark Age wrapped leggings, are all pure Hollywood. Napoleon perpetuates a glorious totemic fraud. Supremely entertaining but no relationship whatsoever to history. The inscription on the base reads:

La Gaule unie, Formant une suele nation,
Animée d'un même esprit, Peut défier l'Univers

[A united Gaul, Formed into a single nation
Stirred by the same spirit, Can defy the world]

Hollywood would love it; shame the Prussians weren't so impressed. But this isn't about Vercingetorix, it is about Napoleon III: a wise craftsman understands his patron. It is a very thin veneer of history overlaid to suit contemporary purposes. Vercingetorix probably wouldn't have had a clue what he was on about.

Choosing the site of heroic defeat rather than defiance (Bibracte) or victory (Gergovia) also tells us something. People often note the Irish tendency to idolise glorious defeat. Perhaps the habit can actually be traced to Napoleon, a perception enhanced by his choice of pose for the statue. He rejected the suggestion of a martial figure, shown thrusting forward into battle, for a more meditative pose. Inviting us, perhaps, to speculate that the hero is contemplating sorrow and loss or is aware of the defeat to come. We are almost encouraged to see him as a man conscious of his impending fate, moving towards it regardless of consequences. There is evidence of profound public interest at the time. The statue was first exhibited in Paris and then processed to Alesia. Crowds flocked to watch it pass, some apparently even genuflecting before it.

Napoleon was of course, aware that the Roman past had also to be incorporated into his scenario. Ceasar's victory was to be presented as a necessary evil, without which France could not have marched into her glorious present. Accomplished by 'streams of blood, to be sure, brought these peoples to a better future'.[22]

After defeat by the Prussians in 1870, the symbolism of Alesia and Vercingetorix began to assume a new significance – resistance to invaders, be they Roman or German. Suddenly a cousin of the German Gauls stood for resistance to the new Germany.

That perception and the delivery of the cult of Vercingetorix were fed by an explosion of artworks, literary pieces, and schoolbooks in which the surrender of Vercingetorix at Alesia became the dominant image. There were surprising participants: 'Moreover, the journal *Pro Alésia*, founded in 1906 to report on the excavations at the site, became a prominent venue for patriotic purple prose'.[23]

The story is one every child learns at school and their memory of Alesia and Vercingetorix is later fed by comic books, novels, historical works, and other media. A recent example is a popular book on Vercingetorix that is subtitled 'With him truly began the history of France'. Dietler is particularly taken by the closing line: 'He was the first resistance fighter of France.'[24]

Alesia has become a place where the French can focus on their patriotic history. A statue of Joan of Arc, another independence fighter, was erected there in 1903. It is commemorated in some surprising aspects of popular culture, giving its name to a Paris metro station (complete with an air duct shaped like a Gaul in a winged helmet).

Nor has Napoleon III been the only politician to understand the potential. Charles De Gaulle, who used the image of Vercingetorix surrendering his arms in a book on the French army, for many years visited the site on the anniversary of the battle.

Gergovia fared less well until 1989. It has been suggested that ceremonies carried out by Maréchal Pétain symbolising the unity of Vichy France with the rest of the country left a sour taste. Although to be fair, an archaeological dig there in 1940 provided cover for a resistance cell. Nonetheless, in 1989, for example, Valéry Giscard d'Estaing and Jacques Chirac chose Gergovia to kick off their campaign for European elections. Their speeches at the site emphasised 'the continuance of French identity'.

President Mitterrand, like Napoleon III before him, provided funding for archaeological investigation and a monument at Bribracte. In 1985 Mitterrand unveiled a monument to Vercingetorix there, calling for national unity as well as European unity (an echo of an earlier Celtic pan-European community). He would follow up ten years later with a substantial museum and research facility on the site. A year later, the sites of Bibracte and Alesia would be symbolically linked by a footpath.

As Dietler puts it, 'Mitterrand's sense of personal identity and his connection to the national collective imagination he strove to construct eventually became so entangled with the mythology of Bibracte that, in an interview in 1995, he claimed to identify personally with Vercingetorix above all other figures of French history, and he expressed the desire to be buried at Bibracte.'[25]

Nor are the French immune to the rituals enacted by those who claim to be descendants of Vercingetorix' Celts – a phenomenon found across the Celtic nations. Like the gatherings at Stonehenge in Britain, visitors to modern Bibracte can also witness 'druids' carrying out fire festivals...

Caesar was not the first to write up military history as memoir and propaganda. Wars have been written about since Ramses II wrote his own, distinctly propagandist, view of the battle of Kadesh (c. 1274 BC). Later Xenophon made the genre his own. What is perhaps the newest form of recording is collecting artefacts and testimony for war museums. It would have been helpful if Caesar had instituted something along the lines of the British National War Museum. Set up in 1917, its curators travelled to both the Western and Middle Eastern Fronts even as titanic battles were still raging. They recognised that whilst the big events would be fully recorded, the everyday stuff might easily be overlooked.

Following the established tradition, a team from what is now the Imperial War Museum (IWM) descended on Camp Bastion, UK Armed Forces central base in Helmand Province prior to the winding down of the Afghanistan campaign. This latter-day fortress had grown since 2006 to be the UK's largest overseas camp constructed since 1945. It was the size of Reading and was described as looking like some desert, hybrid version of Las Vegas, complete with restaurants, runways, shower blocks, hospital complex, water storage and incinerator facilities, temporary home to 30,000 people.[26]

Almost since the initial coalition deployment, a team from the Australian War Memorial Museum had been active, amassing artefacts and film recordings. In 2009, the IWM began recording oral testimony from returning service personnel; so far some 1,600 soldiers from 75 regiments have been interviewed. The IWM curators had the sense to include logistics in their area of interest, showing that they appreciate just how complex and extensive this supply tail is. During the Vietnam era it was said that 30 US personnel were required to keep one 'grunt' fighting in the bush. (For the Vietcong the ratio was one logistician for every two fighters!) To keep the modern Tommy Atkins on patrol or manning a forward operational base requires a vast, thoroughly coordinated organisational supply train.

Camp Bastion, like some fabled caravanserai, was fast disappearing, being progressively disassembled nearly as fast as it had been erected. The IWM team first went out in summer 2013. Using fresh and essentially civilian eyes, they saw the everyday minutiae that troops might take for granted. Hesco, the modern utility equivalent of renaissance gabions, cut up and adapted for many esoteric purposes, including sofas and shoe racks. All of this was to come down and the reality was soon to vanish forever unless it was recorded.

This is not the pomp and chivalry of war, nor is it the horror and tragedy. It is the everyday, the humdrum, the mundane and yet, without these core logistics, there would be no sustainable war at all. Would that Caesar had a similar team sweeping up behind him to record the great siege lines at Alesia. As one modern observer pithily summed up 'It's like Eddie Stobbart on steroids isn't it? It's logistics at its extreme.' We can be sure some legionary managed a very similar quip.[27]

Napoleon III used heritage to stiffen nationalist sentiment. In modern asymmetric conflicts of competing religious and political ideologies, heritage is a weapon. The Taliban in Afghanistan have savagely dese-crated ancient monuments that suggest an alternative brand of cultural heritage. In May 2015, Daesh vandals captured Palmyra, a world heritage site, and went to work with dynamite and bulldozers. The 82-year-old curator Khaled al-Assad, who refused to give up the locations of some of the treasures he had hidden, was horrifically and repeatedly tortured and then, when he still held out, was simply beheaded.

It could always be said that the military naturally subordinate cultural to operational imperatives. The destruction of the great Benedictine abbey of Monte Cassino during the battle to turn the Gustav Line in Italy seventy years ago remains a contentious example. Saving Allied lives, perfectly correctly, was identified as the greater priority. War is hard on heritage.

More recently, in 2011, during the struggle in Libya to oust Gaddafi's tyrannical regime, forces loyal to the dictator deployed half a dozen radar vehicles in the lee of an important Roman site at Ras Almargeb. They reckoned that NATO forces would not risk the PR fallout from damage to such prominent archaeological remains.[28] They were wrong: due to a new and extraordinary partnership between conventional military and heritage professionals, the hostile vehicles were surgically removed with virtually no degradation to the antiquities. The initiative was the brain-child of Professor Peter Stone, a constant advocate of the need to protect the world's heritage from the consequences of conflict. Professor Stone explains how his bespoke software system, 'Arches', operated in Libya:

> We were able to make sure our coordinates which located the site were the same as the military's. It meant they could modify their ordnance and use a different bomb to take out all the vehicles while leaving the fort relatively unscathed.

The Arches programme was launched through a partnership initiative involving the Getty Conservation Institute and the World Monuments Fund. The system will gather and collate information from a range of sources to create a comprehensive database. The project originated, in part, as a response to the wholesale depredations and destruction visited on Iraq in the anarchic wake of the Coalition intervention in 2003. US Defence Secretary Donald Rumsfeld responded unhelpfully with the pithy if blindingly obvious response that 'stuff happens' in such circumstances. Professor Stone has been working towards a more useful response:

> ... Since 2003, I have been involved in drawing up 'no strike' lists for a number of countries which passed to the military with greater or lesser success. One of the issues that we have been grappling with is that the information has been provided in a slightly different way with slightly different technology in slightly different formats. The best way to deal with the military is to deliver information in a way that is most easy for them to lift and drop into their data set, without having to do any translation or do any software modifications... Arches is an open source with software that is free and usable everywhere.[29]

> What I've learnt is not to talk to them about heritage as an academic resource or about the development of civilisation because they just glaze over, but to persuade them that by looking after these places they will not antagonize the local population and not give the enemy great PR that can be used against them. They have begun to acknowledge that by protecting cultural property they are more likely to win the hearts and minds of occupied populations or at least not to alienate them.[30]

The system has additional applications in that it can be gainfully employed in the aftermath of natural disasters to highlight that which has been lost and what survives to be conserved. It can help assess the consequences of an influx of large numbers of tourists, the sheer volume of whom can cause problems. The Arches system was recently used in Jordan to pinpoint just such a threat to ancient sites such as Petra and the great desert fortress of Quseir Amra. In the UK, this resource can assist in the conservation of key sites such as Stonehenge and Hadrian's Wall.

What then is the significance of Alesia today? The siege features heavily in *Asterix and the Chieftain's shield*.[31] The story opens with Vercingetorix surrendering. He lays down all his fabled arms including his magical shield. This gets nicked in an unattended moment by a Roman archer who promptly loses the talisman at dice. The centurion who won the shield trades it in for a jar of wine. A separate plot device draws in Asterix and Obelix who, in the course of an unrelated adventure, end up on the hunt for the shield – Caesar's envoys are hot on the same trail. Asterix gets the better of his opponents and arranges his own triumph with his employer Vitalstatistix being borne aloft on the sacred relic. Gallic honour is thus restored! As always, it's clever and funny but the shield of Vercingetorix is still a great and wonderful thing. The debate over location is a theme that parodies the conflicting viewpoints: *I don't know where Alesia is! No one knows where Alesia is!*

What of Roman Britain's version of Vercingetorix?

> …The whole island rose under the leadership of Boudicca, a lady of royal descent – for Britons make no distinction of sex in their leaders. They hunted down the Roman troops in their scattered posts, stormed the forts and assaulted the colony itself, in which they saw their slavery focused; nor did the angry victors deny themselves any form of savage cruelty.[32]

Tacitus was not likely to see any nobility in Boudicca's revolt in 60 AD although, in his usual discreet fashion, he managed a fair few swipes at the idea of empire. This was another example of total war. Boudicca did not fight in the traditional, limited manner of the Celts. Like Vercingetorix, she forged a coalition with the sole objective of driving Rome out of Britain, a process to be accomplished by a surfeit of 'frightfulness'. Roman veterans, settlers and general collaborators were slaughtered wholesale, striking at the very root of the colony's viability. She wasn't fighting for glory or for loot. The queen correctly saw that she should strike at the economic infrastructure, render the colony bankrupt, make it a place no longer worth fighting for. This was at once both clever and naïve. Whatever the cost, Rome could not allow popular insurrection to succeed. She, like Vercingetorix, was unlucky in her opponent, the finest general of his day, vastly experienced and not prone to panic.

Modern Britons are probably a bit ambivalent about Boudicca, yet she was the British Vercingetorix, brilliant, charismatic and fanatically ruthless. She too was defeated by a commander of steady genius and her survivors suffered for it. Is she admired today? She was definitely admired by the Victorians: like her Gallic counterpart, she had her own impressive statue, on the Embankment in London. Yet she is also a frightening figure, the furious violence of her assault, the massive scale of civilian casualties, are too familiar in another context. Modern observers tend to lean more towards Rome, still buying into the propaganda of 'them' and 'us'. Rome being civilised and ordered (just like modern British society, we tell ourselves) the rest, well, not really. This invented memory came into existence in the 19th century when the British persuaded themselves that Britain was the modern Rome, creating an empire strictly for the good of those already living in the territories we snaffled. That is now starting to change, and the other half of the story is getting told these days. But it is likely to be a while before there is a Boudicca theme park.

Today's battle at Alesia is being fought between the traditionalists and their 'Jurassic' adversaries and that campaign looks set to run for decades. In the popular mind and in the minds of most archaeologists, Alise-Sainte-Reine is definitely where it happened. What can be agreed upon is that the siege of Alesia was one of the most important and dramatic events in European history with profound consequences that continue to resonate today.

GLOSSARY

Ala(e)	The wings of the army occupied in Caesar's day by allied troops, latterly a cavalry formation
Aquila	Legionary eagle, its loss an unimaginable disgrace
Aquilifer	Legionary standard bearer, carries the eagle
Baggage	Tents, general kit, tools, spare gear, officers' effects and, of course, loot
Ballista	Framed timber catapult, like a giant crossbow that came in various sizes, essentially a section or century support weapon
Carnyx	Celtic war trumpet
Century	Company-sized unit of eighty men
Centurion	Company officer
Cippi	'Tombstones', legionaries' black humour; sharpened timber stakes buried in pits in front of defences as an anti-personnel device, Roman barbed wire
Cohort	Battalion-sized unit comprising six centuries or 480 soldiers, ten cohorts made up the legion, essentially a very large brigade
Decurion	Unit commander of cavalry
Equites	Originally gentlemen cavalry, those who could afford their own horse, latterly a social class below those of senatorial rank
Gladius	From *Gladius Hispaniensis* – the short stabbing sword of the infantry

Legate	Ranking officer who commanded a legion
Lorica hamata	Chain mail, as opposed to the later *lorica segmentata*, banded plate defence
Maniple	'A handful'; a larger company-sized formation of 120 men which predates the introduction of cohorts
Montefortino	Form of protective helmet, derived from Celtic patterns, used in Caesar's day
Optio	Non-commissioned officer of the century, subordinate to the centurion
Pilum/pila	Specialised form of javelin intended for throwing, the missile barrage preceding contact, designed to bend on impact and render enemies shields useless
Primus pilus	'First spear', the senior centurion of the 1st cohort, a very important officer
Pugio	A legionary's multi-purpose dagger/fighting knife
Scutum	Distinctive timber laminated curved shield of the legions
Signifer	Unit standard bearer
Spatha	Longer, slashing type sword used by horsemen
Stimuli	'Spurs'; iron points fixed to timber poles which were buried in pits in front of defences; anti-personnel mines in effect
Testudo	'Tortoise', an infantry tactic to facilitate storming, the unit advances with shields either fixed to front or flanks by the external ranks and files whilst those in the centre lock shields overhead
Tribuli	Anti-personnel device, like the later medieval calthrop, a four-spiked iron weapon that, when thrown down, always lay with one point uppermost, used extensively to deter cavalry
Tribune	A gentleman officer, one of six, assigned to the legate's staff, not a cohort commander as such
Vexillation	A commanded detachment from the legion, two or more cohorts detached for a specific purpose or mission

APPENDICES

ORDERS OF BATTLE

Roman Army – Commander Julius Caesar

Legio V – Alaudae
Legio VI – Ferrata
Legio VII
Legio VIII
Legio VIIII
Legio X – Equestris
Legio XI
Legio XII – Fulminata
Legio XIII – Gemina
Legio XIIII
Legio XV

Roman cavalry
Germanic auxiliary cavalry

Peter Inker gives a nominal total of 4,800 men per legion and, perhaps wisely, does not attempt to estimate the size of the cavalry formations. For both we are to a large degree in the field of conjecture. We have gone for an average strength of 4,000 effectives per legion and 4,000 each for the mounted units = 44,000 infantry and 8,000 cavalry. None of these figures can, of course, be verified.

Gallic Army – Commander Vercingetorix

Forces in Alesia
Caesar doesn't give us a breakdown of these forces tribe by tribe but refers to a force (minus cavalry) of 80,000 (*Gallic War* VII, 71). Again, this is both suspiciously large and conveniently rounded up. Nonetheless Caesar is our only authority and we have no revised figure to offer.

The Relief Army★

Aedui (including the Segusiavi, Ambluareti, Aulerci, and Blannovii)	35,000
Arverni (including the Eleuteti, Cadurci, Gabali and Vellavii)	35,000
Sequani	12,000
Senones	12,000
Bituriges	12,000
Santoni	12,000
Ruteni	12,000
Carnutes	12,000
Lemovices	10,000
Bellovaci★★	10,000
Pictones	8,000
Turoni	8,000
Parisii	8,000
Helvetii	8,000
	5,000
Ambiani	5,000
Mediomatrici	5,000
Petrocorii	5,000
Nervii	5,000
Morini	5,000
Nitiobbriges	5,000
Aulerci Cenomani	5,000
Atrebates	4,000
Veliocassi	3,000
Lexovii	3,000

Aulerci Eburovices	3,000
Raurici	2,000
Boii	2,000
Curiosolites, Redones, Ambibarii, Caltes, Osismi, Veneti and Venelli (the Atlantic coast tribes)	30,000

This gives a paper muster of 281,000 and Caesar estimates the actual size of the army as infantry.   24,000

★Figures are based on Caesar's own tally (*Gallic War* VII, 75).
★★The Bellovaci, we are told, declined to send a complement but Commius prevailed upon them to send a token force of 2,000 to swell the muster.

THE BATTLEFIELD TRAIL

Any tour of the wider history of Alesia properly begins at Bourges. The ancient city is a joy for the visitor and forms the apex of the classic triangle, Bourges, Gergovia and Alesia which defines the core of Caesar's campaign. As mentioned in the text, the municipality has prepared a cleared walkway around what would have been the lines of the *murus Gallicus* of 52 BC. Despite the growth of the medieval and modern city, glimpses offered by the circuit give a strong indication of the strength of the Bituriges' capital and the problems facing any besieger.

Though scarcely part of the story the visitor should still visit the magnificent Gothic cathedral of St Etienne, designated since 1992 as a world heritage site. From the height of the north-west tower one gets a very clear view of the surrounding marshes which constituted such an obstacle in 52 BC. The museum too repays a visit, housing many artefacts from the Gallo-Roman era. In terms of atmospheric and comfortable lodgings, I'd recommend the Hotel de Bourbon Mercure on the Boulevard de Republique which began life as a seventeenth-century abbey.

The tour route follows through the heart of France, a glorious shifting chiaroscuro of landscapes. Much has changed since Caesar and Vercingetorix' day yet the feel of the ancient country and a rash of fascinating sites amply repay the time spent travelling. Heading south from Bourges on the A-10, leaving Montlucon to your left and Vichy of evil memory to your right aim for Clermont Ferrand, the nearest large city to Gergovia. The museum there is worth a visit.

Clermont-Ferrand was originally a Celtic *oppidum* and a later Gallo-Roman city, the cathedral was established by the 5th century AD and it was from here Pope Urban proclaimed the First Crusade in 1095. The heart of the place, once one gets past the grim industrial suburbs, built in harsh dark stone, is interesting as is the superb Musée Bargoin which houses an extensive collection of Roman items.

Southwards and the Plateau of Gergovia is a magnificent site, offering superb views of the distinctive, almost lunar landscape of the Auvergne. It was here that Caesar suffered his only real defeat of the campaign, though this might have backfired, giving Vercingetorix hope and reason to put his faith in fortresses. The site is crowned by a stone monument, designed by Jean Teillard and erected in 1903. A reconstructed 'Gallic hut', with an accompanying permanent exhibition (La Maison de Gergovie) is also built on the plateau.

From there it's cross-country, generally moving east to Lyons where the remains of the Gallo-Roman city are certainly worth viewing. Leaving Lyons we head north towards Dijon which, if you can survive the horrors of the one-way system, also has a very fine museum. The small town of Alise-Sainte-Reine, in the lush, calm country of Burgundy lies 17 kilometres south-east of Montbard, 50 kilometres north-west of Dijon. The D905 from Venarey-les-Laumes to Posanges in the south passes through the western part of the commune. Access to the present day village is via the D103, D103J, and D103T from Venaray-les-Laumes in the west which continues east to join the D10.

In terms of the siege of 52 BC, the site is very well served by the visitor centre – the Museo-Parc Alesia – that opened in March 2012. It offers state-of-the-art displays, reconstructions, artefacts, quality reproductions and film. It's a fitting tribute to so important a site and an invaluable resource for the visitor. While in the vicinity, it is definitely a good idea to mount a diversion to nearby Chatillon-sur-Seine, where the Musée de Chatillonnais houses the stupendous Vix cauldron. No tour of the campaign of 52 BC is complete without seeing this. As an insight into the life of ancient Gaul it is without compare.

NOTES

Introduction

1. Anthony King, *Vercingetorix, Asterix and the Gauls: the use of Gallic national symbols in 19th- and 20th century French politics and culture* (University of Winchester, 2015). Neil Faulkner, *Rome, Empire of the Eagles* (Pearson Longman, 2008).
2. Caesar, *The Gallic War*, translated by C. Hammond (Oxford University Press 1995), VII, 85.
3. P. Inker, *Caesar's Gallic Triumph – Alesia 52 BC* (Barnsley, Pen & Sword 2008), p. 104.
4. Caesar, *The Gallic War*, VII, 85.
5. Titus Labienus (100 BC–45 BC), a highly successful professional soldier, Labienus served as Caesar's second in command in Gaul where he proved highly able. At some point, possibly at the time of Alesia, he turned against his commander and fought against him in the Civil Wars, being killed at the battle of Munda in North Africa.
6. Caesar, *The Gallic War*, VII, 86.

Chapter 1

1. https://en.wikipedia.org/wiki/Alise-Sainte-Reine, retrieved 2nd March, 2016.
2. Caesar, *The Gallic War*, VII, 69.
3. Suetonius, *Caesar*, 57.
4. *Druids*, released on 31 August 2001, http://www.imdb.com/title/tt0199481/?ref_=fn_al_tt_1 Retrieved 27th June 2016.
5. Inker, *Caesar's Gallic Triumph*, p. 121.
6. Ibid.
7. Caesar, *The Gallic War*, VII, 69.

8. Hugh Schofield, 'France's ancient Alesia dispute rumbles on' BBC News (Paris, 27 August 2012), http://www.bbc.co.uk/news/world-europe-19167600 retrieved 2nd March 2016.
9. Ibid.
10. Ibid.
11. Ibid.
12. 'Inherent military probability'; in the absence of evidence, how would an experienced commander react in such circumstances.

Chapter 2

1. 'If you seek peace prepare for war'. Or, as President Truman put it in 1945; 'we have learned the importance of maintaining military strength as a means of preventing war... We must be prepared to pay the price for peace, or assuredly we shall pay the price of war.'
2. Tacitus, On Imperial Rome, translated by M. Grant (Middlesex, Penguin 1956) XIV, 14–65.
3. Vegetius, Epitome of Military Science, translated by N. P. Milner (Liverpool University Press 1996), II, 15.
4. Josephus, Jewish War, translated by H. St. J. Thackeray (London 1778) III, () p. 102.
5. Vegetius, Epitome, I, 3.
6. M. Grant, The Army of the Caesars (London, Purnell Book Services 1974), p. xxvi.
7. Ibid., p. xxii.
8. P. Connolly, The Roman Army (London Macdonald Educational 1976), p. 10.
9. Ibid.
10. Ibid., pp. 26–27.
11. Vegetius, Epitome, I, 1.
12. Suetonius, Caesar, 51.
13. Vegetius, Epitome, p. xxxvii et seq.
14. Cataphracts were heavily armoured cavalry – primarily from the east, they did not feature at all in the Gallic War.
15. Vegetius, Epitome, III, 4.
16. Caesar, The Gallic War, I, 51.
17. Ibid.
18. Ross Cowan, Roman Legionary 58 BC–AD 69 (Warrior 71) (Oxford, Osprey 2003), p. 46.
19. Vegetius, Epitome, III, 13.
20. Cowan, Roman Legionary, p. 47.
21. Vegetius, Epitome, III, 16.
22. Cowan, Roman Legionary, p. 15.

23. Both Pullo and Vorenus were granted new fictional lives for the HBO TV Series *Rome* (2005–2007).
24. Caesar, *The Gallic War*, V, 44.
25. Ibid.
26. Ibid.
27. Juvenal, *Satires*, translated by P. Green, XVI, 1–4.
28. Caesar, *The Gallic War*, V, 25.
29. Cowan, *Roman Legionary*, p. 50.
30. Caesar, *The Gallic War*, II, 20.
31. Vegetius, *Epitome*, III, 18.
32. Ibid.
33. Ibid.
34. P. Connolly, 'Roman Legionary 1st Century BC' in *Military Illustrated* (volume 3, no 18), p. 36 et seq.
35. Ibid., p. 37.
36. Ibid., p. 38.
37. Ibid.
38. Ibid.
39. Cowan, *Roman Legionary*, pp. 25–26.
40. Vegetius, *Epitome*, I, 16.
41. Ibid., I, 15.
42. Connolly, *Roman Army*, p. 30.
43. Caesar, *The Gallic War*, I, 13.
44. Connolly, *Roman Army*, pp. 28–29.
45. Vegetius, *Epitome*, IV, 12.
46. Connolly, *Roman Army*, p. 52.
47. Caesar, *The Gallic War*, II, 19.
48. Ibid.

Chapter 3

1. Caesar, *The Gallic War*, I, 1.
2. Tacitus, *Agricola*, translated by H. Mattingly (Middlesex, Penguin, 1960), p. 6.
3. L. Du Garde Peach and John Kenney (illustrator), *Julius Caesar and Roman Britain* (Ladybird history series 561, 1959).
4. Caesar, *The Gallic War*, I, 1.
5. N. Fields, *Alesia 52 BC* (Campaign 269) (Oxford, Osprey 2014), p. 8.
6. Tacitus, *Agricola*, p. 11.
7. Alice Roberts, *The Celts: Search for a Civilisation* (Heron Books, 2015), p. 33.
8. Caesar, *The Gallic War*, I, 1.

9. Tacitus, *Agricola*, p. 11.
10. Fields, *Alesia 52 BC*, p. 9.
11. Caesar, *The Gallic War*, I, 1.
12. Ibid., IV, 1.
13. N. Chadwick, *The Celts* (Middlesex, Penguin 1984), p. 54.
14. Ibid., p. 55.
15. Ibid., p. 56.
16. Ibid.
17. Caesar, *The Gallic War*, IV, 5.
18. Lucan, *Pharsalia*, cited in Maier, Ferdinand, 'The Oppida of the Second and First Centuries BC' in V. Kruta, O. H. Frey, B. Raftery & M. Szabo (eds), *The Celts* (Thames & Hudson 1991), pp. 411–425.
19. Alice Roberts, *The Celts: Search for a Civilisation* (Heron Books 2015), p. 58.
20. Caesar, *Gallic War*, VII, 23.
21. I. Ralston, *Celtic Fortifications* (Stroud, Tempus 2006), pp. 183–184.
22. Ibid., pp. 82–83.
23. Nico Roymans, *Tribal Societies in Northern Gaul: An Anthropological Perspective* (Cingula 12 Amsterdam 1990).
24. Ibid., pp. 31–33.
25. Ibid., p. 35.
26. Ibid., p. 25.
27. Roberts, *The Celts*, p. 142.
28. Tacitus, *Germania*, 13, 31.
29. Caesar, *The Gallic War*, VI, 18.
30. Roymans, *Tribal Societies in Northern Gaul: An Anthropological Perspective*, p. 28.
31. Tacitus, *Germania*, XV.
32. Barry Cunliffe, *The Ancient Celts* (OUP 1997), p. 212.
33. Tacitus, *Germania*, XI.
34. Ibid., XI.
35. Caesar, *The Gallic War*, V, 56.
36. Tacitus, *Germania*, VII.
37. Roymans, *Tribal Societies in Northern Gaul: An Anthropological Perspective*, p. 35.

Chapter 4

1. Caesar, *The Gallic War*, VI, 13.
2. Ibid.
3. Ibid.
4. Ibid.
5. Ibid.
6. Ibid., VI, 16.

7. Ibid., V1, 17.
8. Ibid., VI, 18.
9. Homer, *Iliad*, translated by W. H. D. Rouse (New York, Mentor 1964), XXIII.
10. Caesar, *The Gallic War*, VI, 20.
11. Ibid.
12. Homer, *Iliad*, XXIII.
13. Allen, S., *Celtic Warrior* (Warrior 30) (Oxford, Osprey 2001), p. 20.
14. Tacitus, *Agricola*, 12.
15. Allen, pp. 24–25.
16. Ibid.
17. *Iliad*, VVI.
18. Caesar, *The Gallic War*, V, 16.
19. Suetonius, *Caligula*, 56.
20. Allen, p. 46.
21. Ibid.
22. Ibid.

Chapter 5

1. Michel de Montaigne, VII, *Observation of the Method of Julius Caesar in Making War*, translated by C. Cotton (New York 1910).
2. A. Goldsworthy, *Caesar* (London, Phoenix 2007), p. 222.
3. Suetonius, *Caesar*, 45.
4. Ibid.
5. Montaigne, *Observation of the Method of Julius Caesar in Making War*.
6. Suetonius, *Caesar*, 50.
7. Ibid., 58.
8. Montaigne, *Observation of the Method of Julius Caesar in Making War*.
9. Caesar, *Gallic War*, V, 52.
10. Montaigne, *Observation of the Method of Julius Caesar in Making War*.
11. Suetonius, *Caesar*, 54.
12. Montaigne, *Observation of the Method of Julius Caesar in Making War*.
13. Suetonius, *Caesar*, 1.
14. Ibid., 2.
15. Ibid., 4.
16. Mithridates VI (120 BC–63 BC), king of Pontus and Armenia Minor, formidable adversary of Rome who also fought against both Sulla and Pompey.
17. *Quaestor* – a lower-ranking magistrate with primary responsibility for treasury matters.
18. Publius Clodius Pulcher (93 BC–52 BC) a popularist politician of patrician stock who embarked on a bold reform programme, he died violently at the hands of a rival.

19. Suetonius, *Caesar*, 9.
20. Ibid., 10.
21. Chief Pontiff – *Pontifex Maximus*, high priest of the College of Pontiffs.
22. Suetonius, *Caesar*, 19.
23. Ibid., 20.
24. Ibid., 22.
25. The Sequani occupied what is now Franche-Comté and part of Burgundy.
26. The Aedui inhabited the territories between the Saône and Loire, most of the modern departments of Saône-et-Loire, Côte-d'Or and Nièvre.
27. Caesar, *The Gallic War*, I, 29.
28. Ibid., I, 23.
29. Suetonius, *Caesar*, 25.
30. Caesar, *The Gallic War*, II, 1.
31. Ibid.
32. Ibid., II, 28.
33. Ibid., II, 33.
34. Ibid., IV, 14.
35. Ibid., IV, 37.
36. Ibid., V, 52.
37. Ibid., V, 58.

Chapter 6

1. Caesar, *The Gallic War*, VII, 4.
2. Ibid.
3. Ibid.
4. Ibid.
5. Goldsworthy, *Caesar*, pp. 289–282.
6. Plutarch, *Caesar*, 25.
7. Caesar, *The Gallic War* VII, 1.
8. Goldsworthy, *Caesar*, p. 384.
9. Caesar, *The Gallic War*, VII, 3.
10. Ibid.
11. Ibid.
12. Plutarch, *Caesar*, 26.
13. Goldsworthy, *Caesar*, p. 386.
14. Caesar, *The Gallic War*, VII, 8.
15. Ibid., 10.
16. Ibid., 11.
17. Ibid., 14.
18. Ibid.

19. Ibid.
20. Connolly, *Roman Army*, p. 31.
21. Goldsworthy, *Caesar*, p. 391.
22. Caesar, *The Gallic War*, VII, 18.
23. Ibid., 22.
24. Ibid., 24.
25. Ibid., 28.
26. Ibid., 29.
27. Ibid., 38.
28. Ibid., 42.
29. Ibid., 43.
30. Caesar, *The Gallic War*, p. 239, note 7.44.
31. Caesar, *The Gallic War*, VII, 45.
32. Ibid., 47.
33. Ibid., 65.
34. Ibid., 63.
35. Ibid., 65.
36. Ibid., 66.
37. Inker, *Caesar's Gallic Triumph*, p. 51.
38. Ibid., p. 54.
39. Caesar, *The Gallic War*, VII, 68.

Chapter 7

1. Though authorities like Dr Inker and Dr Fields tend to use the terms slightly differently we will stick with the traditional description, favoured by the *Oxford English Dictionary*, that lines of *circumvallation* are those which enclose the besieged town and lines of *contravallation* are those which surround these inward facing works, looking outwards to shield against external relief. Both together are collectively known as 'lines of *circumvallation*'. For a further discussion, consider the arguments Nic Fields presents in his *Alesia 52 BC* (Oxford, Osprey 2014), p. 54.
2. Plutarch, *Caesar*, 27.
3. Ibid.
4. Caesar, *The Gallic War*, VII, 68.
5. Caesar, *The Gallic War*, VII, 69.
6. Ibid.
7. Inker, *Caesar's Gallic Triumph*, p. 59.
8. Fields, *Alesia 52 BC*, p. 49.
9. Vegetius, *Epitome*, IV, 7.
10. Fields, *Alesia 52 BC*, p. 55.
11. Caesar, *The Gallic War*, VII, 69.

12. Inker, *Caesar's Gallic Triumph*, p. 63.
13. Caesar, *The Gallic War*, VII, 69.
14. Vegetius, *Epitome*, I, 21.
15. Inker, *Caesar's Gallic Triumph*, p. 63.
16. Vegetius, *Epitome*, I, 22.
17. Vegetius, *Epitome*, III, 8.
18. Ibid.
19. Ibid.
20. Ibid.
21. Fields, *Alesia 52 BC*, p. 59.
22. Caesar, *The Gallic War*, VII, 72.
23. Inker, *Caesar's Gallic Triumph*, p. 65.
24. Caesar, *The Gallic War*, VII, 72.
25. Fields, *Alesia 52 BC*, p. 60.
26. Ibid., p. 61.
27. Caesar, *The Gallic War*, VII, 73.
28. Ibid.
29. Inker, *Caesar's Gallic Triumph*, p. 63.
30. Ibid., p. 65.
31. Ibid., p. 67.
32. Ibid.
33. Ibid.
34. Caesar, *The Gallic War*, VII, 70.
35. Caesar, *The Gallic War*, VII, 70.
36. Caesar, *The Gallic War*, VII, 71.
37. Caesar, *The Gallic War*, VII, 71.

Chapter 8

1. Suetonius, *Caesar*, 80.
2. Caesar, *The Gallic War*, VII, 70.
3. Ibid., 72.
4. Ibid., 75.
5. Ibid.
6. Commius of the Atrebates had been a client of Caesar's since 57 BC. He had been entrusted as an ambassador to the Britons prior to Caesar's first expedition. He'd stayed loyal throughout the earlier revolts and Caesar had rewarded the Atrebates with tax concessions and giving them influence over the Morini. In 52 BC he sided with Vercingetorix and kept up the fight even after the fall of Alesia. Next year he was active with the Bellovaci and even recruited Germanic mercenaries to bolster their effort. A wily guerrilla fighter he survived a number of scrapes and

finally agreed terms with Mark Anthony – the prime condition being he never had to see any Roman again (VIII, 48)!

7. Caesar, *The Gallic War*, VII, 76.
8. Ibid.
9. Ibid.
10. Ibid., VII, 77.
11. Ibid., VII, 78.
12. Ibid., VII, 79.
13. This higher ground would be on the ring of knolls, les Collines de Mussy-la-fosse, which rise to some 400 metres west of the level plain.
14. Caesar, *The Gallic War*, VII, 79.
15. Vegetius, *Epitome*, III, 16.
16. Ibid.
17. Caesar, *The Gallic War*, VII, 81.
18. Ibid.
19. Ibid., VII, 82.
20. Ibid., VII, 83.
21. These are in fact 'penthouses' (*musculi*) timber screens like mantlets which allow the infantry to advance in column behind giving considerable shelter from lighter missiles (see Inker, *Caesar's Gallic Triumph*, p. 102).
22. Ibid., VII, 84.
23. Ibid.
24. Ibid., VII, 85.
25. Ibid., VII, 86.
26. Ibid., VII, 86.
27. Ibid.
28. Ibid., VII, 87.
29. Ibid.
30. Ibid.
31. Inker, *Caesar's Gallic Triumph*, p. 108.
32. Ibid.
33. Ibid. VII, 88.

Chapter 9

1. Suetonius, *Caesar*, 81.
2. Ibid.
3. Ibid., 86.
4. Ibid.
5. Goldsworthy, *Caesar*, pp. 596–597.
6. Suetonius, *Caesar*, 81.

7. Ibid., 82.
8. Ibid., 87.
9. Caesar, *The Gallic War*, VII, 89.
10. Plutarch, *Caesar*, XXVII, i–xxxvii 3.
11. Caesar, *The Gallic War*, VII, 90.
12. Uxellodunum is in the modern Dordogne.
13. Gaius Caninius Rebilus, one of Caesar's new men who served initially as a tribune in 52 BC, being promoted to legate and was instrumental in the campaign of 51 BC. He remained loyal during the Civil War and served both in Africa and Spain.
14. Caesar, *The Gallic War*, VIII, 44.
15. K. Gilliver, *Caesar's Gallic Wars* (Essential Histories 43) (Oxford, Osprey, 2002), p.91.
16. Michael Dietler, 'Our Ancestors, The Gauls; Ethnic Nationalism, and the Manipulation of Celtic Identity in Modern Europe', *American Anthropologist* (New Series, Vol. 96, No. 3; Blackwell 1994), pp. 584–605.
17. Ibid and Michael Dietler, 'A Tale of Three Sites: the monumentalization of Celtic Oppida and the Politics of Collective Memory and Identity' in Richard Bradley and Howard Williams (eds), *World Archaeology 30.1: The Past in the Past: The Re-Use of Ancient Monuments* (Routledge 1998).
18. Eric Hobsbawm and Terence Ranger (ed.), *The Invention of Tradition* (Cambridge University Press 1983).
19. Dietler, 'A Tale of Three Sites', pp. 74–77.
20. Ibid., p. 74.
21. Ibid., p. 75.
22. Ibid., p. 77.
23. Ibid., p. 78.
24. Ibid., p. 78.
25. Ibid., p. 79.
26. *The Times* (14th September 2013).
27. Ibid.
28. *The Times* (11th January 2014).
29. Ibid.
30. Ibid.
31. R. Goscinny, illustrated by A. Uderzo, *Asterix and the Chieftain's shield* (first published as a serial in *Pilote* issues 39–421) (1967).
32. Tacitus, *Agricola*, I, v, xi.

BIBLIOGRAPHY

Primary sources

Appian, *History of Rome*
Caesar, *The Gallic War*
Cassius Dio, *Roman History*
Diodorus Siculus, *Library and World History*
Frontinus, *The Strategemata*
Lucan, *The Pharsalia of Lucan*
Paterculus, *History of Rome*
Plutarch, *Fall of the Roman Republic; Six Lives, The Parallel Lives and Lives of the Noble Greeks and Romans*
Strabo, *Geography*
Suetonius, *Lives of the Twelve Caesars*
Tacitus, *Germania*
Tacitus, *On Imperial Rome*
Tacitus, *The Histories*
Vegetius, *Epitome of Military Science*

Secondary sources

Allen, S., *Celtic Warrior* (Warrior 30) (Oxford, Osprey 2001)
Chadwick, N., *the Celts* (Middlesex, Penguin 1984)
Collis, John, *The Celts: Origins, Myths, Inventions* (Tempus Publishing Ltd 2003)

Connolly, P., *The Roman Army* (London, Macdonald Educational 1976)

Connolly, P., 'Roman Legionary, 1st Century BC' in *Military Illustrated – Past & Present* (volume 3, no 18, April/May 1989)

Connolly, P., *Greece & Rome at War* (London, Macdonald Phoebus 1981)

Cowan, R., *Roman Legionary 58 BC–AD 69* (Warrior 71) (Oxford, Osprey 2003)

Cunliffe, Barry, *The Ancient Celts* (OUP 1997)

Cunliffe, Barry, *The Celtic World* (Bodley Head 1979)

Cunliffe, Barry, *The Ancient Celts* (OUP 1997)

Delaney, Frank, *The Celts* (Harper Collins 1993)

Dietler, Michael, 'Our Ancestors, The Gauls; Ethnic Nationalism, and the Manipulation of Celtic Identity in Modern Europe' in *American Anthropologist* (New Series, Vol. 96, No. 3, Blackwell 1994), pp. 584–605

Dietler, Michael, 'A Tale of Three Sites: the monumentalization of Celtic Oppida and the Politics of Collective Memory and Identity' in Richard Bradley and Howard Williams (eds.) *World Archaeology 30.1: The Past in the Past: The Re-Use of Ancient Monuments* (Routledge 1998)

Falx, Marcus Sidonius with Toner, Jerry, *How To Manage Your Slaves* (Profile Books 2014)

Fields, N., *Alesia 52 BC* (Campaign 269) (Oxford, Osprey 2014)

Gilliver, K., *Caesar's Gallic Wars 58–52 BC* (Essential Histories 43) (Oxford, Osprey 2002)

Goldsworthy, A., *Caesar* (London, Weidenfeld & Nicolson 2006)

Grant, M., *Julius Caesar: A Biography*, (Weidenfeld & Nicolson 1969)

Grant, M., *The Army of the Caesars* (London, Weidenfeld & Nicolson 2004)

Hatt, Jean-Jacques, *Celts and Gallo-Romans* (Nagel 1970)

Hobsbawm, Eric & Terence, ed., *The Invention of Tradition* (Cambridge University Press 1983)

Holland, T., *Rubicon – the Triumph & Tragedy of the Roman Republic* (London, Abacus 2006)

Inker, P., *Caesar's Gallic Triumph – Alesia 52 BC* (Barnsley, Pen & Sword 2008)

James, S., *Rome and the Sword* (London, Thames & Hudson 2011)

James, S., *The Atlantic Celts: Ancient People or Modern Invention* (University of Wisconsin Press 1999)

Jones, Peter, *Veni, Vidi, Vici: Everything you ever wanted to know about the Romans but were afraid to ask* (Atlantic Books 2013)

King, Anthony, *Vercingetorix, Asterix and the Gauls: the use of Gallic national symbols in 19th and 20th-century French politics and culture* (University of Winchester 2015)

Kruta, V., Frey, O. H., Raftery, B. & Szabo, M. (eds), *The Celts* (Thames & Hudson 1991)

Laing, Lloyd, *Celtic Britain* (Routledge Paul 1979)

Powell, T. G. E., *The Celts* (London, Thames & Hudson 1958)

Ralston, I., *Celtic Fortifications* (Stroud, Tempus 2006)

Roberts, Alice, *The Celts: Search for a Civilisation* (Heron Books, 2015)

Robinson, H. R., *The Armour of Imperial Rome* (London, Purnell Book Services 1975)

Roymans, Nico, *Tribal Societies in Northern Gaul: An Anthropological Perspective* (Cingula 12 Amsterdam 1990)

Warry, J., *Warfare in the Classical World* (London, Salamander 1980)

INDEX